ISRAEL IN THE BOOKS OF CHRONICLES

To my Mother

ISRAEL IN THE BOOKS OF CHRONICLES

H. G. M. WILLIAMSON

Assistant Lecturer in Hebrew and Aramaic
University of Cambridge

CAMBRIDGE UNIVERSITY PRESS

CAMBRIDGE

LONDON · NEW YORK · MELBOURNE

Published by the Syndics of the Cambridge University Press
The Pitt Building, Trumpington Street, Cambridge CB2 1RP
Bentley House, 200 Euston Road, London NW1 2DB
32 East 57th Street, New York, NY 10022, USA
296 Beaconsfield Parade, Middle Park, Melbourne 3206, Australia

First published 1977

Printed in Great Britain at the
University Press, Cambridge

Library of Congress cataloguing in publication data
Williamson, Hugh Godfrey Maturin, 1947–
Israel in the Books of Chronicles
Based on the Author's thesis, University of Cambridge, 1975.
Bibliography: p.
Includes index
1. Bible. O. T. Chronicles–Criticism, interpretation, etc. 2. Twelve
tribes of Israel.
I. Title.
BS1345.2.W48 222′.6′06 76–56118
ISBN 0 521 21305 3

Contents

Contents

Foreword

This book is based upon a doctoral thesis of the same title presented to the University of Cambridge in May 1975. In preparing it for a wider readership, I have omitted two chapters that bore less directly on the central theme and have further revised parts of the remainder. I am deeply grateful to the trustees of the Tyrwhitt Hebrew Fund and the managers of the Hort Memorial Fund for generous grants to assist in its publication.

It is hoped that the references given in the footnotes, though abbreviated, will be sufficient for readers conversant with the field to recognize at once the book or article cited. In addition, a full bibliography of works referred to is supplied on pages 141–54, so that there should be no difficulty in ascertaining a complete reference where required. It should further be noted that books cited by their author's name alone are also included in the list of abbreviations. Citations of the Hebrew Bible are taken from the third edition of *Biblia Hebraica*, edited by R. Kittel (Stuttgart: 1937). Unless otherwise stated, the English translation of the Bible is that of the Revised Version (1884). The *Loeb Classical Library* is used for the text, translation and system of reference for all classical authors (including Josephus).

In the interests of economy, all Hebrew and Greek script has been transliterated. For the former, the system adopted is that set out in H. H. Rowley (ed.): *The Old Testament and Modern Study* (Oxford: 1951), p. xiii, with the exception that *qōph* is represented by *q*.

Of the many friends and scholars who have helped and advised me in different ways, I should like here to mention three to whom I feel most indebted. Professor J. A. Emerton has carefully read and commented upon every part of this work at each stage of its growth, so that it is difficult adequately to express my gratitude to him for his unfailing encouragement both during my student days and since. My thanks go too to Professor I. L. Seeligmann and Dr S. Japhet, whose kindness contributed much to the enjoyment of the academic year 1973–4 spent at the Hebrew University, Jerusalem, and whose comments on various sections of this book have always been carefully pondered, and often incorporated.

Introduction

Only my wife has shared closely with me during the recent years of absorption in the work of the Chronicler, often sacrificing her own interests in order to facilitate my study. I nevertheless dedicate this book to my mother as a small token of my gratitude for her patient support in every way throughout the period of my school and university education.

List of Abbreviations

This list includes works cited by their author's name alone.
Biblical books are cited in the form:

Gen. Ex. Lev. Num. Dt. Josh. Jd. Ruth Sam. Ki. Chr. Ezr. Neh. Est. Job Ps(s).
Prov. Eccl. Isa. Jer. Lam. Ezek. Dan. Hos. Joel Amos Jonah Mic. Nah. Hab.
Zeph. Hag. Zech. Mal.

AB	The Anchor Bible (Garden City, New York).
AJSL	*American Journal of Semitic Languages and Literatures* (Chicago).
Ant.	Fl. Josephus: *Antiquitates Judaicae.*
AOAT	Alter Orient und Altes Testament (Neukirchen-Vluyn).
AP	A. Cowley: *Aramaic Papyri of the Fifth Century B.C.* (Oxford: 1923).
ASTI	*Annual of the Swedish Theological Institute* (Leiden).
ATD	Das Alte Testament Deutsch (Göttingen).
AUSS	*Andrews University Seminary Studies* (Berrien Springs).
BA	*The Biblical Archaeologist* (New Haven).
Barnes	W. E. Barnes: *The Books of Chronicles* (The Cambridge Bible for Schools and Colleges, Cambridge: 1899).
BASOR	*Bulletin of the American Schools of Oriental Research* (New Haven).
BDB	F. Brown, S. R. Driver and C. A. Briggs: *A Hebrew and English Lexicon of the Old Testament* (Oxford: 1907).
Benzinger	I. Benzinger: *Die Bücher der Chronik* (KHAT, Tübingen und Leipzig: 1901).
Bertheau	E. Bertheau: *Die Bücher der Chronik* (Leipzig: 1854).
BH	Biblical Hebrew.
Bi. Or.	*Bibliotheca Orientalis* (Leiden).
BJPES	*Bulletin of the Jewish Palestine Exploration Society* (Jerusalem).
BS	Biblische Studien (Freiburg und Neukirchen).
BWANT	Beiträge zur Wissenschaft vom Alten und Neuen Testament (Leipzig und Stuttgart).
BZ	*Biblische Zeitschrift* (Paderborn).
BZAW	Beihefte zur *Zeitschrift für die alttestamentliche Wissenschaft* (Giessen und Berlin).
CB	The Century Bible (London).
CBQ	*Catholic Biblical Quarterly* (Washington).
Ch(s).	Chapter(s).
CM	E. L. Curtis and A. A. Madsen: *A Critical and Exegetical Commentary on the Books of Chronicles* (ICC, Edinburgh: 1910).

ix

Abbreviations

CTM	Concordia Theological Monthly (St Louis).
Dr	The numbered list of characteristics of the Chronicler's style in *ILOT*, pp. 535–40.
Elmslie (1916)	W. A. L. Elmslie: *The Books of Chronicles* (The Cambridge Bible for Schools and Colleges, Cambridge: 1916).
Elmslie (1954)	'The First and Second Books of Chronicles', *IB*, III, 341–548.
ET	English Translation.
ET	*The Expository Times* (Edinburgh).
EvTh	*Evangelische Theologie* (München).
Ev(v)	English version(s).
FRLANT	Forschungen zur Religion und Literatur des Alten und Neuen Testaments (Göttingen).
Galling	K. Galling: *Die Bücher der Chronik, Esra, Nehemia* (ATD, Göttingen: 1954).
GK	A. E. Cowley: *Gesenius' Hebrew Grammar as edited and enlarged by the late E. Kautzsch* (2nd edition, Oxford: 1910 = the 28th German edition: 1909).
Harvey-Jellie	W. R. Harvey-Jellie: *Chronicles* (CB, London: 1906).
HAT	Handbuch zum Alten Testament (Tübingen).
HDB	*A Dictionary of the Bible*, edited by J. Hastings (Edinburgh: 1900).
HTR	*Harvard Theological Review* (Cambridge, Mass.).
HUCA	*Hebrew Union College Annual* (Cincinnati).
IB	*The Interpreter's Bible*, edited by G. A. Buttrick *et al.* (New York: 1952–7).
ICC	The International Critical Commentary (Edinburgh).
IEJ	*Israel Exploration Journal* (Jerusalem).
ILOT	S. R. Driver: *An Introduction to the Literature of the Old Testament* (9th edition. Edinburgh: 1913).
Jastrow	M. Jastrow: *A Dictionary of the Targumim, the Talmud Babli and Yerushalmi, and the Midrashic Literature* (London: 1903).
JBL	*Journal of Biblical Literature* (Philadelphia).
JCS	*Journal of Cuneiform Studies* (New Haven).
JNES	*Journal of Near Eastern Studies* (Chicago).
JPOS	*Journal of the Palestine Oriental Society* (Jerusalem).
JQR	*Jewish Quarterly Review* (Philadelphia).
JSS	*Journal of Semitic Studies* (Manchester).
JTS	*Journal of Theological Studies* (Oxford).
KAT	Kommentar zum Alten Testament (Leipzig).
KB	L. Koehler and W. Baumgartner: *Lexicon in Veteris Testamenti Libros* (Leiden: 1953).
Keil	C. F. Keil: *Biblischer Commentar über die nachexilischen Geschichtsbücher: Chronik, Esra, Nehemia und Esther* (Leipzig: 1870).
KHAT	Kurzer Hand-Commentar zum Alten Testament (Tübingen und Leipzig).
Kippenberg	H. G. Kippenberg: *Garizim und Synagoge. Traditionsgeschichtliche Untersuchungen zur samaritanischen Religion der aramäischen Periode* (Religionsgeschichtliche Versuche und Vorarbeiten 30, Berlin: 1971).
Kittel	R. Kittel: *Die Bücher der Chronik* (Handkommentar zum Alten Testament, Göttingen: 1902).
LBH	Late Biblical Hebrew.

Abbreviations

Littmann	E. Littmann: *Safaitic Inscriptions* (Leiden: 1943).
LXX	Septuagint.
MGWJ	*Monatsschrift für Geschichte und Wissenschaft des Judentums* (Breslau).
Mosis	R. Mosis: *Untersuchungen zur Theologie des chronistischen Geschichtswerkes* (Freiburger theologische Studien 92, Freiburg: 1973).
ms(s)	Manuscript(s).
MT	Massoretic Text.
Myers	J. M. Myers: *I and II Chronicles* (2 Vols.; AB, Garden City: 1965).
n.	(foot)note.
NEB	The New English Bible.
NM	Nehemiah Memoir.
ns	new series.
OT	Old Testament.
OTL	The Old Testament Library (London).
Par.	Paralipomena.
PEQ	*Palestine Exploration Quarterly* (London).
PJB	*Palästinajahrbuch* (Berlin).
PSBA	*Proceedings of the Society of Biblical Archaeology* (London).
RB	*Revue Biblique* (Paris).
REJ	*Revue des Études Juives* (Paris).
Rothstein–Hänel	J. W. Rothstein and J. Hänel: *Das erste Buch der Chronik* (KAT, Leipzig: 1927).
RSV	Revised Standard Version.
RTP	*Revue de Théologie et de Philosophie* (Lausanne).
Rudolph	W. Rudolph: *Chronikbücher* (HAT, Tübingen: 1955).
SP	Samaritan Pentateuch.
ST	Samaritan Targum.
SUNVAO	Skrifter utgitt av Det Norske Videnskaps-Akademi i Oslo (Oslo).
SVT	Supplements to *Vetus Testamentum* (Leiden).
ThZ	*Theologische Zeitschrift* (Basel).
US	M. Noth: *Überlieferungsgeschichtliche Studien* I (Halle: 1943).
VT	*Vetus Testamentum* (Leiden).
V(v).	Verse(s).
Welten	P. Welten: *Geschichte und Geschichtsdarstellung in den Chronikbüchern* (WMANT 42, Neukirchen: 1973).
Willi	T. Willi: *Die Chronik als Auslegung. Untersuchungen zur literarischen Gestaltung der historischen Überlieferung Israels* (FRLANT 106, Göttingen: 1972).
WMANT	Wissenschaftliche Monographien zum Alten und Neuen Testament (Neukirchen).
ZAW	*Zeitschrift für die alttestamentliche Wissenschaft* (Giessen und Berlin).
ZDMG	*Zeitschrift der Deutschen Morgenländischen Gesellschaft* (Leipzig und Wiesbaden).
ZDPV	*Zeitschrift des Deutschen Palästina-Vereins* (Leipzig, Stuttgart und Wiesbaden).

1

Introduction

The author of the books of Chronicles lived during a period in which one of the major issues for the Jewish people was the precise definition of the extent of its own community. Before the exile to Babylon, this was less of a problem, because the community was co-extensive for the most part with the nations of Israel and Judah. The loss of sovereignty, however, combined with the divisions caused by the transportation of many of the leaders to Babylon and the later return to the land, created a quite new situation in which the 'terms of membership' had to be redefined. The emergence of the Samaritan sect and the secession of the group responsible for the Dead Sea Scrolls are only two of a number of witnesses which demonstrate that this question was not quickly resolved.

In the present study, an attempt is made to analyse one contribution to the debate. This is not by any means to imply that the Chronicler had only one purpose in writing his history; it is evident, however, that in the circumstances of his day he could hardly avoid giving some attention to this question, and furthermore it will emerge that in fact he does present a distinctive point of view which is of value in the attempt to unravel the lines of thought in a period for which we have notoriously few sources.

The work is divided into two parts. The second is devoted to a presentation of the Chronicler's concept of Israel. At an early stage in the preparation of this study, however, it was discovered that the results of previous studies of 'Israel in Chronicles' had been largely determined by an almost universally prevailing assumption, the common authorship of Chr. and Ezr.-Neh. This assumption is accordingly examined in Part One.

Two main attitudes have dominated the approach of critical scholarship to our topic, the one being a direct extension of the other. The earliest view was propounded in what is now generally regarded as the first modern work on the books of Chronicles, de Wette's *Beiträge*. In this, de Wette included a section on the Chronicler's love for Judah and hatred for Israel (pp. 126ff.), and for obvious reasons this view was adopted without question by all subsequent writers.

Introduction

Our interest here, however, concerns rather the development of this view, an understanding of the Chronicler's ideology that may be said to have begun with Torrey.[1] It does not seem to have been noticed, however, this his starting point for detecting an anti-Samaritan *Tendenz* was a desire to refute Meyer's arguments in favour of the authenticity of the Persian documents in Ezra.[2] Only in a subsequent article did Torrey develop this idea in the books of Chronicles themselves,[3] and then with a reference back to his earlier remarks as justifying this approach in Chr. as a whole.[4]

Torrey's view did not receive much attention for some considerable time,[5] but it finally became accepted by a wide range of scholars through the influence of Noth's study.[6] In dealing with 'Die theologische Leitgedanken' of Chronicles, however, Noth acknowledged his great debt to von Rad's well-known monograph,[7] and it is indeed to the section of this work on 'Das Volk'[8] that we must look for the detailed

[1] According to the English translation of his *Prolegomena*, Wellhausen mentioned the Samaritans once as the real objects of the Chronicler's supposed polemic against the Northern Kingdom (p. 188), but in fact Wellhausen wrote only of 'die Samarier' without any indication that he intended thereby a reference to the later Samaritans; cf. J. Wellhausen: *Prolegomena*, p. 182.

[2] C. C. Torrey: 'Aramaic Portions', in which, on pp. 220ff., he seeks to answer Meyer's argument that there is no discernible *Tendenz* to suggest fabrication of these documents. In reply, Torrey stresses as one of the main purposes of the documents 'the triumph over the Samaritans' (p. 225).

[3] Torrey: 'The Chronicler as Editor'.

[4] *Idem*, p. 157: 'As I have already pointed out, and as will appear still more fully in the sequel, the Chronicler's great task was to establish the supreme authority of the Jerusalem cultus, in all its details (see this *Journal*, vol. XXIV, pp. 223–26).' Thus we can see that, without hesitation, Torrey moved straight back from Ezra to the books of Chr.

[5] The first commentary to appear after Torrey's articles was the ICC volume by Curtis and Madsen (1910). Though they cite the articles in their bibliography (p. 54), they do not seem to have had any material effect on the commentary itself in this respect, except in an odd comment on 2 Chr. 13:7, on pp. 375f. Elmslie's commentary in the Cambridge Bible series (1916) accepts wholeheartedly the viewpoint of Torrey (cf. especially pp. xxxviii–xli) with such remarks as 'it seems very probable that the Chronicler's work was directed specifically against the Samaritans' (p. xxxix), but the major commentary of this period, that of Rothstein and Hänel on 1 Chronicles (1927), relegates the subject to a very minor theme (cf. pp. xxviiff., where again the evidence of Ezra is mainly appealed to, and pp. 376f., where anti-Samaritan polemic is considered possible at 1 Chr. 22:1).

[6] M. Noth: *US*.

[7] At the start of his section on the Chronicler's main theological themes, Noth writes: 'Nachdem G. v. Rad der Theologie des Chronisten eine ausführliche und vorzügliche monographische Behandlung hat zuteilwerden lassen, kann sich die folgende Ausführung kurz fassen, und sich auf die Hauptpunkte beschränken' (Noth: *US*, p. 171).

[8] G. von Rad: *Geschichtsbild*, pp. 18–37.

formulation of what is now so widely accepted as the Chronicler's teaching on the concept of Israel. Whilst the substance of von Rad's exegesis will be dealt with later in our discussion, it is instructive to notice at this point how von Rad set about his task. After asking 'wo muss da die Untersuchung einsetzen?' (p. 18), he acknowledges the problems that the nature of the books of Chronicles themselves pose, and concludes: 'Nicht ebenso liegen die Dinge bei den Quellenschriften von Esra und Nehemia. Hier hören wir die Stimme von Männern, die dem Chronist zeitlich und theologisch ungleich näher standen; hier liegt guter Grund vor, Ansätze und Anbahnungen auch besonderer chronistischer Gedanken vorauszusetzen' (p. 19). Similarly, after his analysis of Ezra and Nehemiah, he concludes: 'Von da aus wird nun die Anschauung des Chronisten über Israel deutlicher' (p. 24). There can be no doubt, therefore, that all the major analyses of the Chronicler's view of Israel that have come up with an exclusivist answer have started from results based on examination of Ezr.-Neh.

In contrast to this, the studies that have produced opposite conclusions have started from examination of Chr. alone. Thus Welch's work[1] tends to stress throughout the continued contacts between Judah and Israel, though without formulating them into the expression of a specific stress by the Chronicler. Danell[2] sees in Chr. a development of 'the idea of pan-Israelism which is undeniably a leading tendency' (p. 280), and if he later tends to modify this view (pp. 284–6), then it is only, as Japhet has correctly observed,[3] because he still maintains the unity of Chr.-Ezr.-Neh.

The four major works that have appeared recently on Chr. all maintain that he is not anti-Samaritan, Japhet[4] on the basis that the author of Chr. is quite separate from Ezr.-Neh., Willi[5] (followed by Welten[6]) on the basis that they are separate works, though written in fact by the same man, and Mosis[7] alone maintaining continuity of authorship. For Mosis, however, the subject is of subsidiary importance only, and he deals with it only in so far as it might clash with his own distinctive approach to Chr. (Along similar lines to these, we may add in passing, statements have been advanced concerning the Chronicler's eschatology,[8] his messianism[9] and his understanding of theocracy.[10])

[1] A. C. Welch: *The Work of the Chronicler.*   [2] G. A. Danell: *Israel*, ch. VI.
[3] S. Japhet: *Ideology*, p. 274.   [4] *Ibid.* p. 4.   [5] T. Willi, pp. 176–84.
[6] P. Welten, pp. 172f. with p. 4, n. 15.   [7] R. Mosis, pp. 11–16 and 205ff.
[8] Cf. Rudolph, p. xxiii, followed notably by O. Plöger: *Theokratie und Eschatologie*; W. Th. In der Smitten: 'Aufnahme der Nehemiaschrift', pp. 215–21.
[9] See, for instance, P. R. Ackroyd: *The Age of the Chronicler*, p. 50, and A.-M. Brunet: 'Théologie'.
[10] E.g. A. Noordtzij: 'Intentions'; Rudolph: 'Problems', where he writes: 'What is the purpose of the Chronicler's work? In answering this question,

Introduction

It is clear, therefore, that if our conclusions about 'Israel in Chronicles' are to be firmly based, the question of the extent of the Chronicler's work must be settled first. This is accordingly undertaken in Part One. A discussion of 1 Chr. 1–9 is also included, since that too has a bearing on the later discussion.

> scholars frequently go astray because they isolate the Books of Chronicles and forget that they are continued in Ezra and Nehemiah. If we look at the *whole* work of the Chronicler, then the question of purpose can only be answered in this way: It is to present the realisation of theocracy in Israel' (p. 404).

PART ONE

The Extent of the Chronicler's Work

For the past 150 years, the view has reigned almost unchallenged that the books of Chronicles, Ezra and Nehemiah were originally all part of a single work. Although there had been some who earlier hinted at this idea,[1] it was in 1832 that L. Zunz[2] set out the evidence which, with later additions and refinements, convinced the overwhelming majority of scholars. Confirmation of this statement may be found by reference to virtually any modern commentary or introduction written from that time down to the present day.[3]

Four main arguments have been advanced in favour of this view:[4]

1. The presence of the opening sentences of Ezr. at the end of 2 Chr.
2. The evidence of 1 Esdras, which starts at 2 Chr. 35 and continues without interruption into Ezr.

[1] Cf. Willi, p. 37.   [2] L. Zunz: *Vorträge*, ch. 2.

[3] The small number of those who have rejected this consensus only emphasizes the point. They include W. M. L. de Wette: *Lehrbuch*, pp. 262 and 265; E. König: *Einleitung*, p. 285; A. C. Welch: *Post-Exilic Judaism*, pp. 185–7; M. H. Segal: 'The Books of Ezra-Nehemiah'; W. A. L. Elmslie (*IB*), pp. 345–8 and 547; E. J. Young: *Introduction*, p. 390; B. Mazar: 'Chronicles'; J. Liver: 'History and Historiography'; R. K. Harrison: *Introduction*, pp. 1149f. More recently, it has been suggested that the Chronicler originally extended his work only as far as the end of Ezr. 6: D. N. Freedman: 'Purpose', V. Pavlovsky: 'Chronologie' and F. M. Cross: 'Reconstruction'. The only major work directed specifically against the consensus, however, is the article by S. Japhet: 'The Supposed Common Authorship'. Whilst some scholars appear to have been influenced by this article (e.g. R. L. Braun: 'Solomonic Apologetic'), no other work, so far as I am aware, has been devoted specifically to this question. (J. D. Newsome: 'Toward a New Understanding', was published only after the completion of this work.)

[4] It is not necessary for our present purposes to discuss the original form of Ezr.-Neh. A number of scholars, for instance, argue that the Nehemiah Memoir was only added much later (e.g. K.-F. Pohlmann: *Studien*), whilst others suggest that parts of the Ezra material are out of order in their present form (e.g. W. Rudolph: *Esra und Nehemia*, p. xxii). Such questions do not immediately affect the question of the extent of the Chronicler's work, for sufficient material remains for analysis without recourse to the disputed material. Naturally, where these points may touch on our discussion in a secondary way, they will be given due attention.

3. The similarity between the books in style and choice of vocabulary.

4. The similarity of outlook, interests and theology.

Whilst it may be argued that these points have a cumulative effect, they must in the first instance, at least, be examined individually. It should be stressed that it is recognized that these books do all treat similar themes and interests, and that there is a chronological continuity that none can gainsay. Whether these themes are treated from the same angle, however, or whether these points are sufficient to prove identity of authorship is another question.

2 Chronicles 36: 22f. and Ezra 1: 1–3a

L. Zunz,[1] and most scholars since, have argued first for the common authorship of Chr. and Ezr.-Neh. from the observation that the ending of Chr. and the beginning of Ezr. are verbally almost identical. It is held that when the books were separated, an overlap was left to make clear the original connection. Representative of the explanations as to why this separation should have taken place at all is that of CM:

> The separation in the Canon is apparently due to the fact that the contents of Ezra-Nehemiah were regarded as the more important, since its narrative was a proper continuation of the sacred history already canonised in 1 and 2 S. and 1 and 2 K., and its narrative chronologically concluded the history of Israel; while Chronicles was only supplementary to 1 and 2 S. and 1 and 2 K., and therefore was not at first very highly valued and was only at a later period received into the Canon.[2]

In a few introductions, almost the whole case for identity of authorship is seemingly made to hang on this point,[3] whilst many scholars list it as being first in significance.[4] However, the evidence in itself, and the explanations of the present text, are ambiguous.

A. INTERNAL CONSIDERATIONS

(1) Identity of authorship is not the only logical conclusion to draw from the fact of the overlap, and indeed, some have taken it to imply precisely the reverse. Welch, for instance, has maintained that 'men do not take the trouble to stitch together two documents, unless they have been originally separate'.[5] Rudolph himself has used just this kind

[1] L. Zunz: *Vorträge*, p. 19.
[2] CM, p. 3.
[3] E.g. W. Rudolph: *Esra und Nehemia*, p. xxii; A. Bentzen: *Introduction*, p. 205.
[4] Notable examples include G. W. Anderson: *Introduction*, p. 215; W. O. E. Oesterley and T. H. Robinson: *Introduction*, p. 110; A. Weiser: *Einleitung*, p. 284; H. H. Rowley: *Growth*, p. 162.
[5] A. C. Welch: *Post-Exilic Judaism*, p. 186.

of argument in order to explain the rather abrupt ending of 1 Esdras: 'Die Worte κ. επισ. aber sind nichts als eine Glosse, die darauf aufmerksam machen wollte, dass der Text anderswo noch eine Fortsetzung hat; hätte es damals schon Kapitel- und Verszahlen gegeben, so hätte es geheissen: Fortsetzung s. Neh. 8 13ff.'[1]

On the other hand, Harrison[2] has suggested that the only real literary parallel we have for this phenomenon is the use of a *Stichzeile* in Babylonian colophons. Harrison gives no documentation to support this view, but we may perhaps point to the work of Hunger, who describes the device thus: 'Die Stichzeile kommt bei Tafeln vor, die Teil einer Serie sind, und ist mit der ersten Zeile (oder wenigstens mit den ersten Wörtern) der folgenden Tafeln identisch. Ihr Zweck ist es, beim Vorlesen den Übergang von einer Tafel zur anderen zu erleichtern ... Sie steht meist vor den eigentlichen Kolophon.'[3] If this is a true parallel to our text, then it must argue in favour of the original continuity of the work.

Before this be conceded, however, it must be observed that it would be unique in the OT,[4] even though there are instances where we might otherwise expect such a device. We know hardly anything about the original materials for the writing of the Biblical texts,[5] but if the Deuteronomic history were indeed conceived in its present form as a single work,[6] it must have been broken up at some points. More pertinently, the same would probably have applied to the books of Chr. themselves. Thus if the *Stichzeile* were the work of the original author, why has no trace of the device survived elsewhere? It seems to be the case of a situation where, if on other grounds the unity were proved, the Babylonian parallel could be adduced as illustration, but in itself the Babylonian material is not strong enough to prove the case in question.

(2) Japhet[7] seems to go much further and suggest that 2 Chr. 36: 22f. represents the original ending of the Chronicler's work, as though the overlap were not a conscious device of any sort, but rather quite fortuitous. This, it must be made clear, is not stated in her article, but it seems to be an inevitable concomitant of her discussion on pp. 338–41. Here she observes that in Ezr.-Neh. there are eighty theophoric names

---

[1] W. Rudolph: *Esra und Nehemia*, p. xv.

[2] R. K. Harrison: *Introduction*, p. 1169.

[3] H. Hunger: *Kolophone*, p. 1.

[4] The suggestion of E. Nestlé ('Zur Frage nach der ursprünglichen Einheit') that the overlap in the LXX of I–II and III–IV Reigns provides a parallel is not convincing because the overlap of Chr.–Ezr. is so very much longer.

[5] Though cf. D. J. Wiseman: 'Books in the Ancient Near East'.

[6] M. Noth: *US*, pp. 3–12, established this widely, though not universally, accepted theory.

[7] S. Japhet: 'The Supposed Common Authorship'.

with the ending -*yh*, mentioned altogether almost two hundred and seventy times. There is only one exceptional case of the longer ending -*yhw*, and this may be due to scribal error (Ezr. 10: 41).[1] In Chr., however, 'the first outstanding fact is the variety of material in which both short and long endings occur'. Japhet concludes her discussion of this point by saying 'in spite of the existence of names with the יה ending it is impossible to deny the general tendency to use the long ending יהו. The difference between Chronicles and Ezra-Nehemiah is clearly expressed in a parallel text:

2 Chr. 36: 22   לכלות דבר ה׳ בפי ירמיהו

Ezra 1: 1   ׳.לכלות דבר ה׳ מפי ירמיה

It seems clear, therefore, that this involves attributing 2 Chr. 36: 22 to the original work of the Chronicler.

Against such a view, however, it must be urged that the form in Chr. might well have been influenced by the preceding verse, where already there is reference to the *dbr yhwh bpy yrmyhw*. Thus, the text of Ezr. 1: 1 might have stood here and later been assimilated by a scribe to the form in the earlier verse. This could explain too the difference between the readings *bpy* and *mpy*. This must have taken place quite early, however, as the LXX seems to support the MT here, reading *dia* for 2 Chr., and *apo* for Ezr. 1. This does not, of course, detract from Japhet's point as a whole; it merely combats the implication that 2 Chr. 36: 22 is necessarily original to the Chronicler.

2 Chr. 36: 22f. has all the appearance of being extracted from Ezr. 1: 1. The break at *weyā'al* would be quite unnatural, and if indeed, as more recent scholars are now willing to agree, a genuine document lies behind the edict of Cyrus,[2] it is difficult to see why the Chronicler did not include it in full. On the assumption that Chr. was written after Ezr.-Neh., it is conceivable that the Chronicler wished to indicate to his readers where the continuation of the story might be found, but we must ask whether he has not already in fact done this without the artificial inclusion of 2 Chr. 36: 22f.

2 Chr. 36: 11–20a gives an account of the fall of Jerusalem at the hands of Nebuchadnezzar. Verses 20b–21, however, already point us forward to the end of the exile, and give a clear indication of the libera-

---

[1] Cf. W. Rudolph: *Esra und Nehemia*, p. 100.

[2] Before 1946, the genuineness of Ezr. 1: 2–4 in containing an original document was widely discounted. In that year, however, E. Bickermann wrote vigorously in its defence ('The Edict of Cyrus'). He has succeeded in convincing a number of scholars, including the two most recent commentators, J. M. Myers: *Ezra. Nehemiah*, p. 5 and L. H. Brockington: *Ezra, Nehemiah and Esther*, pp. 14f. and 48f.

tion to be granted by the Persians (v. 20a). Furthermore, since v. 21 refers to the fulfilment of Jeremiah's prophecy within a specific time limit, the theme of restoration would have already suggested itself to the Chronicler's original readers. This, we would argue, furnishes from every point of view a more satisfying conclusion to the work than the fragmentary v. 23.

We conclude, therefore, that of all the possibilities still open, the one certainty is that if the Chronicler was not responsible for Ezr.-Neh., he was not responsible for 2 Chr. 36: 22f. either.

B. EXTERNAL CONSIDERATIONS

As we have not found it possible to conclude that the overlap automatically demands unity of authorship, external considerations must also be examined.

(1) It is apparently agreed that the kind of explanation represented above by CM is entirely speculative. Eissfeldt, for instance, has to admit after his discussion of this point: 'So lassen sich, ohne dass wir im einzelnen über Vermutungen hinauskommen könnten, schon die Gründe ausfindig machen, die für das Zustandekommen des dritten Teils der kanonischen Bücher unserer hebräischen Bibel massgebend gewesen sind.'[1]

If, then, we are in the realm of 'Vermutungen', it is entirely legitimate to ask whether in fact the theory is inherently probable. Do we have any instance in the process of canonization of a book being divided up and only that part retained which does not repeat material found elsewhere? On the contrary, it is most striking to find that even so close a reproduction of a separate work as is found in Isa. 36–9 is nevertheless faithfully retained, and, again in contrast, if the usual view of the authorship of Isaiah and many other OT books is correct, the tendency was to add to works already established, rather than to subtract from them. Furthermore, whilst indeed Chr. often runs closely parallel to Sam.-Ki., yet it must be at once apparent that it contains a very great deal of its own material which we might suppose a later generation would be anxious to preserve. Finally, if Chr. were originally excluded from the Canon, why was it later introduced?

(2) In a short, but extremely important, section of his recent book,[2] Willi has in fact gone a step further than this. In his view, what evidence we have of the history of canonization points to an original distinction between Chr. and Ezr.-Neh.

Against the normal view, he first points out that in fact the canonicity

---

[1] O. Eissfeldt: *Einleitung*, p. 768.   [2] T. Willi, pp. 176–84.

of Chr. was never disputed, and that there is no evidence to suggest that Chr. was accepted into the Canon later than Ezr.-Neh.: 'Ihre abgeleitete Kanonizität ist dort, wo sie recht verstanden wurde, niemals ange-fochten gewesen, und im Gegensatz zu der üblichen Ansicht wird man es als höchst wahrscheinlich, ja als sicher annehmen dürfen, dass sie mindestens zugleich mit dem anderen Werk wohl desselben Verfassers, Esra-Nehemia, kanonisiert wurde.'[1] The substance of Willi's point holds true, of course, whether or not we accept that both works were written by the same author.

Willi goes on secondly to argue that the works are found separately in the Canon because they were in fact written separately. The modern theory that Chr. was not at first canonized because it contains passages also found in Sam.-Ki. rests on a misunderstanding. Canonization was a *declarative* act, acknowledging the inherent authority of a given work, and not a selective act, based upon the particular contents of that work.[2] Thus, the history of the Palestinian,[3] as well as the Alexandrian, Canon points to the inclusion of two originally separate works.

Finally, Willi makes the point that if Chr. and Ezr.-Neh. had origi-nally been canonized as a single work, there would have been no reason later to divide it up and reverse the order. Rather, the opposite is true: some collections have understandably inserted Chr. before Ezr.-Neh.[4] That the dominant tradition of its in fact being last has come down to us argues for the originality of the order as we have it. For Willi, there-fore, external considerations argue for the original separation of the two books.

(3) To these considerations, we may add a further point. Not only in the MT are the two books separated, but also in the LXX. It is now generally agreed that the Paralipomena should be dated in the second century B.C.[5] If so, we would have to suppose, on the basis of the modern scholarly consensus, that the postulated process of selective canonization took place soon after the composition. However, the further back we push this date, the nearer we come to the very community whose institutions Chr. is thought to legitimize. The theory is thus rendered less probable.

We may conclude, therefore, that whilst on internal grounds there is nothing in the overlap of the end of Chr. and the beginning of Ezr. to demand unity of authorship, the external evidence inclines us to pre-suppose diversity of authorship.

---

[1] *Ibid.* p. 179.   [2] *Ibid.* p. 180.
[3] Reference is made particularly to the well-known section of the tractate Baba Bathra, 14b. For English readers, this can be conveniently found in the Soncino edition of the Babylonian Talmud, edited by I. Epstein, 11, 69–71.
[4] These are listed by Willi at p. 181, n. 12.   [5] Cf. below, pp. 14f.

The Evidence of the Greek Versions[1]

In seeking to determine the extent of the Chronicler's work, the evidence of 1 Esdras has been used in two ways: the fact that it begins at 2 Chr. 35: 1 and continues through into Ezr. without a break (and without the overlap of the end of 2 Chr. and the beginning of Ezr.) is said to show that this is the original condition of the text.[2] Secondly, many scholars have gone further and claimed that 1 Esdras in fact represents for the most part the original ending of the Chronicler's work. Since the latter suggestion naturally involves the former, the two may be dealt with together.

It is fortunate that the recent work by K.-F. Pohlmann[3] sets out to justify precisely this position. The work takes full account of previous discussion and arranges its material in an orderly and coherent manner. It will be simplest, therefore, to follow the order of Pohlmann's work here, though because some sections will need more detailed treatment than others, I shall use my own enumeration.

A. PRELIMINARY CONSIDERATIONS

The first thirty or so pages of Pohlmann's book constitute a clear statement of the problem in hand and a brief survey of the major positions that have been held in the past concerning it. In order to clear the ground of a few of the many suggestions that have been put forward, we may agree that since Nestlé's work[4] it has not been possible to hold to

[1] In view of the different ways in which the books to be considered are named, it will be as well to set out the system of reference used here:

1 Esdras = the Greek apocryphal Esdras, known as Esdras *a* in the LXX, and as 3 Esra in most German scholarship (following the Vulgate). 3 Esra will only be used where it appears in direct quotations, titles of books, etc. Esdras *b* = the Greek translation of Ezr.-Neh. Par(alipomena) = the Greek translation of Chr. It should be further noted that the numbering of verses is often different in the English and Greek versions of 1 Esdras. In what follows, the Greek system will be followed, unless otherwise stated.

[2] E.g. H. H. Howorth: *The Academy* 43 (1893), 60; L. W. Batten: *Ezra and Nehemiah*, p. 2.   [3] K.-F. Pohlmann: *Studien*.

[4] E. Nestlé: *Marginalien*, pp. 23–9. Cf. E. Bayer: *Das dritte Buch Esdras*, pp. 147–61; R. H. Pfeiffer: *History*, pp. 237f.; H. St J. Thackeray: 'Esdras, first book of', p. 759.

Keil's position[1] that I Esdras is dependent upon Esdras *b*. Nestlé produced a number of instances where I Esdras is clearly based on an alternative reading or misunderstanding of the Hebrew text. To give just two examples, Ezr. 4: 14 begins with the difficult phrase *kol qᵉbēl dî mᵉlaḥ hêklaʾ mᵉlaḥnû* ... Esdras *b* omits the phrase altogether, but I Esdras 2: 18 has *kai epei energeitai ta kata ton naon*, which suggests that the translator must have seen (and misunderstood) *hykl'*. Again, at 2 Chr. 35: 10, *kᵉmiṣwat [hammelek]*, I Esdras 1: 10 has read with alternative pointing *bammaṣṣôt = echontes ta azuma*,[2] a misunderstanding that could not have arisen at the Greek stage only.

Furthermore, we may agree that generally speaking I Esdras does give us a translation of our MT. It does not set out to be a literal translation,[3] to be sure, but once that is agreed, the apparent divergences from the Hebrew can nearly all be explained on technical grounds.[4]

Pohlmann is also right in stressing (pp. 29f.) that the age of a translation does not necessarily determine its relationship to the *Vorlage*. He concedes, and we would stress in view of what is to follow, that as far as determining the original form of the work of the Chronicler is concerned, the greater age of I Esdras is not in itself sufficient evidence. Indeed, as Pohlmann again allows (pp. 30f.), it is not even enough to prove that I Esdras is a fragment of an originally larger work, for that larger work itself might have been the subject of change since it left the Chronicler's hand. Thus, if on internal gounds (as in the last section of his book Pohlmann seeks to do) we are satisfied that I Chr.-Ezr. 10/Neh. 8 is an original and unified composition, then I Esdras could be adduced as valuable supporting evidence. If, on the other hand, it was decided that 2 Chr. 36 furnished the original conclusion of the Chronicler's work, I Esdras could not by itself overthrow that decision. It would be necessary only to postulate additions to the Chronicler's work before the translation of I Esdras.

Whilst this latter position is possible, it is not the most desirable, since it rests in part on silence. If, however, I Esdras could be shown to be a secondary work, then that element of doubt would be removed, and we could move with more confidence towards determining the extent of the Chronicler's work on internal grounds alone. We conclude, therefore, that the following examination is justified for our overall purposes.

[1] C. F. Keil: *Einleitung*, p. 704. I have not been able to consult the third edition, where evidently the case is fully set out.
[2] Cf. B. Walde: *Die Esdrasbücher*, p. 75.
[3] W. J. Moulton: 'Überlieferung und Werth'.
[4] Cf. the careful analysis in E. Bayer: *Das dritte Buch Esdras*, pp. 11–86; compare too B. Walde: *Die Esdrasbücher*, pp. 15–26; R. H. Pfeiffer: *History*, pp. 239ff.

The Extent of the Chronicler's Work

Pohlmann deals with the question of the abrupt opening of 1 Esdras on pp. 32f. Against the attempt of Rudolph[1] to justify this, Pohlmann adduces good reasons to suggest the unlikelihood of a Greek book starting with *kai ēgagen*. From this, however, he draws a striking conclusion: 'Dann kann man aber annehmen, dass 3E Fragment einer griechischen Übersetzung war, die ursprünglich auch 1 Chr. bis 2 Chr. 34 umfasste. Das lässt sich zwar nicht beweisen, doch ist es am wahrscheinlichsten zumal sich keinerlei Gründe angeben lassen, die gegen eine derartige Annahme sprechen.'[2]

Apart from the suggestion in a footnote that the reading by Eupolemos of *ktizein* at 2 Chr. 2: 12ff. may reflect knowledge of this original extensive translation, Pohlmann gives no grounds for this sweeping suggestion. This is the more surprising, as in fact there has been a good deal of discussion as to whether 1 Esdras is a fragment of the original LXX of Chr. and Ezr.

Between 1893 and 1910, two long series of articles by Howorth[3] and Torrey[4] presented the case for a late (second century A.D.) date for Par. and Esdras *b*, Torrey stressing in particular the affinities of translation technique with that of Theodotion. Such a late date would *a priori* render very plausible the correlative view that 1 Esdras was a fragment of the 'original Septuagint' translation of Chr.-Ezr.

During the present century, however, a growing number of scholars has attacked this view.[5] First, the undeniable citation of Par. by Eupolemos argues for its existence as early as the second century B.C.[6] Secondly, there is such strong evidence in Par. for Egyptian colouring from the

---

[1] W. Rudolph: *Esra und Nehemia*, p. xiv, n. 8.

[2] In this conclusion, Pohlmann exactly follows Mowinckel, who also argues from silence to suggest that 1 Esdras was originally co-extensive with Chr. Cf. S. Mowinckel: *Studien I*, p. 19.

[3] They are listed in full in the bibliography.

[4] Torrey collected his separate works on 1 Esdras and published them together in *Ezra Studies*.

[5] A full survey may now be conveniently found in L. C. Allen: *The Greek Chronicles, Part I*, pp. 6–17. It was gratifying to find that on these matters Allen's views coincided with those reached independently by the present writer, thus obviating the need here for prolonged discussion of issues that touch only indirectly on our main interest. It need only be added that recently the whole question of transliterations in the LXX and Theodotion has been reopened in a manner that casts grave doubts on the very basis of Torrey's position; cf. E. Tov: 'Transliterations' (and earlier, A. Rahlfs: *Studien 3*, pp. 85f., n. 2).

[6] Cf. M. Rehm: *Textkritische Untersuchungen*, pp. 13 and 32f.; G. Gerleman: *Studies II*, pp. 11–13; L. C. Allen: *The Greek Chronicles, Part I*, pp. 11f.; cf. *Part II*, pp. 162–4. Esdras *b*, whose date need not be considered here, is the work of a separate translator; so B. Walde: *Die Esdrasbücher*, pp. 30–4; Gerleman: *Studies II*, pp. 6f.

Ptolemaic period,[1] that its origins must be sought in Hellenistic Alexandria, not Ephesus of the Christian era.

Pohlmann's silence about all this suggests that he considers it irrelevant, and with this Mowinckel explicitly concurs. He accepts that Walde, Rudolph and Gerleman have given 'recht schwerwiegende Argumente gegen Howorth', but then continues: 'Das ist aber für die folgende Untersuchung nebensächlich, oder richtiger: belanglos. Hauptsache ist, dass 3E die älteste griechische Übersetzung vertritt, die man später durch eine andere hat ersetzen wollen, die des Esdras β.'[2]

However, as far as 1 Esdras being a fragment of the entire work of Chr. is concerned, it is surely *a priori* extremely unlikely that two such translations should have been independently produced within what would have to be considered a comparatively short space of time. The problem becomes the more acute when we realize that both Greek versions show marked signs of Egyptian colouring, and therefore both probably originated in Alexandria. We have already mentioned the widespread acceptance of this conclusion for Par. For the Egyptian origin of 1 Esdras, we may refer to the recent commentary by Myers.[3] Following a suggestion of Pfeiffer[4] to this effect, Myers has produced an impressive collection of words where 1 Esdras differs from Esdras *b*, and has shown that they can be closely paralleled in Egyptian papyri of (mainly) the second century B.C.

Those who argue that 1 Esdras was originally co-extensive with the work of the Chronicler generally assume that our 1 Esdras was preserved because it was the only section of the whole to differ materially from our LXX. Thus Torrey suggests that

> some one, more probably a Jewish scholar, but possibly a Christian, undertook to preserve the older Greek text ... His interest was not in any particular portion of the rejected version, but simply in the matter of its deviation from the history which was now accepted ... From a surviving Greek codex of the old version, the requisite portion was taken.[5]

The difference consists primarily, however, in the inclusion of the story of the three guardsmen, which all except Howorth consider to be a later interpolation. The changes in the order of Ezr. 1–6 are thought to be consequent upon the interpolation. Now it is understandable that a need for Esdras *b* should have been felt after 1 Esdras attained

---

[1] Cf. H. St J. Thackeray: 'The Greek Translators', pp. 276f.; Gerleman: *Studies II*, ch. ii; T. N. D. Mettinger: *Solomonic State Officials*, p. 63; L. C. Allen: *The Greek Chronicles, Part I*, pp. 21–3.

[2] S. Mowinckel: *Studien I*, p. 9.

[3] J. M. Myers: *I and II Esdras*, pp. 12f.

[4] R. H. Pfeiffer: *History*, p. 249.

[5] C. C. Torrey: 'A Revised View', pp. 396f.

its present form. That work, however, as noted above (p. 14, n. 6), is to be attributed to a different translator from Par. We are thus asked to believe that Par. was produced as an alternative translation to a work which *ex hypothesi*, and on the basis of a comparison of 1 Esdras 1 with 2 Chr. 35–6, differed materially from the MT scarcely at all! In our day, new translations of the Bible may be a commonplace occurrence. With this, however, such light as we can gain on the history of LXX origins presents a marked contrast, for in Alexandria at least, and especially as far as the 'Writings' were concerned, it would seem that there was an economy of effort in order to concentrate always upon the chief tasks in hand.[1] A double translation of a book already paralleled for considerable sections in other canonical books produced in the same place and at about the same time does not fit into such a background.

Secondly, it may be suggested that 1 Esdras contains an as yet overlooked clue to the fact that it did not originally include anything like the whole of our books of Chr. There is an addition to the MT in 1: 21f. which reads (RSV, 1: 23f.):

> And the deeds of Josiah were upright in the sight of his Lord, for his heart was full of godliness. The events of his reign have been recorded in the past, concerning those who sinned and acted wickedly toward the Lord beyond any other people or kingdom, and how they grieved the Lord deeply, so that the words of the Lord rose up against Israel.

The presence of these two verses has been variously explained, though Pohlmann's silence must again suggest that he considers them irrelevant at this point. It is necessary first to determine their position in the present text, their relation to MT and Par., and then their meaning within 1 Esdras as a whole.

(1) Walde[2] considers that they constitute a gloss, not only to the MT, but to 1 Esdras itself, and that they should therefore be dismissed from study of this work. This is, first, because they disturb the connection of thought between 2 Chr. 35: 19 and 20, secondly because their estimation of Josiah contradicts that of 1 Esdras 1: 30f., and thirdly because the text of the addition is damaged. The gloss was inserted because a reader found it difficult to understand how the pious Josiah should have lost his life because of one act of disobedience, so he added the observation that not all Josiah's deeds were blameless.

This reasoning scarcely seems cogent, however. The first argument

---

[1] Cf. H. B. Swete: *Introduction*, pp. 23–7; D. Barthélemy: *Les Devanciers*, p. 141; H. St J. Thackeray: *The Septuagint and Jewish Worship*, ch. 1; O. Eissfeldt: *Einleitung*, para. 121; E. Würthwein: *Text*, pp. 36f.

[2] B. Walde: *Die Esdrasbücher*, pp. 88ff.

may show that the verses are secondary to the MT, but in view of some of the later chronological discrepancies in 1 Esdras, it is certainly not hard to believe that they could have been added at this fairly obvious point by whoever was responsible for the work in its present form. The second argument could be rejected for similar reasons, but in fact it is not even necessary to go so far, since it is not Josiah himself who is condemned in v. 22, but those 'who sinned and acted wickedly'. Finally, textual corruption is not enough, it need scarcely be said, to prove the presence of a gloss. There is thus no good reason for rejecting these two verses from the text of 1 Esdras, and sound method demands that we retain them there, unless good evidence to the contrary can be adduced.

(2) 2 Par. 35: 19 also has a long addition to the MT at this point, taken over from 2 Ki. 23: 24ff. This fact has been used by Torrey to suggest that there is a lacuna in the MT here, which can be reconstructed on the basis of the Greek.[1] This too seems to be very improbable, despite the ingenuity of Torrey's conjecture. First, the MT is in itself quite self-consistent; 2 Chr. 35: 19 is clearly the ending by way of summary of the preceding section: 'In the eighteenth year of the reign of Josiah was this passover kept.' It is equally evident that v. 20 begins a new section: 'After all this . . .'. The only point that Torrey can really urge is the reference in this verse to Josiah's temple reform: 'When Josiah had prepared the temple', of which he says: 'The allusion is to some such passage as the one translated by Theodotion (i.e. Par.), which immediately preceded these words.'[2] However, this can quite naturally apply to the whole description of Josiah's activity which precedes, the purpose being, in accordance with the Chronicler's theology, to show how despite all this, his disobedience in the matter of fighting against Neco was sufficient to bring about immediate retribution. There is nothing here to demand that we follow Torrey.

Secondly, fuller study of the text of Par. itself should have made clear that its evidence is not to be taken at face value:

(a) No one has pointed out that such evidence as we have points to the insertion in Par. being in fact in a slightly different position from that in 1 Esdras. After the insertion, 2 Par. 35: 20 starts straight off with *kai anebē pharaō Nechaō* . . ., apparently omitting the introductory time clause, and this remains the witness of the best texts (B A N a h). All the others, however, *before* the insertion, first complete the sentence (which is otherwise awkwardly attached to v. 18) *tō oktōkaidekatō etei tēs basileias Iōseia* with *epoiēthē to phasek touto*, and then use the time clause of 2 Chr. 35: 20 to define this yet more closely: *meta tauta panta*

[1] C. C. Torrey: *Ezra Studies*, p. 87–9; 'A Revised View', pp. 405–10.
[2] Torrey: *Ezra Studies*, pp. 88f.

ha ēdrasen Iōsias en tō oikō. From the point of view of the MT, this positioning is, of course, secondary, but as far as the Greek text is concerned, it constitutes the only evidence we have of the exact position of the addition, and this does not coincide exactly with 1 Esdras.

(b) More significantly, however, it is well known that 2 Par. 35–6 includes a number of substantial additions to 2 Chr. 35–6 that coincide for the most part with 2 Ki. 23. It is probable either that these additions were already in the Hebrew *Vorlage* of Par., or that the translator of Par. interpolated them himself direct from 2 Ki., rather than that they were included from 4 Reigns.[1]

It should thus be quite obvious that the evidence of Par. is almost valueless for these two chapters as a witness to any such lacuna in the text of Chr. as Torrey postulates. 2 Par. 35: 19 is merely the first of a number of such additions and should therefore not be isolated for particular treatment.[2]

By contrast, it is to be observed that 1 Esdras 1: 21f. is a quite different case. First, it is the only significant addition to the narrative of 2 Chr. 35–6 which the book contains. Secondly, it is not a 'natural' addition from a parallel text, but one composed from a number of elements extracted from originally quite different contexts. Since, as we have seen, it is integral to the text of 1 Esdras, but was never included in the Hebrew text of Chr., we feel justified in examining it for any possible light it may shed on the problem of 1 Esdras as a whole.

(3) 1 Esdras 1: 21f. is occasioned by the untimely death of a pious king, and also, as v. 22 makes clear, by the wider problem of the exile itself. For both these events, Ki. and Chr. offer different explanations.

In Ki., the impression is most definitely given of an accumulation of guilt which eventually not even the good deeds of Josiah could counterbalance. This began with Manasseh, who 'seduced them to do that which is evil more than did the nations, whom the Lord destroyed before the children of Israel', 2 Ki. 21: 9. This may be a conscious allusion back to Dt. 9: 4f., where the peoples of Canaan were themselves dispossessed before the Israelites because of their wickedness. The implication is that if Israel surpasses them in this, they can expect the same treatment. Thus, in 2 Ki. 21: 10ff., God promises that He will destroy Jerusalem because of Manasseh and because they 'have provoked me to anger, since the day their fathers came forth out of Egypt', 2 Ki. 21: 15. These twin themes then recur like a refrain

[1] So with L. C. Allen: 'Further Thoughts' and *The Greek Chronicles, Part I*, pp. 213–16, against R. W. Klein: 'New Evidence' and 'Supplements in the Paralipomena'. I had already, in fact, reached this conclusion on other grounds before becoming aware of Allen's work.
[2] Cf. W. Rudolph, p. 330.

through until the exile: 2 Ki. 22: 16f., 23: 26f., 24: 3f., 24: 20. In this context, the early death of Josiah is interpreted as a blessing for him personally, so that he should not see the evil that is about to overtake Jerusalem (2 Ki. 22: 20). This is granted to him because of his personal piety (vv. 18f.).

In Chr., the picture is quite different, in that no guilt is 'held over', if it may be thus crudely expressed, from one reign to another; conversely, as is often remarked, the Chronicler is at pains to draw out the completeness of retribution in each life. Thus, whilst he too records the heinousness of Manasseh's sin, yet he shows that this brought down immediate divine wrath in the form of Manasseh himself being exiled until he repented (2 Chr. 33: 11–13). The exile itself is stated to be due to the sin of Zedekiah and those living in his day alone (2 Chr. 36: 12–17), with only the theme of the exilic period as the land enjoying its Sabbaths (2 Chr. 36: 21) giving any indication of accumulated guilt. In this setting, the death of Josiah naturally acquires new significance: it is true that the Chronicler takes over from Ki. the prophecy of Huldah on the occasion of the finding of the law book in the temple, but he seems to place little weight upon it in comparison with the theme of Josiah's disobedience in the matter of going out to fight against Neco: he 'hearkened not unto the words of Neco, from the mouth of God, and came to fight in the valley of Megiddo. And the archers shot at king Josiah' (2 Chr. 35: 22f.).

The theology of immediate retribution was evidently considered by most people to be either too rigid or too hard to reconcile with experience, and this may account in part for the additions in 2 Par. 35 and 36. Similar considerations too may have occasioned the reinterpretation of the Chronicler's theology by the compiler of 1 Esdras in 1: 21f. Here the emphatic assertion that Josiah was upright (v. 21), is then balanced with the view that the sins of others were still sufficient to condemn Israel (v. 22). The words echo precisely the judgment on Manasseh's reign already mentioned in both 2 Ki. 21: 9 and 2 Chr. 33: 9, and the reference – *en tois emprosthen chronois*[1] – makes it clear that the reader is expected to appreciate this. The question at once arises, however, why the reference is not made explicit. The answer seems clear. Whereas 2 Par. 35: 19 made an addition from Ki. whose theological force is the same as the addition here, he was there able to refer to Manasseh because he had dealt with the events of his reign

[1] The use of *chronos* is superficially ambiguous here, since the word is used in 1 Esdras both of time (which may be the distant past, cf. 1: 20 *apo tōn chronōn Samouēl*, 8: 73 *apo tōn chronōn tōn paterōn hēmōn*) and of written records, 'Chronicles' (cf. 1: 40 *en tē biblō tōn chronōn tōn basileōn*). The context of our verse clearly favours the latter meaning, however, against RSV: 'recorded in the past'.

earlier in the narrative, 2 Par. 33. For our author, however, the situation must evidently have been different: it can only be that his narrative started at some point after the reign of Manasseh. Had 1 Esdras covered, say, the whole of 1 and 2 Chr., as Pohlmann maintains, we should be unable to account either for his veiled reference here, or for the telescoping of the presentation in such a way that the events of Manasseh's day are referred to Josiah's reign, without the kind of interpretation offered by 2 Ki. 23: 26ff. and 2 Par. 35: 19.[1] We conclude, therefore, that if, as seems probable, the opening of 1 Esdras is damaged, yet not so very much has been lost. It may well have started with the accession of Josiah to the throne and the account of his temple reforms (2 Chr. 34: 1), though about this, of course, we can only guess.

In conclusion, therefore, we may say that Par. is to be dated before 150 B.C. It thus seems improbable that 1 Esdras, coming from the same time and place, should have been co-extensive with it.

1 Esdras 1: 21f. is integral to the text of 1 Esdras, but was never part of the MT. It points to a beginning of 1 Esdras later than the reign of Manasseh. Moreover, as against Chr., it introduces a distinct interpretation of the events of the end of the Judean kingdom. Inasmuch as it does not simply follow the Kings' *Vorlage* (as does Par.), it should be seen as a conscious reinterpretation by the author of 1 Esdras of his *Vorlage*.

These two points together show that 1 Esdras is not a fragment of the original LXX of Chr.-Ezr.-Neh. It must therefore have been written for a distinct purpose, which determined (amongst other things) its extent. We should in consequence beware of drawing from it conclusions about the original form and extent of the Chronicler's work.

Par. deviates sharply from its *Vorlage* at precisely the point where 1 Esdras begins. This is based on an independent translation from the Hebrew, and not on the Greek 4 Reigns. Esdras *b* is the work of a separate translator.[2] The additions in 2 Par. 35 and 36 are theologically comparable to 1 Esdras 1: 21f. This leaves Chr. as the unique witness to its particular interpretation of the exile; its message of immediate retribution, however, has the converse of immediate reward for faithfulness, no doubt intended to encourage its original readers. Later, there may have been a need for self-justification in face of the contrast between the glories of monarchical days and the prevailing disappoint-

---

[1] Torrey overlooks the significance of this in his reconstruction, because he too hastily assumes that there is a lacuna in the text before making a full effort to understand it as it now stands. Certainly there is evidence of corruption in the later clause *kai ha elupēsan auton estin* (cf. Rudolph, p. 331), but this does not affect the earlier part of the verse which is our primary concern here, nor does it affect the interpretation offered above.

[2] Or translators; cf. S. Jellicoe: 'Some Reflections'.

ing conditions. If 1 Esdras addressed itself to this task, then we can understand both why there was not felt an earlier need to translate again the Ezra story, and why Par., which otherwise runs close to Chr., could deviate so markedly in its closing chapters.[1]

C. THE ENDING OF 1 ESDRAS AND THE WITNESS OF JOSEPHUS

Pohlmann discusses the ending of 1 Esdras in three sections of his book, first as a problem in itself (pp. 34f.), secondly in the light of the witness of Josephus (pp. 107–12), and thirdly in the context of his understanding of the original conclusion of the Chronicler's work as whole (pp. 127–48). The third of these sections deals with problems rather different from those raised by 1 Esdras. Inasmuch as it builds upon the critical foundations laid in the earlier part of the work, we may set it aside from the present discussion for the reasons given above on p. 13.[2]

1 Esdras ends abruptly with the words *kai episunēchthēsan* 'and they came together'. Hardly a single modern scholar has sought to justify this as the intended conclusion of a self-contained work.[3] Rudolph

[1] There are, in fact, two other deviations of Par. from its *Vorlage* that look as though they might be of significance within the context of the debate in the post-exilic community both about the position Judah should adopt towards its neighbours and towards its Persian, and later Ptolemaic, overlords. It is noteworthy, however, that they again occur within these last two chapters where there is an overlap with 1 Esdras: (a) In 2 Par. 36: 5 *kai tēs Samareias* is added gratuitously to the list of invading bands in 2 Ki. 24: 2. (b) 2 Par. 36: 20 sees the exile lasting until the 'establishment of the kingdom of the Medes', rather than the Persians of 2 Chr. 36: 20.

[2] Nevertheless, it may be noted that actually the chiastic structure upon which Pohlmann builds is not so neat as his table on p. 148 suggests. First, it entirely ignores the Passover celebration at the end of Ezr. 6, even though on any showing this feast is of great significance in the structure of Ezra. Secondly, it does not take into account the fact that the feast in Neh. 8 was Tabernacles, not Passover.

[3] E. Bayer: *Das dritte Buch Esdras*, pp. 89–92, seems to be the only really serious attempt to understand the present ending. He observes first of all that if a stop is put before the final two words (as in most printed editions), the *kai* at the beginning of the verse becomes redundant. He then suggests that the compiler of the book (who worked in Hebrew and Aramaic) misread *wbywm* in v. 13 as *wb'w*. This was then translated at a later stage as in our texts, and should be taken as the conclusion of the sentence, not the start of a new one. Bayer thinks that Neh. 8: 1–12 provides a suitable conclusion in view of the purpose of the work as a whole ('de restitutione templi').

This does not really seem to solve the problem, however, for *wb'w* is as difficult an ending for a Hebrew book as *kai episunēchthēsan* for our present book. If the force of the *ky* is to continue to cover this verb as well as *hbynw* it would need to be repeated. Furthermore, as Pohlmann observes, Bayer's solution demands that one word of Neh. 8: 13 be drawn into consideration; but once this is conceded, *n'spw* provides, as everyone else agrees, the obvious *Vorlage* for *episunēchthēsan*.

himself in effect concedes this point when he suggests that 'die Worte κ. επισ. aber sind nichts als eine Glosse, die darauf aufmerksam machen wollte, dass der Text anderswo noch eine Fortsetzung hat; hätte es damals schon Kapitel- und Verszahlen gegeben, so hätte es geheissen: "Fortsetzung s. Neh. 8: 13ff." '.[1] Three problems arise here, however; first, Rudolph is unable to provide a parallel for this primitive style of footnote, whereas both the Biblical texts themselves and many other writings from the Ancient Near East provide any number of examples to suggest that writers were not afraid of repetition of long sections of their own or other people's works. Secondly, it is not at all certain that *kai episunēchthēsan* would be sufficient as a gloss for a reader to appreciate what was intended. If the reference is to the Hebrew text, we would expect a translation of *wbywm hšny*; if to the Greek text, then we must note that Esdras *b* 8: 13 reads *kai en tē hēmera tē deutera sunēchthēsan* . . ., which is not at all the same. Thirdly, we may question whether Neh. 8: 12 provides in any case a suitable conclusion to the work, as Rudolph supposes. Whilst no doubt much of 1 Esdras is concerned with the temple, this is by no means exclusively so, and certainly not to the extent of excluding as unsuitable (as Rudolph states) the reference in v. 16 to the people celebrating the feast of booths in a number of places, since included in the list is, after all, 'the courts of the house of God'. Nor does the alteration to 'the broad place before the east gate of the temple' from 'the broad place that was in front of the water gate' (Neh. 8: 1) seem sufficient to prove that the narrative could not have extended beyond v. 12. Stronger evidence than this is required to refute the evident implication of our text that the end of 1 Esdras has been broken off.

Thus far, then, we may agree with Pohlmann, who concludes his first section on this subject by maintaining with reference to the views of Bayer and Rudolph, 'dagegen erklärt die Annahme, die sich eigentlich von selbst anbietet, dass nämlich 3E auch am Schluss nur fragmentarisch erhalten ist, den gegenwärtigen Zustand des Textes am besten' (p. 34). To determine the original extent of 1 Esdras, however, Pohlmann then refers us forward to his discussion of the witness of Josephus. To follow him in this will demand first some general remarks as to the use of Josephus in this connection as a whole.

1. *Josephus and 1 Esdras*

Pohlmann's long chapter entitled 'Das Zeugnis des Josephus' (pp. 74-126) may be simply summarized.

(a) In his *Antiquities* XI, 1-158, Josephus followed our 1 Esdras quite closely. This is shown not only by the choice and order of the

---

[1] W. Rudolph: *Esra und Nehemia*, p. xv.

material, but also by the influence on the vocabulary and phraseology in Josephus, which, particularly in the case of 'documents', is often very marked (pp. 76–89).

(b) Where Josephus deviates appreciably from 1 Esdras, there are always internal factors to suggest the reason: he removed some of the worst of the chronological discrepancies, omitted repetitive material and so on. There is no evidence of embellishment from our canonical books of Ezr.-Neh.

(c) The Nehemiah narrative is dealt with in *Ant.* XI, 159–83. This follows Neh. 1–7: 4 quite closely, although it makes Nehemiah responsible for the completion of the temple as well as the city walls (XI, 165, 169). However, Josephus' silence about the events from the remainder of Neh. shows that his *Vorlage* did not contain the events of these chapters. From his presentation of the Nehemiah material, we must conclude that he did not know the books of Ezr. and Neh. in their present form (pp. 114–26).

There is nothing here, therefore, Pohlmann maintains, to overthrow his conclusion that 1 Esdras is independent of the canonical books, and thus can have furnished the original conclusion to the Chronicler's work.

In this, as in other matters, however, Pohlmann neither acknowledges the problems inherent in his own position, nor does full justice to alternative explanations of the facts. The major problem that he passes over concerns the conclusion of Josephus' presentation of Nehemiah. On Pohlmann's view, he had the Nehemiah source in front of him in its original form, and not, as now, interspersed at its conclusion with other material.[1] Why, then, did he not include the later material? It is indeed a coincidence that he should have broken off at just the point where the canonical compiler also broke off; yet on the reconstruction offered below, this can all be quite naturally explained.

Secondly, as is shown below in section D, there is good evidence to support the contention that the compiler of 1 Esdras knew the setting of Neh. 8 after Neh. 7, and not after Ezr. 10. It follows from this that the *Antiquities* should not be brought in as evidence for the earlier form of the literature, except perhaps in matters of detail. How, then, are the facts to be explained? The answer is not far to seek, and I offer the following simple reconstruction as being more satisfactory to the case as a whole than that of Pohlmann.

No one can deny that Josephus used 1 Esdras as his source for the

---

[1] For a recent attempt to isolate the full extent of the original Nehemiah Memoir, cf. U. Kellermann: *Nehemia*, who, after a long and detailed literary analysis (pp. 4–73), isolates the following as belonging to the original Nehemiah source: 1:1 – 7:5ab*a*; 12:27a*a*, 31f., 37–40; 13:4, 5a*a*, 6a, 7ab*a*, 8–10b*a*, 11–21, 22b, 23a, 24a, 25–31 (p. 74).

2-2

history of the return and the career of Ezra, probably because of 'its more elegant Greek style, and a desire not to omit the additional matter contained in it'.[1] That Josephus does not switch from 1 Esdras to Ezra in this section need not surprise us in view of Cohen's conclusion that

> in AJ I–V, the material has been entirely recast, with the object of bringing the Biblical narratives into conformity with the style and psychology of the Greek novel . . . whereas AJ VIff [i.e. to XI] stay much closer to the Bible in order, style and content. Some use is made of these embellishments here too, but unlike AJ I–V, entire chapters are not as a rule moulded anew, but at most only a few sentences at a time.[2]

Josephus followed this source through to its conclusion. Either this included the whole of Neh. 8, or he completed the account on the basis of his understanding of the context (see section 2 below). He then has a notice of the death of Ezra (158), as he is to have later of Nehemiah (183). Neither of these notices is drawn from the Biblical account, which is silent about the fate of these two leaders. If they are set side by side, they leave a strong impression that Josephus is here only adding what he feels to be appropriate, without any documentary, historical justification:

> XI, 158: And it was his fate, after being honoured by the people, to die an old man and to be buried with great magnificence in Jerusalem.
> XI, 183: Then, after performing many other splendid and praiseworthy public services, Nehemiah died at an advanced age.

The lack of concrete detail, the general summarizing of the achievements of the two men and the references to their great age combine to suggest that we are dealing here with a literary convention that Josephus considered suitable to the context.[3]

It need hardly be said that after this point, Josephus will not mention Ezra again! The picture that Pohlmann himself paints of Josephus (pp. 91–114) is of a writer who lays great importance on internal consistency, even at the expense of historical accuracy. Against this background, the rest of Josephus' procedure in this section of the *Antiquities* falls into place.

[1] H. St J. Thackeray: 'Esdras, First Book of', p. 759. Less convincing explanations are offered by C. G. Tuland: 'Josephus, *Antiquities*, Book XI', p. 181.

[2] N. G. Cohen: 'Josephus and Scripture', p. 319.

[3] I am grateful to Prof. I. L. Seeligmann for directing my attention to the works of M. Braun for parallels to this type of literary activity by Hellenistic writers; cf. *History and Romance* and *Griechischer Roman und hellenistische Geschichtsschreibung*.

Quite naturally, having followed 1 Esdras through to its conclusion, he retraces his narrative back to Neh. 1, which 1 Esdras jumps over. As we have already seen, he then follows this source to Neh. 7: 4, where is found the list of which he wrote on its occurrence at 1 Esdras 5: 7–46: 'I have thought it better not to give a list of the families lest I distract the minds of my readers from the connexion of events and make the narratives difficult for them to follow' (*Ant.* XI, 68); he thus omits the list again at Neh. 7. Thereafter, there is hardly anything in Neh. that he would want to include: ch. 8 he has already recorded from 1 Esdras; ch. 9, as Pohlmann agrees (p. 125), would have contained little of interest to him, especially as in many ways it is parallel to 1 Esdras 8: 71–90; much of ch. 10, the whole of ch. 11 and most of ch. 12 are lists such as we have seen Josephus deliberately omits;[1] again, the question of mixed marriages (Neh. 13: 23–30) has already been dealt with once (*Ant.* XI, 140–53), whilst Neh. 13: 15–21 shows Jerusalem in such a bad light that it may have been passed over for apologetic reasons; the second half of ch. 12 deals with the dedication of the walls; Josephus has a short reference to this at 180, and may have refrained from going into detail because of Ezra's involvement in the ceremony (Neh. 12: 33); *Ant.* XI, 181 seems to preserve the substance of Neh. 11, and 182 the substance of Neh. 13: 4–14. Thus we can see that having recorded the events of Neh. 1–8 in detail, Josephus needed thereafter only to summarize in brief fashion the remainder of Neh. before giving the notice of Nehemiah's death. Because he deals with Ezra and Nehemiah separately (a situation that his use of 1 Esdras imposed upon him), Josephus naturally avoids the very passages that provide the most telling evidence of an overlap in their careers. It is this consistency, which we can easily trace on Josephus' part, that has misled Pohlmann into supposing that his work can be used as evidence both for the independence of 1 Esdras and for a knowledge on Josephus' part that Neh. 8 originally followed Ezr. 10, based on sources other than those to which we have access, sources in which, on the other hand, Neh. 9 is presumed not to have followed Neh. 8 (Pohlmann, pp. 113 and 125). However, if the position as outlined in the reconstruction above be correct, we can see at once that the *Antiquities* offer us no help at all in unravelling the early literary history of 1 Esdras, Ezr. and Neh.

2. *Josephus and the Ending of 1 Esdras*

The use by Josephus of 1 Esdras ends at *Ant.* XI, 156. His narrative here continues smoothly, however, and thus it is not surprising that many scholars have asked whether his account preserves material from

---

[1] Further examples of this practice of Josephus are listed in H. J. Cadbury: *Luke-Acts*, p. 124, n. 15.

the original continuation of 1 Esdras, whose present ending, as was established above, is fragmentary.

Well over a century ago, Treuenfels argued in a long series of articles about Josephus and 1 Esdras[1] 'dass er (Josephus) den ganzen Inhalt der Bücher Esra-Nehemia, so weit er im E.A. jetzt noch enthalten ist, aus diesem und nicht aus den kanonischen Büchern geschöpft hat', and further that 'es sich von einer Benutzung der letzteren bei Josephus gar keine Spur findet'. Treuenfels goes on from this to conclude that Josephus must have drawn his account of Nehemiah from the lost ending of 1 Esdras, which must therefore have been considerably more extensive than our fragment.

If, with Treuenfels and now Pohlmann, we conclude that neither 1 Esdras nor Josephus knew our canonical books at all, then it should be said that logically there is nothing against this conclusion. Treuenfels' position, strange as it may appear to us now, highlights the fact that there is really no external control to the problem of the ending of 1 Esdras once we abandon its dependence on Ezr.-Neh.

More recently, Mowinckel argued on the basis of Josephus that 1 Esdras originally contained the whole of Neh. 8, and then concluded with the notice of the death of Ezra.[2] He argues first from the specific reference in *Ant.* XI, 154 to the festival of Tabernacles: this presupposes knowledge of Neh. 8: 13–18. Secondly, it is the Chronicler's practice to include details of his heroes' deaths; thus the notice of *Ant.* XI, 158 is just what we might expect as the conclusion of his work as a whole.

This latter point is without foundation, however. The details of the Chronicler's heroes' deaths are in fact merely taken over from his Kings *Vorlage*, whilst in a case such as Zerubbabel, where we might expect greater evidence of his own practice, there is a notorious, and some have thought suggestive, silence. Moreover, we have already noted reasons for supposing that the account of Ezra's death is to be attributed to Josephus himself (above, p. 24). As to Mowinckel's argument from the explicit reference to the festival of Tabernacles, Pohlmann himself has answered this in his discussion of the witness of Josephus to the ending of 1 Esdras.[3]

Pohlmann maintains that since Josephus was a Jew with priestly connections, he would have known from the date of the events recorded (the seventh month) that reference was being made to the feast of Tabernacles. He would have known too that it was to be celebrated for eight days (*Ant.* XI, 157) as reference to *Ant.* III, 244–7 makes clear.

---

[1] A. Treuenfels: 'Über das apocryphische Buch Esra', *Der Orient* XI (1850), especially 774–7; for a full list of Treuenfels' writings on this subject, cf. K.-F. Pohlmann: *Studien*, p. 163. He was followed in this opinion by H. Bloch: *Quellen*, pp. 76f. and G. Hölscher: *Quellen*, p. 36.

[2] S. Mowinckel: *Studien I*, pp. 25–8.

[3] Pohlmann: *Studien*, pp. 107–12.

Neither of these factors, therefore, proves that his *Vorlage* contained Neh. 8: 13–18. Nonetheless, Pohlmann thinks that Josephus must have known these verses, because he mentions that they kept the festival *en tais skēnais*, whereas in the other passages where Josephus records that the people observed this festival, such an element is lacking. Pohlmann has here to face the problem that if Neh. 8: 13–18 stood in his *Vorlage*, Josephus has abbreviated it drastically. This he explains by reference to 1 Esdras 5: 50=*Ant.* XI, 77. There it is stated that the feast of Tabernacles was celebrated 'in the manner which the lawgiver had ordained', which for Josephus would have included, of course, living in booths for a week. Neh. 8: 17, however, says that this element of living in booths had not been observed 'since the days of Joshua the son of Nun'. Consequently, Josephus had to omit the details of the construction of the booths from vv. 14ff., in order to avoid this contradiction. *Ant.* XI, 157 retains such substance of what remains from these verses that has not been already included earlier in the narrative. Finally, Josephus made the reference to Tabernacles at the start of the narrative rather than at this point because of his abbreviation here and in order to explain to his non-Jewish readers why the people gathered in Jerusalem in the first place.

It is important here to recognize that the evidence being handled is very slender, and that no position is capable of proof. The most that one can hope to show is that one position is more reasonable and hence more probable than another. Pohlmann's position is certainly possible, and definitely the most likely of those mentioned thus far. But does it take full account of what facts there are?

In the first place, Pohlmann has not adequately explained the drastic abbreviation, if Josephus read Neh. 8: 13–18 in his version of 1 Esdras. His explanation from the clash with *Ant.* XI, 77 (assuming that Josephus was aware of it!) accounts only for the omission of the words 'for since the days of Jeshua the son of Nun unto that day had not the children of Israel done so' (Neh. 8: 17b*a*); the rest of the paragraph could have been retained without fear of contradiction.

Secondly, we should notice that there is a difference between *Ant.* XI, 157 and Neh. 8: 13–18 for which there is no apparent reason, namely, the motive for starting the festival: in Josephus, there is a reassurance from Ezra that the people's repentance would act as a safeguard against evil again befalling them, whereas Neh. 8: 14 makes clear that they only celebrated because they found that it was so ordered in the law.

Thirdly, Josephus has introduced into a narrative that he is supposed to be abbreviating drastically the record that after the festival, the people 'returned to their homes, singing hymns to God and expressing thanks to Ezra for rectifying the offences against the laws of the state'. This is not suggested by anything in the *Vorlage*, but is very much of a

piece stylistically with the account of the return home after the celebration of the feast in Solomon's day in *Ant.* VIII, 124:

> And when they had had enough of these things and had omitted
> nothing that was required by piety toward God, the king dismissed
> them and they went away, each to his own home; and giving thanks
> to the king for his care of them and for the display he had made,
> and praying to God to grant them Solomon as king for a long time,
> they set out on their way with joyfulness and mirth and singing
> hymns to God, so that by reason of their delight, they all accom-
> plished the journey homeward without fatigue.

This is clearly an amplification of the notice in 1 Ki. 8: 66 (cf. 2 Chr.
7: 10):

> On the eighth day he sent the people away, and they blessed the
> king, and went unto their tents joyful and glad in heart for all the
> goodness that the Lord had showed unto David his servant, and to
> Israel his people.

This close parallel, where such factors as hymn singing are similarly
introduced, suggests that Josephus is also composing freely in our
passage. This confirms our earlier suggestion about the account of the
death of Ezra, which immediately follows.

Fourthly, the broken-off ending of 1 Esdras – *kai episunēchthēsan* –
is sufficient in view of the whole context to suggest that the account of
the festival itself was to follow. In short, every element of the generalized statement in *Ant.* XI, 157 can be shown to be either his own composition, or a natural inference from the context to a writer like Josephus,
or else to be quite unrelated to, and not even suggested by, Neh. 8:
13–18, whilst in this latter passage there are many references that he
could well have included without contradicting his earlier work, which
would have enhanced his portrait of the law-abiding community, and
which he yet omits for no reason.

The only exception to this is the phrase *en tais skēnais*, of which we
must ask, is it sufficient to demand, in view of the contrary evidence
we have outlined, that Josephus here be following Neh. 8: 13–18 as a
Vorlage? There are reasons for returning a negative answer; it seems
that Josephus is trying here as he does elsewhere to bring his account
into closer conformity with the requirement of the law. This would
explain why he refrains from mentioning the day of the month on which
these events occurred: 1 Esdras 9: 37 gives the date as the new moon
of the seventh month; however, since Josephus knew that the feast of
Tabernacles was to start on the fifteenth of the month (cf. *Ant.* III, 244),
he simply dates our passage 'in the seventh month' (*Ant.* XI, 154).
Ant. III, 244–7 shows that Josephus knew that dwelling in booths was an

essential part of the festival; he could, then, easily have included this element here in order to show that the celebration was carried out as required in the law, without his having to have derived the information from a *Vorlage*. That he does not mention this element in other descriptions of the feast of Tabernacles (e.g. *Ant.* IV, 209; VII, 100; VIII, 123, 225; XI, 77) is for the simple reason that in not one of these instances does his *Vorlage* (about which there is no doubt in these cases) mention it either. In our passage, however, if he was not following a particular text, he may have added it in because he felt that it was appropriate.

We may thus conclude this discussion of the ending of 1 Esdras and the witness of Josephus to it by agreeing with Pohlmann that the original ending has been lost. Josephus' use of 1 Esdras, however, tells us nothing about the original composition of the work in general, nor about the ending in particular; it would appear that by his time, it was already in the state that we know today. There is nothing to prove either way, therefore, whether its compiler stopped with Neh. 8, or whether in fact he continued further through Neh. Since Pohlmann rates the evidence of Josephus too highly, we cannot follow him in using the *Antiquities* to prove that the compiler of 1 Esdras did not know that Neh. 9 followed Neh. 8.

D. 1 ESDRAS AND THE CANONICAL BOOKS OF EZRA AND NEHEMIAH

Pohlmann turns next (pp. 35–52) to consider the story of the three guardsmen at the court of Darius. This section is not found in the MT, and, as may be imagined, a good deal of attention has centred on it in discussions of 1 Esdras. Only Howorth and Marquart seem to have defended the view that it was an integral part of the Chronicler's original work.[1] As far as I can see, however, every other writer agrees that it is secondary to the context, and hence an interpolation so far as the original composition of Ezr. 1–6 is concerned.[2] The dispute centres rather around the stage at which the story was interpolated. Unless he wishes to take Howorth's line, Pohlmann is naturally obliged to argue that the story is secondary not just to the Chronicler, but to 1 Esdras itself, since, as we have seen, he holds that 1 Esdras is the earliest Greek translation of the Chronicler's work. On the other hand, In der Smitten[3]

---

[1] H. H. Howorth: 'A Criticism of the Sources', pp. 68–85; J. Marquart: *Fundamente*, p. 65.

[2] In addition to the works on 1 Esdras already cited in this chapter, cf. A. Büchler: 'Das apocryphische Esrabuch'; W. Th. In der Smitten: 'Zur Pagenerzählung'; R. Laqueur: 'Ephoros', which study is taken by many more recent writers as the definitive work in isolating this story as an interpolation; W. O. E. Oesterley: *The Apocrypha*, p. 137; F. Zimmermann: 'The story of the three guardsmen'.   [3] In der Smitten: 'Zur Pagenerzählung'.

has argued (specifically in refutation of Pohlmann) to defend the alternative view that the story was interpolated by the compiler of 1 Esdras himself.

Neither of these positions could in any way challenge our view that 1 Esdras is secondary. If In der Smitten is right, then 1 Esdras must indeed be a later compilation; if Pohlmann is right, then that would still only prove that this particular section is later, and it would have no bearing on the nature of the original composition. Since the whole subject is therefore peripheral to the main line of our investigation, we can move straight on to an area where we may hope to achieve some firmer results, namely the relation between 1 Esdras and the present form of Ezr.-Neh.

It is clearly of vital importance to Pohlmann to show that 1 Esdras betrays no knowledge of Neh. 1–7, for if it did, this would at once prove beyond reasonable doubt that 1 Esdras is a compilation, selecting its material to suit some particular purpose, and not just a translation of the Chronicler's work in its original form. Pohlmann deals with this question on pp. 53–73. He introduces the discussion with the legitimate observation that it is not enough simply to explain why the supposed compiler of 1 Esdras might have omitted this material. Bayer[1] did this, arguing that there was nothing in these chapters that suited the 'temple theme' of 1 Esdras. Pohlmann quite correctly replies that this by no means proves that 1 Esdras in fact knew these chapters at all. He then turns to consider the passages from which such knowledge has been adduced.

1. *Inconclusive Passages*

According to Pohlmann (p. 66), 1 Esdras 9: 37 provides the strongest case against his position. We shall therefore consider it in detail below. Here, we would rather point to another article by In der Smitten,[2] part of which has some observations pertinent to our purpose. We may leave out of account the first part of this article, which argues that the compiler of the Ezra story must have known the Nehemiah source, because it seeks to heighten the glory of the return under Ezra over against the journey of Nehemiah. As has been observed in connection with Kellermann's similar argument,[3] 'if much of the narrative in Ezra 7–10 and Neh. 8–13 was invented by the Chronicler with the aim of making Ezra overshadow Nehemiah, it is surprising that the task was not fulfilled more efficiently'.[4]

In der Smitten moves on to suggest, against Pohlmann, that had the

---

[1] Bayer: *Das dritte Buch Esdras*, pp. 92f.
[2] In der Smitten: 'Die Aufnahme der Nehemiaschrift'.
[3] U. Kellermann: *Nehemia*, pp. 94f.
[4] J. A. Emerton: in a review of Kellermann: *JTS* ns 23 (1972), 183.

Chronicler known the Nehemiah source, he could hardly have expected his contemporaries to accept his work if he left it out of account. This leads him to consider Pohlmann's arguments against the knowledge in 1 Esdras of the Nehemiah source.

(a) Walde[1] had argued that the list in 1 Esdras 5: 7ff. was not exclusively dependent on Ezr. 2, but also drew some of its details from Neh. 7. For instance, at the head of the list in 1 Esdras there are twelve names, as at Neh. 7: 7, whereas Ezr. 2: 2 has only eleven. Pohlmann suggested that either one name had been lost from Ezra, or that there had been a later expansion in 1 Esdras 5 and Neh. 7. In der Smitten rejects the latter suggestion, because it is improbable that both recensions should add the same name, but he has nothing to offer against the first, and more plausible, alternative that Pohlmann offers, unless it be his rather lame conclusion: 'Hat 3E die Liste von Neh. 7 wirklich nicht gekannt?'

The lesson from such an exchange as this is that the material being discussed is by its very nature unlikely to provide evidence that will convince anyone unless his mind is already made up. As Allrik has picturesquely expressed it in a comment on this chapter from a rather different angle, 'lists like this . . . were obviously testing stones for the patience of the saints in any scriptorium; one need only glance at the apparatus of variant readings in editions like Swete or Rahlfs – which easily doubles or trebles in size on the pages which reproduce lists'.[2] Both sides of the discussion here, then, are inconclusive.

(b) In der Smitten also deals with the reference to the *Attaratēs* in 1 Esdras 9: 49. Pohlmann's explanation (pp. 64–6) is that this is an addition by a later worker who sought to bring 1 Esdras into line with the Hebrew text of Ezr.-Neh., which by then was in its present form. The singular verb *wy'mr* in Neh. 8: 9, however, shows that in the original form of the Hebrew text, there was no reference to Nehemiah or the Tirshatha. Only after Neh. 8 was joined to Neh. 7 did it become necessary to include him in the ceremony of reading the law, and at first he was included by use of this title only. It was from this form of the Hebrew text that a correcting marginal gloss was made in 1 Esdras, and from there the word was incorporated into the text.

To this, In der Smitten replies that he can only visualize the gloss being first added to the Hebrew text. That must, of course, have been after the combining of the Ezra and Nehemiah records. It was in this form that the Hebrew text lay in front of the redactor of 1 Esdras.

Here again, it seems to me, there is no meaningful discussion at all. Either position is possible, but neither is able to establish one possibility or discredit the other. In der Smitten's discussion of Pohlmann's

---

[1] B. Walde: *Die Esdrasbücher*, pp. 142–54.
[2] H. L. Allrik: '1 Esdras according to Codex B and Codex A'.

work thus fails completely, because he does not answer Pohlmann's points, but merely states alternative possibilities. In der Smitten does not even mention Pohlmann's other two sections here. One of these – the relationship of Ezr. 2 to Neh. 7 in their respective contexts – is also likely to be inconclusive for the specific question of whether 1 Esdras knew Ezr.-Neh. in its present form. The other, however, seems to me to offer positive evidence. Since In der Smitten has not answered Pohlmann here, it is necessary now to deal with this in greater detail.

2. *1 Esdras 9: 37 and its Knowledge of Neh. 7: 72 (Ev 7: 73)*

Comparison of the last three verses of Neh. 7 and the first phrase of 8: 1 with Ezr. 2: 68–70 and the first phrase of ch. 3 suggests that the time reference (*wyg' hḥdš hšby'y*) originally belonged with the preceding section, and not with the contents of ch. 8 as in the present arrangement. It appears that 1 Esdras 9: 37 translates this heading, and thus could only have been effected after Neh. 8 had been combined with the preceding material.

(a) Mowinckel seeks to answer this point on pp. 21–5 of his *Studien I*. He recalls first of all that 1 Esdras sometimes betrays double translations of the Hebrew. The origins of this feature are glosses designed to bring 1 Esdras into closer conformity with the (by then established) MT. The verse in question presents an example of this. The evidence for this suggestion is drawn first from the observation that 1 Esdras 5: 45f. has correctly rendered the verse from the identical Ezr. 2: 70. 1 Esdras 9: 37, however (ignoring for the moment the omission of the singers, porters and Nethinim), has made a syntactical error in joining the time phrase to what precedes rather than to what follows, as the MT demands. Mowinckel then asks: 'Ist es überhaupt denkbar, dass ein Übersetzer der in 5: 45 richtig übersetzt hat, in 9: 37 eine solche falsche Übersetzung gegeben habe?' Moreover, the translations of the two passages are quite different, which also suggests that a second hand has been at work.

The use of *tē noumēnia* is also noteworthy, since in 1 Esdras 8: 6 it is used to translate *bywm 'ḥd lḥdš*, whereas *wyg' hḥdš hšby'y* is elsewhere (5: 46) correctly rendered by *enstantos tou hebdomou*. Here, however, the secondary writer felt obliged to follow the *noumēnia* of v. 40.

Finally, the history of the MT itself shows that 1 Esdras 9: 37 must be a later interpolation. The position of the chapter's original time phrase in 8: 2 arouses suspicion. We should have expected it at the start of v. 1. In fact, Mowinckel thinks that this was its original position; it was only removed to v. 2 by a later redactor, after Neh. 8 had been joined to Neh. 7. Inasmuch as 1 Esdras 9: 37 follows this feature, it too must be an interpolation.

Whilst Mowinckel's ingenuity in this argument cannot be gainsaid, there remain two objections to his solution.

(i) First, as Mowinckel emphasizes, the sole purpose of the postulated secondary worker was to align 1 Esdras more closely with the MT (p. 24). It is, then, curious that he should have altered the whole sense of the passage by misunderstanding, as Mowinckel thinks, the syntax of the time phrase so as to construe it with what precedes; it is incomprehensible that he should have omitted the reference to the singers, porters and Nethinim; most of all, it is impossible on this hypothesis to explain why he has used *tē noumēnia*. Mowinckel suggests that he felt obliged to follow the translation of v. 40, but since the Hebrew texts are different, and *ex hypothesi* this interpolator is trying to bring the work into conformity with the Hebrew, we should have expected him rather to use a different phrase. This assimilation points rather to the work of one man.

(ii) Secondly, Mowinckel's case runs into difficulty over the position of the time phrase in v. 40. As we have seen, he thinks that it stood originally at the head of the section, and so presumably it stood there too in the earliest version of 1 Esdras. We must suppose, therefore, that the later corrector would have found it there. As far as the sense of the Hebrew goes, the MT also has the same date in the same position, but expressed in slightly different words. Why then should the 'corrector' have had any cause to alter what must have been to him a quite satisfactory rendering of the Hebrew? We should have expected him rather only to add the new material, and leave the correct phrase untouched. On the other hand, since 1 Esdras can at this point be fully understood on the basis of our MT, it is simplest to suppose that this is in fact what was read, and this must have been, as shown above, after Neh. 7 and 8 had been combined.

(b) Whilst Pohlmann concedes that Mowinckel's position is possible, he claims to have a better explanation to offer (pp. 68–71). First of all, he maintains on the basis of an examination of the vocabulary used that the translator of 9: 37 is the same as for the rest of 1 Esdras. Secondly, however, he questions whether we should take Neh. 7: 72 in its connection with the list in Neh. 7: 6–71 as the Hebrew equivalent of 1 Esdras 9: 37. Not only, as we have seen, are there certain differences between the Hebrew and its supposed Greek rendering, which contrasts with the accurate rendering of Ezr. 2: 70/3: 1, but also the verse is indispensable as a link between Ezr. 10 and Neh. 8. It is thus certainly in its original position, and cannot have been added later. We have therefore no grounds, according to Pohlmann, for linking 1 Esdras 9: 37 with Neh. 7. After the list of Ezr. 10, we expect some transition passage to introduce the events of Neh. 8, and our verse precisely supplies this. 1 Esdras 9: 18, 23 and 26 had shown that some of the priests, Levites and men of

Israel had been involved in marrying foreign wives; our verse neatly shows that the problem had been settled. Furthermore, it makes clear to the reader that the following events were not confined to the inhabitants of Jerusalem, and this is in line with the Chronicler's conception of the true Israel (cf. 2 Chr. 30: 11f., etc.).

Next, Pohlmann claims that the verse is not in its original form: the time phrase stands out at once, not only because of its syntactical irregularity, but mainly because it is superfluous in view of v. 40. It can, he thinks, be most easily explained as a marginal gloss: a later scribe had noticed that the dating of the passage came late (i.e. in v. 40), and his marginal correction was then mistakenly adopted into the text. So Pohlmann conjectures that the *Vorlage* of the verse might have originally read: *wyšbw hkhnym whlwym wmn h'm byrwšlm wbmdynh wbny yśr'l b'ryhm.*

There are three main objections to this reconstruction by Pohlmann:

(i) It is based entirely upon the prior assumption that Neh. 8 originally followed Ezr. 10, but in fact this is the very point that Pohlmann is seeking to prove. If on the other hand the writer of 1 Esdras had our books before him in their present form, then it is equally possible to argue that he used Neh. 7: 72 precisely because it suited his purpose at this point. It seems quite as likely as Pohlmann's theory that the references to priests, Levites and 'those of Israel' (in vv. 18, 23, 26) led him to mention only these three classes in v. 37, and so to omit the other temple servants. I cannot see the force, therefore, of Pohlmann's main point, namely the suggestion that because the verse suits the context well it cannot have been drawn from Neh. 7: 72.

(ii) Pohlmann's implied history of the text leads him logically to postulate an absurdity. On the one hand, his reconstructed Hebrew text must, *ex hypothesi*, have stood at one stage immediately in front of Neh. 8. Neh. 7: 72, as is shown by Ezr. 2: 70/3: 1, is equally firmly tied to the preceding verses. We must therefore assume, on Pohlmann's view, that when Neh. 7 and 8 were combined by the later redactor, he found that one section ended and the next fortuitously began with verses of almost identical wording: a remarkable coincidence indeed![1]

(iii) Pohlmann's relegation of the time phrase to the status of a marginal gloss is entirely unconvincing, bearing as it does all the marks of a desperate expedient. *wyg' hḥdš hšby'y* could well be rendered *tē noumēnia tou hebdomou mēnos* if we bear in mind that *ḥdš* has the well attested meaning of 'new moon'. Again we have to observe that it is in exactly the position which it holds in the MT, which must on Pohlmann's

---

[1] This is only increased by the fact, not mentioned by Pohlmann, that the parallelism of text in fact runs on further to include *wy'spw kl h'm k'yš 'ḥd 'l* . . . Ezr. 3: 1, Neh. 8: 1.

view be yet another coincidence, since he thinks its position is due to its accidental inclusion from the margin.

In conclusion, therefore, we find that the only observation of Mowinckel and Pohlmann to have any substance is the fact that this verse is rendered differently from the same verse in Ezr. 2: 70/3: 1. This need not surprise us, however, since any number of examples have been shown in the past of passages where 1 Esdras either handles its *Vorlage* freely, or makes mistakes in translation.[1] I cannot find anything in 1 Esdras which could not be explained in this way if Neh. 7: 72 were its basis.

On the other side, it must be stressed that to postulate such a *Vorlage* for our verse is by far the simplest solution. The absurd lengths to which Mowinckel and Pohlmann are forced to go to get round this only strengthen our conclusion. The simplest explanation remains the best, and we may thus conclude that 1 Esdras knew Neh. 7. It follows that the work cannot have been a simple translation, but must in some sense be a compilation.

E. CONCLUSION: THE GREEK VERSIONS AND THE EXTENT OF THE CHRONICLER'S WORK

We have now examined all the sections of Pohlmann's book that have a direct bearing on the question of the original status of 1 Esdras. His final chapter builds on the preceding discussion and stands or falls with it. We may summarize the chief points that we have sought to maintain:

(a) Par. is the early Greek translation of Chr. Esdras *b* is an independent work. Though the beginning of 1 Esdras has been lost, it probably started at some point after the reign of Manasseh. It was never intended, therefore, to be a translation of the whole of the Chronicler's work. The existence of 1 Esdras may have been the reason for the delay in the translation of Esdras *b*.

(b) The use of these writings by Josephus should not be used to support either side of the discussion.

(c) We do not know the original extent of 1 Esdras. Josephus offers us no help here either, since it was already in its present shape by his time. It may have stopped at Neh. 8 or it may have included later material.

(d) 1 Esdras 9: 37 shows clearly that the compiler was following a *Vorlage* in which Neh. 8 followed Neh. 7, not Ezr. 10.

I therefore conclude that 1 Esdras is a secondary work. Pohlmann seems to suggest that we must hold that it is *either* a compilation *or* a

---

[1] Cf. Bayer: *Das dritte Buch Esdras*, pp. 11–36. Pohlmann is quite willing to accept this kind of argument when it suits his case; cf. pp. 54f.

fragment. Our investigation has shown that in fact it is both, and that Pohlmann's way of setting up this antithesis is false.

The results of this for the study of the original extent of the Chronicler's work are thus almost entirely negative. 1 Esdras cannot be used to support the view that Chr. was originally continued by Ezr. 1–10 and Neh. 8. All we can say positively is that by the second century B.C., Chr. was being treated separately from Ezr.-Neh. (as Par. shows). There is nothing from the Greek versions to say whether they were originally joined or always separate, however.

4

Vocabulary and Style in Chronicles, Ezra and Nehemiah

One of the arguments most frequently advanced in favour of the unity of authorship of Chronicles, Ezra and Nehemiah is that of linguistic or stylistic similarity. In most of the modern Introductions and Commentaries, this is usually stated without any evidence being advanced in its support.[1] The reason for this is no doubt that the case is generally held to have been established by scholars of an earlier generation, so that it is unnecessary merely to repeat their work.

A pioneering attempt in this direction was made by Zunz,[2] who was followed in particular by Bertheau[3] in the introduction to his commentary on Chr. Of more lasting influence, however, has been the numbered list included by S. R. Driver in his *Introduction*.[4] This material was later repeated and expanded by Torrey,[5] Brown[6] and by Curtis and Madsen,[7] the latter being most widely known.

In fairness to these scholars, it must be said that it was not the primary purpose of them all to prove by their lists the common authorship of

[1] The following is a random selection of examples, not intended in the least to be exhaustive: B. W. Anderson: *The Living World*, p. 432; G. W. Anderson: *Introduction*, p. 215; O. Eissfeldt: *Einleitung*, p. 720; G. Fohrer: *Einleitung*, p. 257; R. H. Pfeiffer: *Introduction*, p. 831; H. H. Rowley: *Growth*, p. 162; A. Weiser: *Einleitung*, p. 284; L. W. Batten: *Ezra and Nehemiah*, p. 2; J. M. Myers: *I Chronicles*, p. xviii; Rudolph, p. iii.

[2] L. Zunz: *Die gottesdienstlichen Vorträge*, pp. 19–30.

[3] E. Bertheau, pp. xv–xxiii.

[4] *ILOT*, pp. 535–40.

[5] C. C. Torrey: *Composition*.

[6] F. Brown: 'Chronicles, I. and II.'.

[7] CM, pp. 27–36. Reference should also be made here to the influential work of A. S. Kapelrud: *The Question of Authorship in the Ezra-Narrative*. Kapelrud's main purpose, to establish uniformity of style in the Ezra narrative, does not, of course, affect our present discussion. In further identifying the author of this narrative with the Chronicler, he first presupposed that some other passages of Ezr.-Neh. were from the Chronicler (cf. pp. 22 and 95), which begs the whole question. Inasmuch as he secondly supported this by reference to the books of Chr. themselves, his arguments will in any case be covered by the general discussion which follows.

the various books. Driver, for instance, made quite clear that his list was to illustrate some of the 'peculiarities and mannerisms' of the style of the books of Chr., in which 'the occurrences in Ezr.-Neh. are included'.[1] Similarly, it is evident that the list in CM was not to prove unity of authorship from the fact that many of the words appear only in one of the books under discussion. It thus emerges that these lists have been used by later scholars for a purpose slightly different from that of their original compilers. Though the unity of authorship was maintained by all the earlier writers, they did not always advance their lists directly to establish this point. This leads us to pose the question: is the evidence presented in these older works nevertheless sufficient to bear out the assertions of more recent scholars?

The need to answer this question has become more acute in recent years, since the whole question of similarity of style in the Chronicler's work has been thrown wide open. This new situation has been caused in the main by Japhet's fine article on the subject.[2] Under the headings 'linguistic opposition', 'specific technical terms' and 'peculiarities of style', she has sought to show that there are in fact not only differences, but even points of opposition between the styles of the two books.

Japhet's reasoning has evidently convinced some that we are here dealing with separate works.[3] For others, it has merely reopened the question,[4] whilst a third group remain, apparently, unconvinced.[5] As far as stylistic considerations on their own are concerned, Japhet's position could be challenged on two grounds. First, it has been argued[6] that she does not pay sufficient attention to the various layers of composition to be found within the books of Chr. Only those parts that derive from the Chronicler himself should be used in an attempt to establish opposition between the two parts.

Whilst this reasoning is quite evidently sound in itself, it is by no means clear that Japhet's article can be criticized on such grounds. As far as Ezr.-Neh. is concerned, Japhet made clear that she would only make use of 'the general edition of Ezr.-Neh. which is regarded as "chronistic", and those portions which are not subject to debate and are accepted as "chronistic" by general consensus'.[7] As to Chr., Japhet often makes reference to changes introduced by the Chronicler over against his *Vorlage*; a number of peculiarities of style and expression in Ezr.-Neh. are totally absent from Chr., and again, many of the

[1] *ILOT*, p. 535.
[2] S. Japhet: 'The Supposed Common Authorship'.
[3] E.g., R. L. Braun: 'Solomonic Apologetic'. Willi, pp. 176–84, argues that they are separate works, but in fact written by the same man.
[4] E.g. P. R. Ackroyd: *I and II Chronicles, Ezra, Nehemiah*, pp. 22f.
[5] E.g. R. Mosis, pp. 11–16 and 205ff., and K.-F. Pohlmann: *Studien*.
[6] Mosis, p. 214, n. 23, and P. Welten, p. 4, n. 15.
[7] Japhet: 'The Supposed Common Authorship', p. 333.

traits listed from Chr. but absent from Ezr.-Neh. are drawn from passages generally recognized as being the Chronicler's own composition. It would seem, therefore, that Japhet's argument is sound in the face of such criticism.

Secondly, however, it could be urged that she has not done justice to the similarities of style.[1] These might be of such a nature as to overrule any evidence of opposition that could be adduced. It is imperative, therefore, that we examine the evidence for similarity of style with this question in mind. It is necessary first to establish briefly the criteria for determining unity of authorship on this basis, and secondly to see whether the evidence that has been advanced satisfies these criteria.

B

(1) Regardless of which specific date we assign to the work of the Chronicler, the amount of Hebrew known with any certainty to us from the same period is really quite small. At the same time, however, it has been established beyond doubt that it is possible to draw distinctions between the Hebrew of this post-exilic period and that of earlier classical or later Mishnaic Hebrew.[2] This means, of course that extreme caution is needed before we can designate as 'peculiarity of style' phenomena which may in fact reflect only the style of a particular literary period for which we are so scantily informed. As a general, preliminary point, therefore, we are justified in demanding that a substantial number of words or stylistic peculiarities be produced before common authorship can be supported on these grounds alone. It is the differences that are more likely to be significant.

(2) It ought not to need saying that these peculiarities must be drawn from both Chr. and Ezr.-Neh. before they have value as evidence for our purposes.[3] The reason for making this very obvious statement is that, as will be seen below, a substantial number of examples listed do not satisfy this criterion. Whilst it was quite legitimate to list these

---

[1] This argument is advanced against Japhet by Willi, p. 183, n. 19, who thinks that the lists of Driver and CM 'behalten doch ihr Gewicht und ihr Recht'.

[2] Cf. especially A. Hurvitz: *The Transition Period in Biblical Hebrew*. The first chapter of this book (pp. 13–63) is given over to a most helpful and lucid discussion of sound method in the attempt to reach firm conclusions on the isolation of late features in Biblical Hebrew. On the transition to the later Mishnaic Hebrew, cf. A. Bendavid: *Biblical Hebrew and Mishnaic Hebrew*.

[3] Some of Torrey's examples open themselves to circular reasoning on this basis. Having established to his own satisfaction that certain passages of Ezr.-Neh. are from the Chronicler, he then compares other sections with these passages (e.g. *ḥth ḥsd* on p. 16, *šnym 'šr* on p. 17, *ḥrd* on p. 19, *wyqm . . . wybnw* on p. 37, *mdh šnyt* on p. 38, *bny 'bdy šlmh* on p. 40, etc.). It is clear, however, that this will convince no one who is not already convinced that these books are substantially a single composition.

words in a discussion of literary characteristics, one senses that often the sheer magnitude of the lists is appealed to by those who go on to maintain unity of authorship, without observing that a considerable amount has no value whatever in this more specific connection.

(3) The evidence adduced should be confined exclusively, or at least overwhelmingly, to the books under discussion. Since, as has been said, our knowledge of the language of this period is so scanty, any distribution of the phenomena outside these books stimulates the suspicion that we are dealing with late Biblical Hebrew (LBH) characteristics in general, rather than individual stylistic peculiarities.

(4) The words or expressions in question should preferably be expressed in other literature of the same period in a different way.[1] It is clear that Chr. and Ezr.-Neh. often deal with similar interests (though whether from the same point of view is, of course, open to question). Since these interests are often not reflected in other post-exilic literature, occurrences, for instance, of technical cultic language in these books may be no more than a coincidence.[2] This criterion of 'opposition' guards against consequent misuse of such evidence. It naturally applies to vocabulary rather than to grammatical or syntactical peculiarities.

(5) Words that are found to satisfy the above criteria should further be checked to determine that they are used with the same meaning in both Chr. and Ezr.-Neh.[3] Examples will be adduced below where this is found not to be the case. Naturally, these too cannot then support unity of authorship.

In order to gain as wide a basis for agreement as possible, the following discussion has drawn on every layer of the books of Chr. If there is thus included material that is not from the Chronicler himself, that can only be to the advantage of those who *support* unity of authorship, since we are here concerned with features that are common to both

---

[1] For the importance of this criterion in a slightly different context, cf. Hurvitz: *The Transition Period*, pp. 20–4.

[2] Driver himself expressed strong reservations over the use of technical vocabulary in determining the date of the priestly sections of the Pentateuch in his article 'On Some Alleged Linguistic Affinities of the Elohist', for instance: 'Technical terms ought to be disregarded in any comparison of the vocabulary of Q with that of other writers', p. 216, and cf. pp. 209, 214f., 220f. The same reasoning holds good too in our present discussion.

[3] This point too was recognized by Driver:

Enough will have been said to show the precarious nature of conclusions, based on an unchecked application of the method of arithmetical computation. The use of that method implies that the units summed *are of equal value*; but in the facts of language with which we are now dealing, this is constantly not the case: they differ by the presence of factors, variable and subjective, of which the arithmetical computation can take no account (*ibid*. p. 220, and cf. pp. 203 and 217).

Chr. and Ezr.-Neh. For similar reasons, it has seemed safest only to isolate the Nehemiah Memoir (NM) from Ezr.-Neh. as being from a separate hand.[1] It is generally agreed that this memoir reflects accurately the style of its original author, being incorporated into the present book of Neh. without substantial alteration.[2] It thus becomes an exceedingly valuable alternative witness to the characteristics of LBH.

The analysis is based primarily on the numbered entries in Driver's list (hereafter referred to as Dr). Secondly, reference is made to the numbered list in CM, and all entries there which are not found in Dr are included. Since between them these two lists incorporate all the significant items that other scholars have analysed, it has seemed best to work on this basis alone, without confusing the discussion by a multiplicity of references.

C

Forty-seven entries in these lists are of words or usages that occur either in Chr. or in Ezr.-Neh. alone. For our purposes, they may therefore be eliminated straight away. This number does not include those words which occur so frequently in one book only as to favour diversity of authorship (see section F below). A number of these words are also found elsewhere in LBH.

(1) *lᵉma* (Dr 31; CM 121): 1 Chr. 15: 13, 2 Chr. 30: 3.

(2) *ldbry ywm bywmw* (Dr 42; CM 131): 1 Chr. 16: 37, 2 Chr. 8: 14, 31: 16.

(3) *'rgwn* (CM 5): 2 Chr. 2: 6; cf. Dan. 5: 7.16.29.

(4) *bwṣ* (CM 9): 1 Chr. 4: 21, 15: 27, 2 Chr. 2: 13, 3: 14, 5: 12, Est. 1: 6, 8: 15, Ezek. 27: 16.[3]

(5) *byrnywt* (CM 13): 2 Chr. 17: 12, 27: 4.

(6) *gdwd* (CM 17):[4] 1 Chr. 7: 4, 2 Chr. 25: 9.10.13, 26: 11, Job 29: 25, Mic. 4: 14.

[1] We have chosen to follow U. Kellermann's definition of the extent of the NM, as set out with full analysis in his book *Nehemia*, pp. 4–74. Most dissent from this view centres on the place of Neh. 13. P. R. Ackroyd, for instance, *The Age of the Chronicler*, pp. 28f., suggests that much of this chapter is the work of a later imitator. This does not affect our position, however, since either way the language represents an alternative witness to that of the Chronicler for the characteristics of LBH.

[2] Compare, for instance, the two major modern commentaries: W. Rudolph: *Esra und Nehemia*, pp. xxiv and 211–13, and J. M. Myers: *Ezra. Nehemiah*, p. li. For a discussion of some aspects of Nehemiah's style, cf. A. Bendavid: *Biblical Hebrew and Mishnaic Hebrew*, I, 64f.

[3] For a full discussion, cf. Hurvitz: 'The Usage of שׁשׁ and בוץ' and 'The Evidence of Language', pp. 33–5.

[4] With the general meaning of *band, troop*, this word is common in BH. The more specific meaning of divisions of the army of Israel is thought to be late, however; cf. BDB, p. 151 A.

(7) *gwph* (CM 18): 1 Chr. 10: 12.

(8) *gnzk* (CM 19): 1 Chr. 28: 11 (and 28: 20?).

(9) *dḥp* (Niph.) (CM 21): 2 Chr. 26: 20, Est. 6: 12.

(10) *drkmwnym* (CM 22): Ezr. 2: 69, Neh. 7: 69.70.71.

(11) *mdrš* (CM 24): 2 Chr. 13: 22, 24: 27.

(12) *hdrt qdš* (CM 25): 2 Chr. 20: 21 (prose); 1 Chr. 16: 29, Pss. 29: 2, 96: 9 (poetry).

(13) *hyk* (CM 26): 1 Chr. 13: 12, Dan. 10: 17.

(14) *zn* (CM 29): 2 Chr. 16: 14, Ps. 144: 13 (twice); cf. Dan. 3: 5. 7.10.15.

(15) *znḥ* (Hiph.) (CM 30): 1 Chr. 28: 9, 2 Chr. 11: 14, 29: 19.

(16) *z'p* (CM 31): 2 Chr. 26: 19 (twice).

(17) *mzqq* (CM 32): 1 Chr. 28: 18, 29: 4, Isa. 25: 6, Ps. 12: 7.

(18) *zrḥ* (CM 33): 2 Chr. 26: 19.

(19) *mḥbrwt* (CM 34): 1 Chr. 22: 3, 2 Chr. 34: 11.

(20) *ḥzqh* (of royal power) (CM 39): 2 Chr. 12: 1, 26: 16, Dan. 11: 2.

(21) *ḥl'* (CM 40): 2 Chr. 16: 12.

(22) *mḥlyym* (CM 41): 2 Chr. 24: 25.

(23) *ymn* (Hiph.) (CM 51): 1 Chr. 12: 2.

(24) *yšš* (CM 52): 2 Chr. 36: 17 (*yšyš* occurs four times in Job).

(25) *kbš* (CM 53): 2 Chr. 9: 18.

(26) *mkrbl* (CM 58): 1 Chr. 15: 27.

(27) *krmyl* (CM 59): 2 Chr. 2: 6.13, 3: 14.

(28) *l'b* (CM 62): 2 Chr. 36: 16.

(29) *tlmyd* (CM 64): 1 Chr. 25: 8.

(30) *ml' yd* (CM 66): this phrase has a wide distribution, including four occurrences in Chr., but it is not found at all in Ezr.-Neh.

(31) *ndn* (CM 71): 1 Chr. 21: 27; cf. Dan. 7: 15.

(32) *htḥ hsd* (CM 72): Ezr. 7: 28, 9: 9.

(33) *nksym* (CM 73): 2 Chr. 1: 11.12, Josh. 22: 8, Eccl. 5: 18, 6: 2.

(34) *nškh* (CM 77): Neh. 3: 30, 12: 44, 13: 7.

(35) *s^epār* (CM 80): 2 Chr. 2: 16.

(36) *'dr* (CM 83): 1 Chr. 12: 34.39.

(37) *m'rb* (CM 93): seven times in Chr. and often elsewhere, but not once in Ezr.-Neh.

(38) *'tyq* (CM 95): 1 Chr. 4: 22; cf. Dan. 7: 9.13.22.

(39) *pṭr* (CM 97): 1 Chr. 9: 33, 2 Chr. 23: 8.

(40) *prbr* (CM 98): 1 Chr. 26: 18 (twice).

(41) *mpš'h* (CM 99): 1 Chr. 19: 4.

(42) *ṣrk* (CM 102): 2 Chr. 2: 15.

(43) *šhyth* (CM 112): 2 Chr. 30: 17.

(44) *šlh* (Niph.) (CM 113): 2 Chr. 29: 11.

(45) The relative *še* combined with the prep. *bᵉ* (CM 122): 1 Chr. 25: 4, 27: 27.

(46) *ll'* (CM 133; cf. Dr 43): 2 Chr. 15: 3 (three times).

(47) *kᵉ'al* (CM 135): 2 Chr. 32: 19, Ps. 119: 14; cf. Isa. 59: 18, 63: 7.

D

A further twenty-seven entries may also be eliminated without discussion, since it is at once apparent that their distribution is so extensive that they cannot be regarded as idiosyncratic of a single author. It has not seemed necessary to itemize all the references in full.

(1) *mlkwt* (Dr 9; CM 67): twenty-six times in Est., fourteen times in Dan., etc.

(2) *qibbēl* (Dr 11; CM 103): both lists make clear that this word is as common generally in LBH as in Chr. and Ezr.-Neh. in particular.[1]

(3) *rkwš* (Dr 20; CM 107): there are sixteen occurrences of this word outside Chr. and Ezr.-Neh.[2]

(4) *'mr = to purpose, to promise that* (Dr 33; CM 4).[3]

(5) 'Words repeated, often strengthened by כל, to express the idea of *all* considered distributively, i.e. *every*' (Dr 35; CM 124): both lists show the very wide distribution of this usage. For instance, it apparently occurs more in Est. than in the whole of Chr.! It is thus quite general in LBH, and common too in post-Biblical Hebrew.

(6) *'d l* before a verb (Dr 38b; CM 127): whilst this usage is common in Chr. (occurring there nine times), the fact that it is found only once in Ezr. and three times in other writings renders it inconclusive for our purposes.

(7) *lkl = as regards all . . . (=namely, in brief)* (Dr 45; CM 130): frequent also in 'P'[4] and elsewhere.[5]

(8) *'bl* (CM 1): with adversative force, this word occurs twice in Dan. as well as three times in Chr. and once in Ezr. It is therefore to be regarded as general LBH.[6]

(9) *'grt* (CM 2): twice in Chr., six times in the NM (Neh. 2: 7. 8.9, 6: 5.17.19) and twice in Est.

(10) *'ḥzh* (CM 3): this word has a very wide distribution outside the books under discussion.

(11) *byrh* (CM 12): of the temple – twice in Chr.; of a fortress near

---

[1] Cf. Hurvitz: 'The Evidence of Language', pp. 43–5.
[2] Driver also includes this word in his list of characteristics of P: *ILOT*, p. 132, no. 17.
[3] Cf. *ILOT*, p. 506, no. 3 (characteristics of Dan.), which makes clear that this is a LBH idiom generally.
[4] Cf. *ILOT*, p. 132, no. 14.
[5] H. Ewald: *Lehrbuch*, para. 310a and BDB, p. 514 B.
[6] And so BDB, p. 6 A.

the temple – twice in the NM; of Shushan the palace – once in the NM, ten times in Est. and once in Dan. Hence this word is to be regarded as LBH generally.

(12) *bzh* (CM 10): this word has an equally wide distribution, including the NM, Dan. and Est.

(13) *byt 'bwt* (CM 14): the fact that Driver chooses rather to include this expression in his list of characteristics of 'the priestly narrative of the Hexateuch'[1] indicates that it cannot be used to demonstrate the common authorship of our books.[2]

(14) *ḥdš = month* numbered not named (CM 36).

(15) *ḥṣṣrh* (CM 44a): whilst this word is frequent in Chr. itself (fifteen times), its three occurrences in Ezr.-Neh. are quite in line with its distribution elsewhere in the Bible (on the verb, cf. below, section F).

(16) *ydh* (Hiph.) (CM 46a): this is also used particularly frequently in the Pss. (on the use of the hithp., cf. below, section F).

(17) *kns* (Qal) (CM 56): a widely scattered distribution.

(18) *kᵉtāb* (CM 60).

(19) *lᵉg* (Hiph.) (CM 63).

(20) *lškh* (CM 65): a rather specialized word, whose quite wide distribution suggests that we are dealing with the actual name of a room of the second temple. This being the case, there seems to be no force behind CM's observation that it is used in the sense of 'storeroom' only in Chr. and Ezr.-Neh.

(21) *'md = rise* (for earlier *qwm*) (CM 88): as the dictionaries show, *'md* assumes in LBH generally quite a number of the meanings of *qwm*.[3] This particular meaning occurs frequently in Dan., as well as at Est. 4: 14, Ps. 106: 30 and Eccl. 4: 15.

(22) *'md 'l 'omed* (CM 90): three times in Chr., once in the NM (Neh. 13: 11) and twice in Dan.; with *qwm* for *'md*: Neh. 9: 3; without the verb: Neh. 8: 7.

(23) *ṣpyr* (CM 101): 2 Chr. 29: 21, Ezr. 8: 35, Dan. 8: 5 (twice). 8.21; cf. Ezr. 6: 17 (Aramaic).

(24) *r'šy 'bwt* (CM 104, and cf. 14): the concentration of usage of this term in Chr., Ezr.-Neh. and 'P' suggests that its distribution is caused rather by the authors' interests and the circles in which they moved than by any individual idiosyncrasy.

(25) *rbw, rbw'* (CM 106).

(26) *rš'* (Hiph.) (CM 108).

(27) *šlḥ* (CM 114): though limited, the distribution of this word points firmly to its general LBH usage.

---

[1] *ILOT*, p. 133, no. 30.
[2] For a detailed discussion of this phrase, cf. J. P. Weinberg: 'Das *BĒIT 'ABŌT*'.
[3] Cf. BDB, p. 764 and KB, p. 712.

The remaining entries in the lists all require an element of discussion. It will emerge from this that the majority are also inconclusive as evidence for common authorship, that others point rather to diversity of authorship, whilst only a very few actually support it on the basis of the criteria established. We shall deal first with the inconclusive items.

(1) *htyḥś* (Dr 1; CM 49): this root is used twenty-one times in Chr. and Ezr.-Neh., and nowhere else in the OT. It would therefore appear strongly to support unity of authorship. However, there are other factors to be considered. First, Hurvitz has recently successfully shown that this word came into general use in post-Biblical Hebrew;[1] it was the word commonly used in Rabbinic literature in discussion of questions of pedigree. Since, however, different expressions with similar meanings are used in the books of the law themselves (derivatives of the roots *śph*, *yld*, *pqd* and *spr*), it becomes clear that √*yḥś* must have had wider currency in the post-exilic period than our literature shows.

Secondly, this contention is borne out by the word's occurrence at Neh. 7: 5, for this is generally regarded as an integral part of the NM.[2] The list, parallel with Ezr. 2, does not start until the following verse. It has been well argued, however, that were the word *lhtyḥś* (and perhaps also *spr hyḥś*) not already found in the NM, there would have been nothing to cause a later editor to insert the repetitive list at this point.[3]

Thirdly, were this word to be used as solid evidence for common authorship, we should expect to find an alternative expression being used elsewhere in the post-exilic literature. This, however, is not the case.[4] Of the four roots mentioned above, and as listed by Hurvitz, *śph* is used at Est. 9: 28, Zech. 12: 12.13.14, 14: 17.18, but not one of

---

[1] Hurvitz: 'The Evidence of Language', pp. 26–9, and cf. M. Jastrow, p. 575.

[2] So, for instance, U. Kellermann: *Nehemia*, pp. 23–6; M. Noth: *US*, p. 148; W. Rudolph: *Esra und Nehemia*, p. 211. L. H. Brockington: *Ezra, Nehemiah and Esther*, p. 159, thinks that only with *w'mṣ* may the editorial insertion start. The comments of J. M. Myers on this passage (*Ezra. Nehemiah*, p. 146) are confusing: he seems to suppose that as early as Neh. 7: 4 the parallel with Ezr. 2 begins. If that were the case, v. 5 could not, of course, be attributed to Nehemiah himself. However, since the parallel passage begins only at v. 6, his position cannot be maintained.

[3] There is thus no reason to follow L. W. Batten (*Ezra and Nehemiah*, pp. 264f.) in his preference for the LXX version at this point. On the basis of the Greek *eis sunodias* he wants to emend *lhtyḥś* and *hyḥś* to *l'ṣrwt, for a conference*.

[4] Orthodox criticism might wish to use the language of P here for this purpose. However, it is precisely on the basis of its language that Hurvitz has suggested a pre-exilic date for P: 'The Evidence of Language'. To this may be added many other arguments in favour of an earlier date for this material, conveniently summarized by R. J. Thompson in *Moses and the Law*, especially pp. 120ff. Sound method therefore demands that we leave out of account for our purposes material whose date is at the very least disputed.

these furnishes a true parallel in meaning to *htyḥś*. *pqd* is used twice in Est. 2: 3, but with the sense 'to appoint', at Isa. 60: 17 as a title and at Ezek. 43: 21 for 'an appointed place' belonging to the temple. The hithp. of *yld* occurs only at Num. 1: 18 in the OT; nor was it apparently used in later Hebrew (on *twldwt*, see below).[1] For *spr* as well, there are no certainly post-exilic passages outside the books under discussion. This all strongly suggests that at no other point in LBH was there cause for the authors to use *htyḥś* or its alternatives. That it occurs only in Chr. and Ezr.-Neh. is thus seen to be the result merely of their holding certain interests in common. This fact is, of course, readily acknowledged, but it does not amount to proof of unity of authorship.

(2) *h'myd=establish, appoint* (in earlier books: *station*) (Dr 4; CM 89): this weakened meaning is certainly found at quite a number of places in both pre- and post-exilic literature, such as 1 Ki. 12: 32, 15: 4, Pss. 105: 10 (with a parallel in Chr.), 148: 6, Dan. 11: 11.13.14. Moreover, several of the passages in which it occurs in Neh. are certainly from the NM: following Kellermann's analysis, Neh. 4: 3, 6: 7, 7: 3, 12: 31, 13: 11.30. This in fact only leaves two other references in Ezr.-Neh. (3: 8 and 10: 33 respectively). The result is that we can draw no conclusions from so widely attested a usage.

(3) *byt h'lhym* (Dr 5; CM 15): it is argued that this was a designation for the temple peculiar to the Chronicler, in contrast to the usual *byt yhwh*. Three pieces of evidence, however, suggest that this name was a regular alternative in the period of the second temple. First, it occurs in quite a number of passages outside the books under discussion. Whilst many of these probably do not refer to the temple in Jerusalem (Gen. 28: 17.22, Jd. 9: 27, 17: 5, 18: 31, Josh. 9: 23, Hos. 9: 8, Amos 2: 8 and Joel 1: 13.16), those that *do* come in their present form from the post-exilic period for the most part:[2] Pss. 42: 5, 52: 10, 55: 15, 84: 11, Eccl. 4: 17, Dan. 1: 2, 5: 3. Furthermore, we find once again that there are several references included from the NM: Neh. 6: 10, 13: 4.9.11.14.

Secondly, the use at Dan. 1: 2 is especially instructive. Commentators have often argued that the author was here drawing on 2 Chr. 36: 7.[3] If that is so, *byt h'lhym* would indeed appear as a common post-exilic alternative, for 2 Chr. 36: 7 actually reads *byt yhwh*!

Thirdly, confirmation of this contention comes from quite a different source. The Jewish colonists at Elephantine consistently referred to

---

[1] No examples of its use are listed by Jastrow, pp. 577f.

[2] For the post-exilic dating of a number of the Pss. on linguistic grounds, cf. Hurvitz: *The Transition Period*, part II.

[3] So, for instance, J. A. Montgomery: *Daniel*, p. 114; R. H. Charles: *Daniel*, p. 5; A. Bentzen: *Daniel*, p. 17; J. Barr: 'Daniel', p. 592; N. W. Porteous: *Daniel*, pp. 25f.; M. Delcor: *Le Livre de Daniel*, p. 60.

their temple as *'gwr' zy yhw 'lh'* (and equivalents).[1] One of the documents that has been preserved for us, however, is a memorandum addressed to the colonists from Bigvai and Delaiah, whose style we may take to reflect more nearly the language of Jerusalem and Samaria at the time. They, by contrast with the colonists' practice, refer to the temple as *byt mdbḥ' zy 'lh šmy'*.[2] Although this is admittedly not an exact equivalent to *byt h'lhym*, it approaches it closely both in its use of *byt* and of *'lh*, and adds weight to the view that *byt h'lhym* is inconclusive for establishing the common authorship of Chr. and Ezr.-Neh.

(4) *nqbw bšmwt* (Dr 12; CM 75): the full list of Biblical occurrences of this expression is 1 Chr. 12: 32, 16: 41, 2 Chr. 28: 15, 31: 19, Ezr. 8: 20, Num. 1: 17 and cf. Isa 62: 2b – *wyqr' lk šm ḥdš 'šr py yhwh yqbnw* (not noted in either Dr or CM). Thus, though the expression is a rare one, it is yet found once exactly, and another time nearly, in other literature. Because of its technical meaning, we would not expect necessarily to find it outside our books and P. The evidence is thus unreliable for arguing identity of authorship.

(5) *hwdwt whll* (Dr 16; CM 47): four of the canonical Pss. begin with the words *hllwyh hwdw lyhwh ky ṭwb ky l'wlm ḥsdw* (Pss. 106: 1, 107: 1, 118: 1, 136: 1). This is clearly a form of words that was familiar to the authors of Chr. and Ezr.-Neh., cf. 1 Chr. 16: 41, 2 Chr. 5: 13, 20: 21, Ezr. 3: 11. Whilst certainty on such a matter is impossible, it is attractive to suppose that this formula was associated in its origins with Ps. 100: 4f.:

b'w š'ryw **btwdh** *ḥṣrtyw* **bthlh**
hwdw *lw brkw šmw.*
ky ṭwb yhwh l'wlm ḥsdw

It would thus appear that we are dealing here with a standard expression in temple worship, which in a narrative such as Chr. has been appropriately altered to the third person form. It is in no way surprising to find this form in books which have temple worship as a common interest (Pss., Chr. and Ezr.-Neh.), whereas there are no other postexilic books where we should expect to find it.

(6) *ḥdwh* (Dr 17; CM 35): this is an Aramaic loan-word (cf. Ezr. 6: 16). In Hebrew, it occurs only twice, at 1 Chr. 16: 27 (where Ps. 96: 6 has *tp'rt*) and Neh. 8: 10. Thus it cannot in any sense be termed part of the characteristic style of an author.[3] Chr. and Ezr.-Neh. both use commonly the normal OT word for joy: *śmḥh*. Furthermore, it is not clear why the Chronicler has introduced this change from Ps. 96: 6,

---

[1] *AP* 13: 14, 25: 6, 30: 6.24, 33: 8 and E. G. Kraeling: *The Brooklyn Museum Aramaic Papyri*, 3: 9–10, 4: 10.
[2] *AP* 32: 3f.
[3] See further Hurvitz: *The Transition Period*, pp. 23f.

since he in fact uses *tp'rt* elsewhere in his narrative (e.g. 1 Chr. 29: 11). It may be, therefore, that he already found *ḥdwh* in the particular *Vorlage* that he was using as an Aramaism that had come in under the general influence of the period. Either way, there can be no case made out for its appearance as a stylistically tendentious change.

(7) *nṣḥ* = *to oversee* (Dr 21; CM 74): as well as occurring six times in Chr. and twice in Ezr., this word is found in fifty-five of the Ps. headings and at Hab. 3: 19. The situation is thus comparable to *hwdwt whll* discussed above (no. 5). It is an apparently late expression, used in association with the temple only, where it came to have a specific meaning associated with singing. We would thus again not expect to find it used elsewhere in LBH, nor does there in fact appear to be any satisfactory alternative term.

(8) *htndb* (Dr 23; CM 70): the hithpa'el is found only in Chr. and Ezr.-Neh. (and twice in Jd. 5, but not with the specifically cultic meaning that characterizes these later references).[1] Hurvitz has sought to show, however, that this was a common word in the second temple period, being found in Rabbinic literature, the Targums and the Dead Sea Scrolls.[2] Its close association with the temple may once again account for its distribution in LBH.

(9) Sentences without a subject or verb (Dr 27; CM 117): as far as the omission of a subject is concerned, Ewald has set this feature into a wider context,[3] showing it to be a development of an earlier, widely known phenomenon, and thus a characteristic of LBH generally (cf. Dan. 8: 19.26). As for sentences without a verb, all the examples listed are from Chr. alone, and thus irrelevant for our present discussion.

(10) Inf. constr. used freely, almost as a subst. (Dr 28; CM 118): according to Ewald,[4] this again is a general late development; cf. Est. 1: 7 as a good example. Several of the references as listed by Dr prove to have parallels as to their use of the inf. constr. with uses in other books: for instance, with 2 Chr. 24: 14, Neh. 12: 46, compare Eccl. 3: 4, Gen. 2: 17; with Ezr. 1: 11, compare Num. 35: 19, Gen. 27: 45. This syntactical feature is thus inconclusive for our purposes.

(11) The relative omitted (rare in prose) (Dr 30; CM 120): though it is true that this feature usually characterizes Hebrew poetry, *GK* 155d–n[5] lists also a large number of passages apart from our books where the relative is omitted in prose: e.g. Gen. 39: 4 (but text dub.),

---

[1] For the occasional occurrence of an apparently late word in unquestionably early texts, cf. Hurvitz: *The Transition Period*, pp. 24–6.

[2] Hurvitz: 'The Evidence of Language', pp. 29–32.

[3] H. Ewald: *Lehrbuch*, para. 303b.
Ibid. para. 236a.

[5] And cf. A. Sperber: *A Historical Grammar*, p. 285.

Ex. 4: 13, 9: 4, 18: 20, Lev. 7: 35, Jd. 8: 1, 20: 15, 1 Sam. 6: 9, 14: 21,[1] 26: 14, 1 Ki. 13: 12, 2 Ki. 3: 8, Isa. 6: 6, Jer. 36: 2. In addition, Neh. 13: 23 is from the NM. It seems that this feature also continued into the prose of Mishnaic Hebrew.[2] We are thus left with three occurrences in Ezr.-Neh. against many in Chr. This, therefore, does not allow us to argue for a single author.

(12) *l* with the inf. at the end of a sentence (Dr 32; CM 126): a check through the book of Est. (chosen only at random as a piece of literature from the right period) reveals that this phenomenon is quite common there too: cf. Est. 2: 9 (where *ltt lh* is placed *after* its object), 3: 8.13 (again with inversion), 4: 7, 7: 4a, 8: 11 and 9: 24. Some of these references compare quite closely with the kind of constructions found in the passages listed from Chr.,[3] e.g. compare 1 Chr. 15: 19.21 with Est. 3: 13, 8: 11; 1 Chr. 25: 5 with Est. 3: 13, 4: 7 (the content of a decree or promise); 2 Chr. 22: 3b with Est. 9: 24 (plot/counsel). Furthermore, 2 Chr. 36: 19 is an inverted form of the inf. with *l* continuing a finite verb, a construction found 'especially in the later books'.[4] We may conclude that this is by no means a feature peculiar to the Chronicler.

(13) *'l-yd*, *'l-ydy = according to the guidance of* (Dr 34; CM 86): since this is found eight times in Chr., twice in Jer. (5: 31, 33: 13) but only once in Ezr., there is not sufficient evidence to argue that this is characteristic of Ezr.-Neh., as it may be of Chr.

(14) *wkklwt* (Dr 37a; see also no. 15 following): this form, with its position first in the sentence, is found (as listed) three times in Chr., once in Ezr. and (*not* listed by Dr) once at Dan. 12: 7. Also to be compared are Ezek. 43: 23 – *bklwtk mḥṭ'* – and 2 Sam. 11: 19 – *kklwtk . . .* (not listed). No conclusions, therefore, can be drawn from this.

(15) Order of clauses: 'Subordinate temporal and causal clauses are placed at the beginning of the sentence (where in the earlier language either they were introduced later, or, if placed at the beginning for sake of greater prominence, ויהי was prefixed)' (Dr 37b; CM 125): CM find this twenty-one times in Chr., four times in Ezr., twice in Est. and nine times in Dan. There is thus ample justification for Delitzsch to classify this construction as LBH generally.[5] It was not unknown, however, even in pre-exilic times: e.g. 1 Sam. 17: 55, Gen. 27: 34.

(16) *l* as the mark of the accus. (Dr 39; CM 128): reference to the grammars and dictionaries which treat this feature[6] shows clearly that

---

[1] S. R. Driver: *Samuel*, pp. 84f.   [2] M. H. Segal: *Grammar*, para. 477.

[3] Both lists include 1 Chr. 22: 5; however, the inf. under consideration (*lhgdl*) comes neither at the end of a sentence nor even at the end of its clause. It may therefore be left out of consideration.   [4] *GK* 114p.

[5] Cf. Delitzsch's letter cited by S. R. Driver in *Samuel*, at 1 Sam. 17: 55.

[6] Cf. *GK* 117n, BDB, pp. 511f., F. Giesebrecht: *Die hebraeische Praeposition Lamed*, pp. 79–83 and Segal: *Grammar*, para. 351.

it is a late phenomenon generally. Moreover, in the detailed classification supplied by both Dr and CM, it will be noticed that for each category, either there are examples drawn from passages outside our books or that the references do not occur frequently enough (if at all) in both Chr. and Ezr.-Neh. to draw any firm conclusions as to authorship.

(17) *l* with the inf., expressing *necessity, purpose, intention* (Dr 40; CM 129): it is widely recognized that there is to be found an increasing frequency of this usage generally in LBH[1] which continued on also into Mishnaic Hebrew.[2] Thus, using Est. alone once more as a sample, it occurs at Est. 2: 11, 3: 15, 4: 4.5.7.8 (five times), 7: 1.7 and 9: 2.

(18) *b* expressing concomitance (without a verb) (Dr 41; CM 136): according to the examples as listed, this occurs only once in Ezr.-Neh., at Ezr. 3: 12b. There, however, there is uncertainty about the text itself, so that Batten, for instance, wishes to emend *btrw'h* into a verb: *mry'ym*.[3] But even retaining the text as it stands, it is difficult not to construe the *b* with *lhrym qwl*,[4] so that this verse must be discounted as an example of this particular usage. There will then be no instance of it in Ezr.-Neh., making it irrelevant for this discussion. The construction also occurs elsewhere, e.g. at Hag. 2: 3.

(19) *l'yn = in the condition of none* . . . *= without* (Dr 43; CM 132): *l'yn* is found only once in Ezr., at 9: 14, but the sense there seems to be rather different from its five occurrences in Chr. In these latter, it is equivalent to the English 'without'. The verse in Ezr., however, reads *hl' tn'p bnw 'd klh l'yn š'ryt wplyṭh* . . . This does not so much mean '. . . till thou wouldest consume us without a remnant . . .' as '. . . consume us *until* there was no remnant . . .'. The force of the '*d* carries over to the *l*.[5] The verse was clearly understood thus by its earliest Greek translator:

ouchi ōrgisthēs hēmin apolesai hēmas heōs tou mē katalipein hrizan kai sperma kai onoma hēmōn 1 Esdras 8: 85. This means that we cannot group the uses of *l'yn* to support common authorship.

(20) *lhrbh* (Dr 44; CM 134): since this is found only twice in Chr. and once in the NM (Neh. 5: 18), it does not contribute at all to our purpose.

(21) *l* of 'introduction' (Dr 45b; CM 130b. There is some confusion in CM at this point, for some of the instances cited here are also found at 128b, cases where *l* marks the end of an enumeration!): the list of

---

[1] Cf. *GK* 114l, S. R. Driver: *Tenses*, paras. 202–6, and, specifically for *l' l* . . ., *'yn l* . . ., A. B. Davidson: *Syntax*, para. 95b.

[2] Segal: *Grammar*, paras. 344ff. and 514.

[3] L. W. Batten: *Ezra and Nehemiah*, p. 125.

[4] Compare no. 12 above for the word order.

[5] There is thus no need actually to emend the text at this point, *contra* Batten: *Ezra and Nehemiah*, p. 339.

passages where *l* is used in this way at BDB, p. 514 B shows that it is not confined to Chr. and Ezr.-Neh. It is also found in Aramaic at Ezr. 6: 7. Thus, though its occurrence is unusually frequent in Chr., its one appearance only in the Hebrew of Ezr.-Neh. (at Ezr. 7: 28) does not allow us to conclude that these latter books present it as a stylistic peculiarity over against other OT writers.

(22) *mšwrr* and *šw'rym* (Dr 46; CM 111 and 116): it is not at all surprising that these two terms for minor cultic officials are found only in Chr. and Ezr.-Neh. Since without doubt they reflect the actual situation in the second temple at least (if not the first), their appearance only reflects the interests of these books, and has no bearing on the question of authorship. In this connection, it is therefore of far more significance that for a comparable group, the *ntynym*, Chr. and Ezr.-Neh. reflect *contrary* traditions concerning their origins.[1] Moreover, whereas they occur frequently in Ezr.-Neh., they are mentioned only once in Chr. (1 Chr. 9: 2), and that in a list which has been incorporated from a separate source.

(23) *brwrym, -wt* (CM 16): being found only three times in Chr., and once in the NM, these words do not contribute at all to our discussion.

(24) *'drknym* (CM 22): this word is found at 1 Chr. 29: 7 and Ezr. 8: 27. Though anachronistic in Chr., no conclusions can be drawn from its single occurrence. Words of this kind hardly give themselves over to stylistic variation!

(25) *hll (l)yhwh* and *hll* (abs.), of technical levitical function (CM 27): since so particular a definition has been put on this expression, it is difficult to imagine where else in LBH we might expect to find it. In the direct speech of the Pss., however, *hll* with the direct object occurs frequently.

(26) *ḥasdê = good works, pious deeds* (CM 43): the only instance of the word with this meaning in Ezr.-Neh. is in the NM (Neh. 13: 14). Moreover, this development of meaning may be traced into the post-Biblical period generally,[2] and may be compared with the shift of meaning in *ṣdqh* possibly found at Dan. 4: 24.[3] Isa. 57: 1 has these two words in parallel in a passage that may also reflect this development. On grounds of distribution alone, however, the word is discounted for our purposes.

(27) *kpwr* (CM 57): the extremely bizarre distribution of this word

---

[1] Cf. S. Japhet: 'The Supposed Common Authorship'.

[2] Cf. Jastrow, p. 486.

[3] Theodotion translated this as *en eleēmosunais*, which A. A. Bevan considers 'possibly right': *Daniel*, p. 94. This meaning is supported by, for instance, R. H. Charles: *Daniel*, p. 97, and N. W. Porteous: *Daniel*, pp. 71f. Other commentators disagree as to how far in this direction the author of Daniel had reached, but all agree that he had moved that way.

shows that it is of such a technical nature as to render it worthless for a discussion of the characteristics of an author's style: I Chr. 28: 17 (six times), Ezr. 1: 10 (twice), 8: 27. We may note that it does not occur in 2 Chr. 36, which we might have expected on the basis of the reference in Ezr., were this a favourite word of a single author.

(28) *lḥm hm'rkt* and equivalents (CM 61): the earlier *lḥm hpnym* gives way in LBH to a number of related terms: *lḥm hm'rkt, m'rkt lḥm, šlḥn hm'rkt* and *m'rkt tmyd*. It would again be hazardous to base any conclusions upon this very specialized terminology, the more so as *m'rkt* in fact occurs also at Lev. 24: 6 and 7.

(29) *nś'=take* as a wife (usually with *l*) (CM 76): appearance of this idiom at Ruth 1: 4 and in the NM (Neh. 13: 25) suggests that it had a general distribution in LBH.

(30) CM 78 groups a number of similar expressions *ntn yd l, ntn yd tḥt, ntn ydm lhwṣy'* and *ntn lb l*. The first three only occur once each, and so cannot help our enquiry at all. The last expression, the only one to use *lb*, is not found at all in Ezr.-Neh., but twice in Chr., once in Dan. and five times in Eccl. It, too, is therefore inconclusive for our discussion.

(31) *lh'byr qwl* (CM 82): this idiom is found at 2 Chr. 30: 5, 36: 22= Ezr. 1: 1, Ezr. 10: 7, Neh. 8: 15, Ex. 36: 6. Since 2 Chr. 36: 22 is probably added later from Ezr. 1: 1, only one reference remains for Chr., the same as for Ex. This can hardly satisfy the criterion of distribution.

(32) *'l-yd=next to* (in a series) (CM 85): this meaning occurs many times in Neh. 3 and at Neh. 13: 13 (both from the NM). It is therefore not the mark of a single author. The definition of *'l-yd* as having this meaning is in any case a false one to some extent, and is such as to include only works that show an interest in lists. In its sense of *beside* (which it really retains here too), its distribution is rather wider.[1]

F

Up to this point, an attempt has been made to show that much of the published evidence for the use of style in the question of the extent of the Chronicler's work is totally irrelevant, or at best quite inconclusive. Only thirty-five entries remain of the lists under consideration, and it will next be argued that the majority of these in fact favour the view that separate authors were responsible for Chr. and Ezr.-Neh. Where these have already been treated by Japhet in her article, a reference to that discussion will suffice. More attention will be given to those items which she has not included in her work.

(1) *lrb=abundantly* (Dr 2; CM 105).[2]

[1] Cf. BDB, p. 391 B.
[2] Japhet: 'The Supposed Common Authorship', p. 358.

(2) *m'l* (Dr 3; CM 68): this word is not only frequent in our books, but also in Ezek., P[1] and elsewhere. However, it appears to be used in different ways in Chr. and Ezr.-Neh. In the former, its precise content is not always made clear (e.g. 2 Chr. 33: 19), but whenever it is, it nearly always refers to an offence against the Jerusalem temple and the purity of its service. A striking example of this is the case of Uzziah, whose entry into the temple was boldly denounced: 'When he was strong, his heart was lifted up so that he did corruptly, and he trespassed (*wym'l*) against the Lord his God, for he went into the temple of the Lord to burn incense upon the altar of incense' (2 Chr. 26: 16). The rebuke of the priests confirms the point: 'Go out of the sanctuary; for thou hast trespassed (*m'lt*)' (v. 18). The examples could be multiplied. We read of 'all the vessels which king Ahaz in his reign did cast away when he trespassed' (2 Chr. 29: 19), and of Hezekiah, who ordered the priests to cleanse the holy place 'for our fathers have trespassed' (2 Chr. 29: 5f.), and so on: cf. 2 Chr. 28: 19.22, 30: 7, 36: 14.

In Ezr.-Neh., however, *m'l* is used with but one exception for the people's infidelity in the matter of mixed marriages (Ezr. 9: 2.4, 10: 2.6.10, Neh. 13: 27). The exception – Neh. 1: 8 – is very general in reference and is thus neutral for the purposes of the present discussion.

Now it would be possible to argue that a single author was in fact here making a very important point for his readers by thus stressing the serious nature of these mixed marriages: he puts them on a level with the infidelity of the period of the monarchy against the temple, an infidelity which in fact led directly to the exile (1 Chr. 9: 1, 2 Chr. 36: 14). This seems rather too subtle, however, for it is doubtful if his original readers would have appreciated the point. It is therefore perhaps more satisfactory to admit that the same word is being used in different ways in the two books. This makes diversity of authorship more probable.

(3) *hkyn* (Dr 6; CM 54): as set out in both lists, the evidence in favour of unity of authorship provided by this word looks compelling. Fuller investigation, however, alters the picture in three main ways.

(a) *hkyn* is used in many other books of both the pre- and post-exilic periods with meanings identical to those found in Chr. and Ezr.-Neh. Just a few of the many examples possible may be listed:

of establishing the kingdom, etc.	1 Sam. 13: 13, 1 Ki. 2: 24, 2 Sam. 5: 12 (parallel with 1 Chr. 14: 2), 2 Sam. 7: 12 (parallel with 1 Chr. 17: 11)
of place (*mqwm*)	Ex. 23: 20; cf. 1 Chr. 15: 1 and 3
of buildings	1 Ki. 6: 19
of gallows	Est. 6: 4, 7: 10
of an image	Isa. 40: 20. In usage, this is identical with Ezr. 3: 3, where the altar is set up.

[1] Cf. *ILOT*, p. 134, no. 43.

(b) Both lists single out the use of *hkyn* with *lb* as being especially significant. This too is found elsewhere, however: cf. 1 Sam. 7: 3, Job 11: 13 and Ps. 78: 8.

(c) *hkyn* is used only twice in Ezr. (never in Neh.), and as we have seen, both instances are in senses that have close parallels in other parts of the Bible. This, then, is in no way exceptional for either BH or LBH. In the books of Chr., however, the word is used some forty times. This is far more than might normally be expected, suggesting that it was a favourite word of the Chronicler. Since this feature is not reflected in the books of Ezr. and Neh., it would seem to favour the work of separate authors.

(4) *drš* 'to seek to, to enquire of* (God), in a general sense, of seeking Him in the various exercises and offices of religion', weakened from the earlier sense of a special enquiry, especially by a prophet (Dr 7; CM 23): though not indicated by the evidence as presented in the lists, this 'weakened' sense seems to have been a general development in LBH.[1] In the Pss., it is found at 9: 11, 14: 2 (=53: 3), 24: 6 (where vv. 3–5 make clear that it is used in the sense as defined by Dr), 22: 27 (cf. v. 26), 34: 5.11, 69: 33, 77: 3, 78: 34 (cf. 2 Chr. 20: 3), 105: 4 (paralleled at 1 Chr. 16: 11), 119: 2.10. Since the Psalms are generally thought to have had some kind of cultic setting, the use of *drš* in this context may be assumed to mean to seek God 'in the various exercises and offices of religion'. As indicated above, some of the passages make this clear in any case.

There are other passages that may have the same sense too, e.g. Isa. 9: 12, 31: 1, 55: 6, 65: 10 (where, as often in Chr., there is a contrast with *'zb* in v. 11) and Job 5: 8. Without doubt, this word was a favourite of the Chronicler, for it occurs very frequently in Chr. In Ezr., however, it occurs only three times, which reflects more accurately the general level of distribution for the period. The situation is thus analogous to that of *hkyn* treated above, and so may be said to imply diversity of authorship.

(5) *hthzq* (Dr 8; CM 38): nearly all the occurrences of this word are found in Chr. alone (fifteen times), as the lists clearly show. It occurs only once in Ezr. (7: 28), and that, as CM makes clear, with a meaning slightly different from the one normally found in Chr., but one that *is* paralleled elsewhere in the Bible (cf. Dan. 10: 19). Thus, as Dr implies, the really distinctive uses (such as those followed by *lpny* and *'l*) are peculiar to the Chronicler alone, where the distribution is also much higher, whilst Ezr. once more fits into the more normal BH practice. This word too, therefore, supports diversity of authorship.

(6) *'zr = help* of divine assistance (Dr 10; CM 84): this meaning of *'zr* is frequent in Chr., and is also found extensively in the Psalms and

[1] Cf. C. Westermann: 'Die Begriffe für fragen und suchen'.

Deutero-Isaiah.[1] Thus, though by no means unique to the Chronicler, it would seem to be another of his favourite words. This contrasts strongly with Ezr.-Neh., however, for despite ample opportunity, it is not found even once in that work.

(7) *lmʿlh* (Dr 13; CM 87).[2]

(8) *'rṣwt* and *ʿmy h'rṣwt* (Dr 14; CM 6 and 91):

(a) Used in a purely general way as a plural meaning 'lands', this is a largely late form, but one that is then quite common, as Dr concedes.[3] It is found, for instance, seven times in Jer., twenty-six times in Ezek. and three times in Dan., as well as elsewhere.

(b) As an explicit designation for Israel or for districts of Israel (i.e. where Israel or the districts are mentioned by name), it is used by Chr. alone in the OT: 1 Chr. 13: 2, 2 Chr. 11: 23, 34: 33.

(c) The expression *ʿmy h'rṣwt* is used differently in our two books. In Ezr.-Neh., it occurs at Ezr. 3: 3, 9: 1.2.11, Neh. 9: 30, 10: 29. Its meaning there has been summarized by Vogt as 'die heidnische Bevölkerung im Umkreis der Provinz Juda'.[4] It is important to notice that, with the possible exception of Neh. 9: 30, it always refers to non-Jews living within the borders of Israel.

At 2 Chr. 32: 17 (and cf. v. 13), the reference is quite clearly to the inhabitants of other lands. Whilst this fact is not made explicit at the phrase's only other appearance in Chr. (2 Chr. 13: 9), we should, to be consistent, give it the same meaning there, a meaning which in any case makes the best sense in that passage.

This expression, as is well known, was of great importance for the post-exilic community in its efforts to establish a sense of self-identity. We may therefore consider it very unlikely that a single author would have confused the issue by using it in two different ways.

(d) We may note finally that the expression *mmlkwt h'rṣwt* is peculiar to Chr: 1 Chr. 29: 30, 2 Chr. 12: 8, 17: 10, 20: 29.

(9) *mbyn* (Dr 15; CM 11): we should distinguish two related meanings of this word in a way that is not done in either list:

(a) It is used for men of understanding generally at 1 Chr. 27: 32, Ezr. 8: 16, Neh. 10: 29, Prov. 8: 9, 17: 10.24, 28: 2.11. This sense, therefore, is not peculiar to our books.

(b) It has also the meaning of those with a specific technical skill, and often governs the preposition *b*: 1 Chr. 15: 22, 25: 7.8, 2 Chr. 26: 5, 34: 12. Here again, we might have expected to find this usage also in

---

[1] Pss. 10: 14, 28: 7 (passive), 30: 11, 37: 40, 46: 6, 54: 6, 79: 9, 86: 17, 109: 26, 118: 7.13, 119: 86.173, Isa. 41: 10.13.14, 44: 2, 49: 8, 50: 7.9.

[2] Japhet: 'The Supposed Common Authorship', pp. 357f.

[3] Cf. his cross-reference to *ILOT*, p. 297, no. 4.

[4] H. C. M. Vogt: *Studie*, p. 154. Vogt discusses the phrase in detail on pp. 152–4.

Ezr.-Neh., but in fact it is confined to Chr. Once more, a careful examination suggests that we are dealing with separate authors.

(10) *nkn'* (Dr 18; CM 56).[1]

(11) *šm'wny* (Dr 22; CM 115).[2]

(12) *'šr wkbwd* (Dr 24; CM 94).[3]

(13) *hmwn* (Dr 25; CM 28).[4]

(14) *hyh phd yhwh 'l* (Dr 26; CM 96).[5]

(15) *mhlqt* (Dr 46; CM 42).[6]

(16) *bdl* (Niph.)=*separate oneself* (reflex. of Hiph.) (CM 8): this is found at Num. 16:21, 1 Chr. 12:9, 23:13 and seven times in Ezr.-Neh. Once again, we should note a difference in usage. At 1 Chr. 12:9, it is followed by *'l*, and the RSV renders: 'From the Gadites there went over to David . . .'. At 1 Chr. 23:13, the thought is of being set apart for an office (followed by *l* with the inf.).

In Ezr.-Neh., on the other hand, it is normally followed by *mn* in the sense of separation from the heathen. This is quite clear at Ezr. 6:21, 9:1, 10:11, Neh. 9:2, 10:29. At Ezr. 10:16, it is used absolutely, though with the same sense. However, many of the commentators prefer to follow the LXX at this point, and so to read *wybdl (lw)*, in which case it should not be included in our discussion. At Ezr. 10:8, the word is used to express exclusion from the community, which is a different sense again. We can see, then, that it is Ezr.-Neh. who use the word in a distinctive manner, but in this they are not followed by Chr.

(17) *mgrš* (CM 20).[7]

(18) *hzh* (CM 37): in the sense of a *seer*, *hzh* has a wide distribution, though this is especially marked in Chr. As applied to a singer, it is found only in Chr.: 1 Chr. 25:5, 2 Chr. 29:30, 35:15. By contrast, it is not found at all with either meaning in Ezr.-Neh., despite their interest, shared with the Chronicler, in the musical aspects of the cult.

(19) *hṣṣr* pi'el and hiph. (CM 44b): this verb comes six times in the Bible, all of them in Chr. Since it is again a term associated with the music of the cult, we might have expected also to find it in Ezr.-Neh., were the same man responsible for these books, particularly at Ezr. 3:10, Neh. 12:35.41, where there is mention of the priests with their trumpets.

(20) *kyd 'lhy htwbh 'ly* (CM 45).[8]

(21) *ydh* (Hithp.)=*give thanks* and *confess* (CM 46b): as seen above (section D, no. 16), the hiph. of *ydh* is commonly used for *to praise* in ritual worship. This appears also to be the sense of the only occurrence of the hithp. in Chr., at 2 Chr. 30:22. In Ezr.-Neh., by contrast,

[1] Japhet: 'The Supposed Common Authorship', pp. 359f.
[2] *Ibid.* pp. 358f.   [3] *Ibid.* p. 366.   [4] *Ibid.* pp. 365f.
[5] *Ibid.* pp. 360f.   [6] *Ibid.* pp. 344–8.   [7] *Ibid.* pp. 348–50.
[8] *Ibid.* pp. 366f.

the hithp. is used for confession of sin (Ezr. 10: 1, Neh. 1: 6, 9: 2.3).
Acts of confession occur several times in the Chronicler's narrative
(e.g. 2 Chr. 12: 6, 28: 12–13, 29: 5–11, 33: 13, 34: 27), but not once
does he use the hithp. of *ydh* to describe them. Rather, he often uses as
a circumlocution one or another of his favourite words as grouped in
2 Chr. 7: 14.

(22) *twldwt* (CM 50): this word comes nine times in Chr., but never
in Ezr.-Neh., despite a number of lists of names where it might have
been expected.

(23) *mṣ'* (Niph.)=*be present* (CM 69): whilst this usage is common
in Chr. (ten times), it is found only once in Ezr.-Neh. (Ezr. 8: 25). As
shown by CM, it is also found in other OT passages. Once more, this
puts Ezr.-Neh. in line with the normal Biblical practice, whilst Chr.
stands out as the exception.

(24) *ntynym* (CM 79).[1]

(25) *'bwdh*=*service* of God (CM 81): this sense of *'bwdh*, whilst
common in P and occurring elsewhere too, is an especial favourite
of the Chronicler, CM listing thirty-six instances of its usage in Chr.
In Ezr.-Neh., by contrast, it is found with this meaning only once,
at Neh. 10: 33.

(26) *'ṣr kḥ* (CM 92).[2]

(27) *śr*=*prince, chief, ruler*, of religious office (CM 110): the various
uses of *śr* in this sense may be itemized in more detail:

(a) *śry hkhnym*	2 Chr. 36: 14, Ezr. 8: 24.29, 10: 5
(b) leaders of Levites: *śr hlwym*	1 Chr. 15: 22
śry hlwym	1 Chr. 15: 16, 2 Chr. 35: 9
hśr	1 Chr. 15: 5.6.7.8.9.10
hśr hmś' hmśrrym	1 Chr. 15: 27
(c) other: *śry qdś wśry h'lhym*	1 Chr. 24: 5 (cf. Isa. 43: 28)

It is quite likely that we are here dealing with actual titles of the second
temple period. It is thus not so surprising to find *śry hkhnym* used in
both Chr. and Ezr.-Neh. as to observe that only in Chr. is *śr* used in
connection with the Levites (ten times) where Ezr.-Neh. have instead
an apparently alternative title, *r'śy hlwym* (Neh. 11: 16, 12: 24), a title
which in turn is not found in Chr.

(28) 'The combination of two plural forms (contrary to better usage)'
(CM 123): instances have been noted by Kropat[3] where the Chronicler
may even alter his *Vorlage* to effect a combination of two plural forms,
or else uses two plurals for a phrase which occurs elsewhere in the OT

---

[1] *Ibid.* pp. 351–4.   [2] *Ibid.* p. 360.
[3] A. Kropat: *Syntax*, pp. 8f., and cf. A. Bendavid: *Biblical Hebrew and Mishnaic Hebrew*, I, 70.

with one part in the singular.[1] In Ezr.-Neh., however, such combinations are used nearly always in titles or stereotyped expressions only, e.g. r'šy h'bwt,[2] bny 'bdy šlmh,[3] kwkby hšmym,[4] etc. The rather curious effect of the Chronicler's style in this regard is thus not reflected in these other books.[5]

It is not suggested that all the twenty-eight items listed here are of equal force in a discussion of the authorship of Chr. and Ezr.-Neh. Should some (the majority of which were collected by Japhet) appear convincing, however, the remainder may add a certain corroborative weight to the argument.

G

It remains finally to present the few items from the lists of Dr and CM that apparently satisfy the criteria set out at the beginning of this chapter. Even here, however, reservations must be drawn concerning some of them. It is submitted that they are not sufficient to outweigh the contrary evidence.

(1) 'šmh (Dr 19; CM 7): this word is used seven times in Chr. and six times in Ezr. Even so, we should observe that it is also found at Lev. 4: 3, 5: 24, 22: 16, Amos 8: 14 and Ps. 69: 6. Thus, though not fully satisfying the criterion of distribution, it is at least nearer what we would expect of a single author.

(2) ywm bywm (Dr 29; CM 48): this expression is found four times in Chr. and three times in the Hebrew of Ezr.-Neh. kywm bywm is found with the same meaning at 1 Sam. 18: 10.

(3) h for the relative[6] (Dr 36; CM 119): according to the MT, this phenomenon occurs in quite a number of passages outside our books.[7] However, Ewald,[8] GK[9] and Driver[10] all seek to explain these away, leaving only five references in Chr. and three in Ezr.

If they are right in so doing, this example would fully satisfy the criteria. We should note, however, that according to Davidson, 'Dan. 8: 1, being late, is doubtful',[11] a recognition that this may be a more general late development, so that we should not attempt automatically to exclude all possible occurrences of it.[12]

---

[1] E.g. 'nšy šmwt at 1 Chr. 5: 24, 12: 31; gbwry ḥylym at 1 Chr. 7: 5.7.11.40, 11: 26; 'ry mṣwrwt at 2 Chr. 11: 10.23, 12: 4, 21: 3, etc.

[2] Ezr. 1: 5, 2: 6, 3: 12, 4: 2.3, 8: 1, 10: 16, Neh. 7: 70, 8: 13, 12: 12.22.23.

[3] Ezr. 2: 55.58, Neh. 7: 57.60, 11: 3.   [4] Neh. 9: 23.

[5] CM refer to L. Zunz: *Die gottesdienstlichen Vorträge* for this characteristic. However, Zunz compared only 'my h'rṣwt in Ezr.-Neh. with gbwry ḥylym in Chr. (p. 22), which does not alter the results of our analysis.

[6] The intention here is to exclude usage with the participle which is, of course, quite common.   [7] Cf. GK 138i and k.   [8] H. Ewald: *Lehrbuch*, para. 331b.

[9] GK 138k.   [10] S. R. Driver: *Samuel*, at 1 Sam. 9: 24.

[11] A. B. Davidson: *Syntax*, para. 22, R 4 (p. 30).

[12] Cf. A. Sperber: *A Historical Grammar*, p. 285.

(4) *'d l* before a subst. (for *'d* or *l* alone) (Dr 38; CM 127): in BH, this combination is found only in Chr. (fifteen times) and Ezr. (four times),[1] though *'d lpny* is found at Est. 4: 2. It thus forms the strongest argument for unity of authorship on the basis of these lists,[2] though as is apparent, it stands rather isolated in this regard.

(5) *mṣltym* (Dr 46; CM 100) occurs eleven times in Chr. and once each in Ezr. and Neh. Its equivalent, *ṣlṣlym*, is found at 2 Sam. 6: 5 and Ps. 150: 6 (twice). Thus it would be possible to argue that it is idiosyncratic of a single author, but on the other hand its distribution may be accounted for on the basis of its being a rather specialized word, with its form as merely a later development of the earlier *ṣlṣlym*.

(6) *śmḥh gdwlh* (CM 109) comes twice in Chr., three times in Ezr. and twice in Neh. With these should be compared 1 Ki. 1: 40, Jonah 4: 6 and (less exactly) Isa. 9: 2. Thus its use in our books is not unique, though it constitutes a better example in favour of unity of authorship than most.

H

Having now presented all the evidence relating to the two lists in Dr and CM, we may briefly summarize by observing that for the specific purpose of demonstrating the unity of authorship of Chr. and Ezr.-Neh. on the basis of style, the large majority of the entries are found to be irrelevant or quite inconclusive. Of the remainder, most in fact favour diversity of authorship, and serious questions can be raised about at least four of the six items that might favour unity.

It should be stressed that the discussion of this chapter is not in itself intended in any way to be conclusive. It has been limited strictly to the evidence as published in two works, even though it seems that most scholars have subsequently based their arguments on these works. The intention rather has been to show that the evidence from style now available does not compel us to accept that these books are the work of a single author; the validity of Japhet's reasoning to the contrary is thus enhanced. Moreover, the arguments concerning theological outlook remain to be examined. Nevertheless, as far as the argument from style is concerned, the onus now rests on those who favour unity of authorship to produce more compelling new arguments to support their position.

---

[1] Cf. F. Giesebrecht: *Die hebraeische Praeposition Lamed*, p. 16.

[2] 'This combination of prepositions is one of the most characteristic marks of the Chr.'s style', C. C. Torrey: *Composition*, p. 19. By contrast, however, it is worth observing that, on the basis of the material analysed by Giesebrecht, there are also some aspects of the use of *lamed* in Chr. that distinguish it from Ezr.-Neh. Thus, for instance, the use of *l* for 'becoming': 'Besonders die Sprache der Chronik und der Poesie', p. 56; the use of *h'myd l*, p. 57; of *'śr l*, p. 71 and cf. some especially idiosyncratic uses of *lpny* on p. 19.

5

Ideology

The fourth main argument usually adduced in favour of the unity of Chr. and Ezr.-Neh. is that they reflect the same interests, outlook and theology. So many different topics could be included that we have felt it best to gather them all under the general heading of ideology. The treatment here is not meant to be exhaustive, and where other scholars have dealt satisfactorily with aspects of the issue under review, discussion will be kept to a minimum.

We have already several times admitted that in many respects our books do share certain interests in common. This in itself, however, as has been stressed by Segal,[1] does not prove that they were written by the same man. These interests are often those that would doubtless have been shared by most of the Jews living in Jerusalem at the time.

For our present purposes, therefore, it has seemed likely that if differences of outlook between the books could be detected, these would be of greater significance. Accordingly, it is hoped in this chapter to show that there are such differences, and that if these be added to the evidence of the previous chapters, the conclusion will be that separate authors were responsible for these books.

A. MIXED MARRIAGES

One of the central features of the reforms of both Ezra and Nehemiah was their insistence on the finishing of marriages between the Jewish population of Judah and others. There are certain well-known differences over the exact identity of these 'others' (e.g. contrast Ezr. 9: 1 with Neh. 13: 23) and concerning the courses of action adopted by Ezra and Nehemiah to deal with these marriages.[2] The basic problem and the urgent need for its solution remain, however, among the characteristics of these books.[3]

The strong contrast between this outlook and that of Chr. may be

---

[1] M. H. Segal: 'The Books of Ezra-Nehemiah', p. 83.
[2] Cf. H. H. Rowley: 'The Chronological Order', pp. 162f.
[3] In addition to the commentaries, cf. the brief treatment of H. C. M. Vogt: *Studie*, pp. 155f.

indicated first on the basis of some words of Nehemiah. In his exhortation against such marriages, Nehemiah argues:

> Did not Solomon king of Israel sin by these things? yet among many nations there was no king like him, and he was beloved of his God, and God made him king over all Israel: nevertheless, even him did strange women cause to sin (Neh. 13: 26).

When we turn with this in mind to the Chronicler's account of Solomon's reign, however, far from using such a golden opportunity of driving home this important lesson to his readers, we find that he actually omits from 1 Ki. 11: 1ff. the very account to which Nehemiah refers. It is usually argued that this passage was omitted by the Chronicler because he wanted to make of Solomon an ideal figure.[1] However, if Ezr.-Neh. is an integral part of his work, that argument completely breaks down in view of Neh. 13: 26. It seems far more sensible to see here the divergent emphases of separate authors.

This conclusion is strengthened when we realize that in fact the Chronicler nowhere condemns mixed marriages, but if anything rather condones them. We find that several of the ancestors of the tribes were involved in such marriages: Judah married Bathshua the Canaanitess (1 Chr. 2: 3); David's sister Abigail bore a son by Jether the Ishmaelite (1 Chr. 2: 17); Sheshan gave his daughter to his Egyptian slave (1 Chr. 2: 34f.); Manasseh had children by an Aramaean concubine (1 Chr. 7: 14), and so on (1 Chr. 4: 17, 8: 8). Furthermore, David himself married foreign wives (1 Chr. 3: 1), as did other influential figures mentioned in the Chronicler's narrative (cf. 2 Chr. 2: 13, 8: 11, 12: 13, 24: 26). In the face of such evidence, it seems hard to believe that the Chronicler condemned mixed marriages with the same vigour as Ezr.-Neh.

On the basis of Neh. 13: 26 primarily, therefore, with these other factors fully in support, we suggest that a difference of outlook over an issue of central importance is thus reflected between Chr. and Ezr.-Neh.

B. THE EARLY HISTORY OF ISRAEL

Neither Chr. nor Ezr.-Neh. deals directly with the early history of their people. As we would expect, both books show by numerous incidental references that they are fully conversant with the whole range of Pentateuchal traditions. Nevertheless, when full allowance has been made for that fact, there remains a significant divergence of emphasis.

In Ezr.-Neh., as Vogt has successfully shown,[2] the community is

---

[1] So, amongst recent writers, R. Mosis, p. 158; R. L. Braun: 'Solomonic Apologetic', p. 512.

[2] Vogt: *Studie*, especially pp. 55–9.

presented as standing in the direct succession of the Israel of the Exodus and Conquest of the land. Of the passages which he mentions, we should single out in particular Neh. 1:10 and Neh. 9. In Neh. 1:10, the Exodus is made the basis for appeal to God in prayer. In Neh. 9, there is recorded the confession and statement of faith that lies at the basis of the covenant (Neh. 10) which should perhaps be regarded as the climax of the books as a whole.[1] In this confession, the election of Abraham marks the beginning of God's dealings with his people (vv. 7f.), whilst the Exodus and associated events dominate the presentation as a whole (vv. 9ff.).

In Chr., by contrast, there is a marked emphasis on Jacob, probably because he was in an immediate sense the father of the children of Israel. This emphasis comes to expression in a variety of ways. First, as is well known,[2] the Chronicler nearly always uses the name Israel instead of Jacob for the patriarch: 1 Chr. 1:34, 2:1, 5:1 (twice), 5:3, 6:23, 7:29, 16:13.17, 29:10.18 and 2 Chr. 30:6, twelve times in all.[3] In no case is there in fact a precisely parallel passage in which this change is made, but on the other hand most of the instances are in stereotyped formulae which use the name Jacob elsewhere in the Bible.

The only occasion where the Chronicler changes his *Vorlage* to Israel=Jacob is 1 Chr. 16:13, where Ps. 105:6 has Abraham. The citation of this Psalm furnishes the only two times where the Chronicler actually mentions the name Jacob (vv. 13 and 17), and in both cases it is parallel to Israel.

This consistent and distinctive practice of the Chronicler, we may at once point out, is totally absent in Ezr.-Neh.

Secondly, the Chronicler's viewpoint is expressed in the arrangement of the genealogy in 1 Chr. 1:1 – 2:2. The material for these verses is taken from Gen., but its schematic presentation is the Chronicler's.[4] From Adam to Noah (vv. 1–4a) he gives the direct line of descent only,

---

[1] There have been many suggestions as to the original source of this chapter. A. C. Welch, for instance, argued forcefully that it was a litany of the Northern Israelites who remained in the land after the downfall of the Northern Kingdom (*Post-Exilic Judaism*, pp. 25–45). Others think more in terms of a well-known liturgical prayer (e.g. L. H. Brockington: *Ezra, Nehemiah and Esther*, p. 172) or an eclectic composition (e.g. J. M. Myers: *Ezra. Nehemiah*, p. 166). Be that as it may, however, and regardless of the original order of Ezra and Nehemiah, all reconstructions agree in making these chapters the climax of the work of the two reformers. Rudolph summarizes: 'Damit ist die Jahwegemeinde neu konstituiert', *Esra und Nehemia*, p. xxii.

[2] Cf. G. A. Danell: *Israel*, p. 270, *et al.*

[3] In view of this consistency, textual changes on the basis of the LXX (e.g. at 1 Chr. 1:34) should not be entertained.

[4] Cf., in addition to the commentaries, E. Podechard: 'Le Premier Chapitre des Paralipomènes' for discussion of the textual problems of the chapter, and defence of its attribution to the Chronicler.

since of course for him, Noah represented a completely fresh start in genealogical terms. Thereafter, he gives some details of secondary lines, but always treats them first, and thus finishes each section with the stress on the line that was to lead eventually to Israel. Thus: Noah's three sons (Shem, Ham and Japheth, v. 4) are treated in reverse order: Japheth in vv. 5–7, Ham in vv. 8–16 and Shem in vv. 17–23. Even within this latter section, Eber's second son Joktan is treated first (19–23), before (with partial recapitulation) the direct line is traced from Shem to Abraham (24–7).

In this respect, Abraham does not cause any change or division; of his two sons, Isaac and Ishmael (28), Ishmael is treated first (29–33), and then Isaac (34). Here again, the same procedure is followed, with Esau's line detailed first in vv. 35–54, and Israel's in 2: 1ff. Whilst, as we have seen, the same system is used within the section on Shem, since it forms part of the main line, within the secondary lines we find by contrast the more usually expected presentation of genealogical material. Thus in vv. 5–7, the sons of Japheth are treated in the order Gomer, Javan, following v. 5; in vv. 8–16, the sons of Ham in the order Cush (9–10), Egypt (11–12), Canaan (13–16), following v. 8; in 32–3, the sons of Keturah in the order Jokshan (32b), Midian (33), following v. 32a; and in vv. 36–7, the sons of Esau in the order Eliphaz (36), Reuel (37), following v. 35.[1]

By retaining the material that he does, and by presenting it in this abbreviated and systematic form, the Chronicler succeeds in emphasizing that the line he is following is not one of natural descent, but rather must be of election. Of significance for us, however, is the observation that the break in the scheme does not occur with Abraham, but with Israel (Jacob), after which the genealogies are arranged on quite a different principle. It seems that this is an intentional device to stress that it is to this point that the people of Israel should trace its historical beginnings.[2]

Thirdly, attention may be drawn to the Chronicler's handling of

[1] It is not clear how the Chronicler associated Seir (38–42) with the foregoing, the more so if the link through Timna (39b) is secondary (so Rudolph: *ad loc.*).

[2] A parallel situation is provided by some of the Samaritan Chronicles and their 'chain of pure ones', that start with Adam. For the Samaritans
the process in the election of Israel they conceived to have begun with the first Adam, that is, man before the fall from whom the light was transmitted through righteous men until Abraham, the progenitor of Israel. Thus the *realization* of election in the history of a people begins from Abraham properly, because Abraham was a 'new root'. Figures like Abel and Noah belonged to the history of election, but these men could not be regarded as elect Israelites, for Israel as a distinctive unit was born only with Abraham (J. Macdonald: *The Theology of the Samaritans*, p. 277).
With the substitution of Jacob for Abraham, the same could be said of the Chronicler.

Solomon's request when God appeared to him in a dream at Gibeon (2 Chr. 1: 8–10). As well as abbreviating his *Vorlage* drastically at this point (forty-five words as against eighty-one), he introduces an interesting change in his description of the people: *'m rb 'šr l'ymnh wl' yspr mrb* (1 Ki. 3: 8) becomes *'m rb k'pr h'rṣ* (2 Chr. 1: 9). We may suggest that he has substituted for a description that is first used in Gen. for Ishmael and his descendants (Gen. 16: 10) one that was used in God's promise to Jacob during his dream at Bethel (Gen. 28: 14).[1] This again points us to the significance of that patriarch in the Chronicler's thought.

Fourthly, mention should be made of the only occasion on which the Chronicler uses the root *bḥr* in connection with the people as a whole, 1 Chr. 16: 13: *zr' yśr'l 'bdw bny y'qb bḥyryw*. In this verse, Israel (parallel to Jacob) has been introduced for Abraham in Ps. 105: 6. This indicates to us that the verse was of significance in the eyes of the Chronicler. It is therefore no coincidence that 'his chosen ones'[2] is postulated specifically of 'the sons of Jacob'.

The force of these four points is cumulative. In a variety of incidental ways, the Chronicler has betrayed his high estimation of the role of Jacob in his nation's history. This is a distinctive feature of his work, but one that is totally lacking in Ezr.-Neh.

This contrasting situation is further highlighted by the Chronicler's handling of the events of the Exodus. That these events receive less stress in the Chronicler's work has often been noted before, and a number of explanations offered (as conveniently summarized by North).[3] In seeking to elucidate this problem, we may observe first with Brunet[4] that this change of emphasis is most marked in the account of the dedication of the temple in 2 Chr. 6, where the references at 1 Ki. 8: 21.51 and 53 have been reduced or altered (though not in every case completely suppressed). Verses 52 and 53 have been replaced by a citation of Ps. 132: 8–10. The main theme of this Ps. is a prayer for David, whose

---

[1] This seems more likely than a reference to Gen. 13: 16 on several counts: (a) if specific reference to Abraham were intended, we would have expected an allusion either to Gen. 12: 1–3 or to the more characteristic 'stars of heaven' and 'sand on the seashore' (Gen. 15: 5, 22: 17). In the case of Jacob, however, there are no such alternatives; (b) the Chronicler may have been influenced by the parallel dream situation; (c) in view of what has already been seen of the Chronicler's *Tendenz*, an allusion here to Jacob is comprehensible, whereas one to Abraham would seem to have no force.

[2] Though the original form of the Ps. probably read the singular – *bḥyrw* – referring to Jacob as chosen rather than Esau (so C. A. Briggs: *Psalms, ad loc.*), it is now impossible to determine which form constituted the Chronicler's *Vorlage*.

[3] R. North: 'Theology of the Chronicler'; more recently, P. R. Ackroyd: 'History and Theology', pp. 510–12.

[4] A.-M. Brunet: 'La Théologie du Chroniste'.

appeal is based both upon his faithfulness in caring for the Ark (2 Sam. 6) and upon God's promise to him of an eternal dynasty (2 Sam. 7). The Chronicler has retained the essence of both these themes in the verses he has cited. This is most certainly not a matter of chance, for they are themes which are highlighted also in other parts of his work.

One of the distinguishing marks of Chr. against Ki. is its emphasis upon the new role which David assigned to the Levites and its interest in their performance of that role. The reason given for this change, however, is precisely the observation that they need no longer act as bearers of the Tabernacle, and the Ark in particular (cf. 1 Chr. 6: 16f., 16: 7.37–42, 23: 24–32, 2 Chr. 7: 6, 8: 14f. and especially 35: 3), since the temple is to be the final resting place of the Ark (1 Chr. 22: 19, 28: 2, etc.). It is therefore only natural that the Chronicler should have wished to stress the fulfilment of this in his account of the dedication.

The Chronicler also stresses over against Sam./Ki. that it is especially in the building of the temple that the promises to David mediated through Nathan will have their initial fulfilment. This is the main purport of the speeches of David in 1 Chr. 22: 7–19, 28: 2–10, 29: 1–5 and his prayer in 29: 10–19, all of which are peculiar to Chr., and when this is linked with the Chronicler's well-known emphasis on the Davidic dynasty itself, it is again not surprising that he should go beyond the Kings account of the temple dedication in pointing to this fulfilment also.

In both accounts, Solomon's prayer ends with an appeal to God. In 1 Ki. 8: 52–3, the appeal is that God will hear the prayer of his people, and it is based on the fact that they were separated out for God at the time of the Exodus. It thus adds nothing to what has already been said in the substance of the prayer as a whole. In 2 Chr. 6: 40–2, however, whilst the request that the people's prayer be heard is retained, the final appeal is *zkrh lḥsdy dwyd 'bdk* – 'remember the mercies of David thy servant'. This adds a new request to the prayer, but one that is fully in accord with the Chronicler's understanding of the significance of the dedication of the temple, namely that as God's promises have found an initial fulfilment in these events, so they will continue to be realized in like measure thereafter. The basis for this appeal, of course, must therefore be sought in the covenant of 1 Chr. 17.

It is hoped that this brief sketch of the Chronicler's familiar stance on these issues will be sufficient to support the contention that in his description of the dedication of the temple, he has a point of his own to make, and one that inevitably detracts from the emphasis of the Deuteronomist on the Exodus events. It is not just that he takes a deliberately polemical attitude against the very occurrence of those events.[1] That he does not do so would seem to be clear from his presentation in 1 Chr. 17 of David's prayer in response to Nathan's oracle. There, at the establishment of the dynasty, the basis is the previous saving events in the nation's history, namely the Exodus and Conquest, which are given all due attention and emphasis (cf. especially vv. 21f.). Now at the dedication of the temple, however, that basis has for the Chronicler to lose ground to the stress on the new, Davidic covenant.

In Ezr.-Neh., by contrast, there is not reflected any such development in the covenantal basis of God's relationship with Israel.[2] As we have seen, the community is presented as being in the direct succession of the generation of the Exodus, in which the covenant with David plays no part whatever.[3]

C. THE FALL OF THE NORTHERN KINGDOM

In Ezr. 4, two traditions related to the fall of the Northern Kingdom that are not directly recorded elsewhere in the OT are preserved. The first concerns resettlement of the land in the days of Esarhaddon (v. 2), and the second, in one of the Aramaic documents, resettlement by 'the great and noble Osnappar'[4] (v. 10). The most closely related Biblical account is found in 2 Ki. 17: 24, where the context suggests that the king of Assyria involved was Shalmaneser (v. 3), although his successor Sargon II may be intended.[5] Although there is no other direct attestation to these successive waves of repopulation, there is no reason necessarily to doubt them, since they appear to fit satisfactorily with what is known of contemporary Assyrian policy.[6]

[1] *Contra* S. Japhet, who, in *Ideology*, especially pp. 14–19, 93–130 and 367–88 develops the thesis that the Chronicler wished to present a view of Israel in which its origins were timeless and which was marked by continuity of inhabitation of the land. She therefore dispenses almost entirely with historical election, Exodus, Conquest and Exile, since these all imply absence from the land. This extreme view, however, does not stand up to careful scrutiny.
[2] Cf. A. C. Welch: *Post-Exilic Judaism*, pp. 219–25; M. H. Segal: 'The Books of Ezra-Nehemiah', p. 85; J. Liver: 'History and Historiography', p. 225, and D. N. Freedman: 'The Chronicler's Purpose', who calls this 'a complete reversal of the Chronicler's treatment of the tradition' (p. 440).
[3] I am thus not persuaded by P. R. Ackroyd's attempts to harmonize these two approaches: 'History and Theology', pp. 510–13 and 'The Theology of the Chronicler', pp. 113f. The point is not whether Chr. knows of the Exodus or not: he clearly does; it is rather that he presents a development from this basis which is absent in Ezr.-Neh.
[4] Usually identified with Ashurbanipal.
[5] For a reconstruction of the events surrounding the fall of Samaria from the viewpoint of Assyrian history, cf. H. Tadmor: 'The Campaigns of Sargon II of Assur', pp. 33–9, and 'On the History of Samaria', pp. 69–72.
[6] So, for example, A. Malamat: 'The Historical Background of the Assassination of Amon'; contrast S. Talmon: 'Biblical Traditions'.

Within the whole presentation in Ezr.-Neh. of the relationship of the returning Jews to their neighbours, these verses play a most important role. They may be said to give the rationale for the exclusivist attitude that dominates these books.

On the theory of unity of authorship, it is therefore extremely surprising to find that the Chronicler passes over these matters in complete silence. As will be explained in greater detail in Part Two below, not only does he fail to reproduce 2 Ki. 17 or the alternative traditions of resettlement that he is supposed to have included in Ezr. 4, but he even goes so far as to make clear that the North was still populated by genuine Israelites in the period after the Assyrian conquest (2 Chr. 30: 5–11.18. 25), without any suggestion of the presence of a new foreign population. In fact, the only record that he preserves of the Northern exile is in 1 Chr. 5: 26, where the two and a half Transjordanian tribes are exiled by Tilgath-Pilneser. It will be suggested below (p. 82), however, that this paragraph may in any case be secondary. Either way, the account is clearly unrelated to those which have been under discussion.[1]

We shall seek to show later that within the framework of Chr. itself, all these features can be naturally explained. It is most uncertain, however, that they can fit into the ideology of the compiler of Ezr. 4.

D. IMMEDIATE RETRIBUTION

It has for long been recognized that one of the most prominent and characteristic features of the Chronicler's theology is his emphasis upon the doctrine of immediate retribution.[2] The fortunes of the individual monarchs (and through them usually, though not invariably, those of the people) are directly related to their obedience to the law of God. Often, a change for evil or repentance from wickedness causes a dramatic change of status. The basis of this doctrine is furnished by 2 Chron. 7: 14, which establishes the vocabulary through which its development may be traced in Chr., and shows that it is intended to be generally applicable to the people and not just reserved for certain specific cases.

It is noteworthy, therefore, that no trace of this doctrine is to be found in Ezr.-Neh. The piety of the leaders and/or the people is not reflected in sudden up-turns of fortune, but on the contrary may entail an increase of opposition (Ezr. 4, Neh. 4), neither is there any indi-

---

[1] A. Spiro: 'Samaritans, Tobiads and Judahites in Pseudo-Philo', p. 316, suggests that these verses may reflect anti-Tobiad polemic.

[2] Cf. J. Wellhausen: *Prolegomena*, pp. 198–205; R. North: 'Theology of the Chronicler', pp. 372–4, who cites further literature; R. L. Braun: 'The Message of Chronicles', pp. 510f. The most serious attempt to do justice to this doctrine is G. von Rad: *Theologie*, I, 345–7.

cation that confession of sin leads to restoration (Ezr. 9, Neh. 9). Rather, the problems of mixed marriages, tithing and Sabbath profanation seem merely to recur regardless (Neh. 13). The characteristic vocabulary of 2 Chr. 7: 14 does not hold the programmatic significance that it clearly does in Chr.

This contrast is hard to explain if these books are indeed all part of a single work.[1]

E. HISTORIOGRAPHY

There are two aspects of the manner of presentation of history that distinguish between Chr. and Ezr.-Neh. The first concerns the Chronicler's interest in prophecy and the prophets. The point here is not just that he often mentions them: that might be no more than a reflection of the circumstances of history. It is rather that their words are so built into the structure of the narrative that the work as a whole may be termed a prophetic history.[2] It seems that the Chronicler could not conceive of his people's history without the influence of prophecy upon it.

In Ezr.-Neh., by contrast, the prophetic influence has virtually ceased; only the work of Haggai and Zechariah (Ezr. 5: 1–2, 6: 14) could be compared here, but even their influence is qualified (Ezr. 6: 14b), and they are by no means sufficient to obliterate the contrast in this respect between the two works.[3]

The second distinguishing aspect, in line with the first, has been pointed out briefly by Liver:[4] on the one hand, we have a history in which miracles abound, numbers are exaggerated, circumstances are idealized into black and white situations where right and wrong are immediately recognizable. On the other hand, Ezr.-Neh. presents a modest and matter of fact account of the return and later reforms. Here again, the contrast is not inherent in the events themselves, but in the differing approaches to history of separate authors.[5]

[1] Cf. Willi, p. 183, n. 18.

[2] The material itself has often been collected; cf. J. M. Myers: *I Chronicles*, pp. lxxv–lxxvii; Willi, pp. 216–29, and, to a lesser extent, von Rad: 'Die levitische Predigt'. Y. Kaufmann: *History*, 4, 457–79, and Willi in particular have stressed the importance of prophecy in the Chronicler's understanding of history.

[3] Cf. Freedman: 'The Chronicler's Purpose', p. 440. [See now J. D. Newsome: 'Toward a New Understanding'.]

[4] Liver: 'History and Historiography', p. 225.

[5] For a detailed examination of the issues involved in these differing approaches as found in other parts of the OT, cf. I. L. Seeligmann: 'Menschliches Heldentum und göttliche Hilfe'.

Ideology

(a) Mention should further be made of the Nethinim and the sons of Solomon's servants, who feature amongst the cultic personnel throughout Ezr.-Neh. Japhet has shown not only that they are absent from Chr., but that the Chronicler has included variant traditions about the origins and functions of an apparently identical group. We may refer to her convincing presentation for fuller details.[1]

(b) Welch has argued strongly that a difference between the two works may be detected in their attitude to the status of the Levites.[2] Whilst part of this might be due to their association with the Ark, which of course ceased at the time of the exile, it remains true nevertheless that they are more prominent in Chr. as a distinct group than in Ezr.-Neh., and that they are sometimes given teaching (2 Chr. 17: 8, 35: 3), judicial (2 Chr. 19: 8.11) and even prophetic (2 Chr. 20: 14) functions[3] not paralleled in Ezr.-Neh.

(c) A dominant concern of Nehemiah was the correct observance of the Sabbath; cf. Neh. 10: 31, 13: 15–22. He states plainly his reasons for this concern:

> What evil thing is this that ye do, and profane the sabbath day? Did not your fathers thus, and did not our God bring all this evil upon us, and upon this city? Yet ye bring more wrath upon Israel by profaning the sabbath (Neh. 13: 17f.).

In contrast, the Sabbath plays no significant role in Chr., and is most noticeably absent at 2 Chr. 36: 11–16,[4] where we should have expected a reference to it on the basis of Nehemiah's words.

(d) In Part Two below, an attempt will be made to present the Chronicler's concept of Israel. Without anticipating our analysis, it may be claimed here that the picture to emerge will differ most markedly from that in Ezr.-Neh.[5] The idea of the 'holy seed' (Ezr. 9: 2) has no part there, the concept of the remnant is presented in a distinctive manner (cf. pp. 125f.) and there is a stress on a twelve-tribe Israel[6] which contrasts with the concept of Ezr.-Neh. in which 'Israel ist jetzt Juda und Benjamin'.[7]

---

[1] S. Japhet: 'The Supposed Common Authorship', pp. 351–4.
[2] A. C. Welch: *Post-Exilic Judaism*, pp. 227–41.
[3] For further details, cf. Myers: *I Chronicles*, pp. lxixf.
[4] The reference in 2 Chr. 36: 21 to the land enjoying its Sabbaths concerns the Sabbath year, and is not to be associated directly with the question of a weekly Sabbath.
[5] On this latter, the present writer has nothing of significance to add to the work of von Rad: *Geschichtsbild*, pp. 19–25; G. A. Danell: *Israel*, pp. 281–6 and H. C. M. Vogt: *Studie*, especially pp. 47–65.
[6] Cf. Japhet: *Ideology*, pp. 283–313.   [7] von Rad: *Geschichtsbild*, p. 24.

The Extent of the Chronicler's Work

G. CONCLUSION: THE END OF THE CHRONICLER'S WORK

We have now examined all the evidence that has been presented in favour of the view that Chr., Ezr. and Neh. were originally a single composition. It was established that the Greek versions could not contribute anything of substance to the discussion, except that I Esdras makes clear that already by the time of that work's compilation, the NM had been incorporated into the whole. It is thus not possible to follow Mowinckel, Pohlmann and others, who cite I Esdras as evidence for the form of the original ending of the Chronicler's work.

The remaining arguments were shown in fact rather to favour diversity of authorship. The overlap between the two works tells us nothing in itself, but on the other hand raises the question of the history of the formation of the Canon. As far back as we can go, the books have always been treated separately.

Discussion of the choice of vocabulary and of style set us on to rather firmer ground. Granted that both works originate from a comparable period in the development of LBH, they nevertheless display also certain contrasting characteristics. A number of such characteristics were added to those already collected by Japhet.

The ideology of the two works was also found to contrast at certain points which were central to the interests of the post-exilic community. These are, of course, more significant than the interests which the authors inevitably held in common.

On this basis, we may conclude that it is most reasonable to accept the view that the work of the Chronicler originally ended at 2 Chr. 36:21. By accepting this as a working hypothesis, we hope to show that study of Chr. in isolation from Ezr.-Neh. can produce very positive results.

6

The Start of the Chronicler's Work

In 1 Chr. 1–9, genealogies of the tribes of Israel are presented. Ch. 1 traces the line of election from Adam to Jacob, whilst the remainder deals, with considerable variation in the amount of attention given, with most of the tribes of Israel. Zebulun and Dan, however, appear to be omitted.

Three approaches have been adopted towards this material in critical scholarship. A few deny all nine chapters to the Chronicler, arguing that they are entirely a later addition to his work. Others, however, argue that all or most of these lists were put into substantially their present shape by the Chronicler, whilst the third group take a position between these two. They concede that the Chronicler may have included a brief summary of tribal genealogies in his original work, but argue that much of the material as we now have it represents later additions.

The first of these approaches, championed in particular by Welch,[1] has now been generally abandoned.[2] It has been shown that there are too many points of contact with the central interests and theology of the Chronicler's narrative to enable us to deny these chapters to him. Fortunately, Johnson has dealt with the issue directly in his monograph on the Biblical genealogies,[3] so that we may be content for the most part to refer to his discussion. We would merely single out as of particular importance the concern throughout for the full complement of twelve tribes,[4] which contrasts with the more exclusivist attitude of the Jerusalem community as reflected in Ezr.-Neh. Also, in addition to those points of the Chronicler's doctrine which Johnson mentions, we would, first, add in particular 1 Chr. 5: 20, a note that coincides very closely with accounts of battles in the Chronicler's narrative, especially 2 Chr. 13: 14–18, 14: 11–14, 18: 31 (where *wyhwh ʿzrw* is added by the Chronicler to his *Vorlage*) and 32: 20–2.

[1] A. C. Welch: *Post-Exilic Judaism*, pp. 186f.
[2] Its revival by F. M. Cross: 'Reconstruction', as part of the complicated literary history which he discerns behind Chr., cannot be supported in view of our arguments concerning the secondary nature of 1 Esdras in ch. 3 above.
[3] M. D. Johnson: *The Purpose of the Biblical Genealogies*, pp. 44–55.
[4] Cf. S. Japhet: *Ideology*, pp. 283–313.

Secondly, the genealogies show the same interest in Jacob as the Chronicler's narrative does. Here too, he is consistently called Israel (1 Chr. 1: 34, 2: 1, 5: 1 [twice], 5: 3, 6: 23, 7: 29), and we have already noted above (pp. 62f.) how the genealogy in ch. 1 focuses attention upon him as the real progenitor of Israel.

If, then, we are justified in assuming that part, at least, of these chapters was included by the Chronicler, our concern must be to ask whether, as so many have thought, these chapters have been subjected to substantial later editorial activity, or whether they have reached us in more or less the form in which they left the Chronicler's hand.

Research into the original form of 1 Chr. 1–9 has been closely linked with the question of the order in which the tribes are listed. Noth, for instance, has argued that the Chronicler followed Num. 26 as his *Vorlage* for this section,[1] so that any deviation from this is considered secondary. Following ch. 1, which Noth accepts as essentially authentic, the original form can therefore be seen in 1 Chr. 2: 3–5, 4: 24, 5: 3, 7: 1, 7: 12.13, 7: 14–19, 7: 20, 7: 30, 8: 1.[2] Apart from the line in Judah to David and the high priestly family, 'die grosse Masse dessen, was jetzt in 1. Chr. 2–9 steht, ist ein Gewirr von sekundären wilden Textwucherungen'.[3]

Rudolph, on the other hand, develops in his commentary the view that the Chronicler mainly followed the order of the tribes as listed in 1 Chr. 2: 1–2.[4] He too is then faced with certain passages that do not fit this scheme, and has to argue that they are secondary.[5]

Since the work of these two scholars is the most influential in this field, their arguments may be regarded as representative, and examined accordingly.

A. AN EXAMINATION OF THE POSITION OF M. NOTH

Noth's starting point in his discussion is 1 Chr. 7: 12f. He argues that the text can be restored in such a way as to bring it closely into line with Num. 26: 39ff. It is important to notice that the whole of his subsequent discussion is built upon this conjecture. Since his argument is progressive, rather than cumulative, everything stands or falls on the correctness of this conjecture.

Elsewhere, I have subjected Noth's conjecture to careful examination, and suggested that with but one slight emendation to the consonantal text, 1 Chr. 7: 12 can best be understood as a fragment of the Ben-

[1] M. Noth: *US*, pp. 118–22. [2] *Ibid.* p. 118.
[3] *Ibid.* p. 122.
[4] Rudolph, pp. 9ff., especially pp. 65f.
[5] Rudolph helpfully includes a table in which the results of his discussion are clearly set out: pp. 1f.

jamite genealogy in which it now stands.[1] It is unnecessary to rehearse the arguments again here.

Further objections, however, may be raised against Noth's development of his arguments.

(a) Even if he has been able to establish that Num. 26 provided the Chronicler with the structure of his genealogical introduction (which it is possible to accept in any case on other grounds), why should that mean, as Noth appears to assume without giving any reasons, that the Chronicler did not supplement that framework with material drawn from other sources? In 1 Chr. 1, for instance,[2] the Chronicler seems to have used all the material he could cull from his source, namely our book of Gen. Why then should we suppose that for a later period he should have abandoned this method, and dealt more scantily with matters for which he almost certainly had more extensive information?

(b) Perhaps most important of all, we must ask Noth what purpose he supposes this introduction served in the work as a whole, for we are left on this hypothesis with genealogies which do not even reach down to the time of the opening of the history with the death of Saul, let alone down to the writer's own time. This point alone is sufficient to show that Noth's literary critical arguments tend in themselves towards a *reductio ad absurdum*.

(c) Noth in fact concedes that the Chronicler used other sources in one or two cases. With most commentators, he accepts that 1 Chr. 2: 1f. is based on Gen. 35, and remarkably he allows to stand the Davidic line (1 Chr. 2: 9–15) and the list of high priests in 1 Chr. 6: 34–8. These exceptions appear to be allowed merely because they would be of particular interest to the Chronicler. However, as the whole drift of Noth's discussion is to establish that the greater attention paid to some tribes in these chapters is *not* evidence of the Chronicler's own interest, he seems to be in danger here of self-contradiction.

In addition to these general difficulties which Noth's theory fails to meet, more specific problems arise when we turn to see whether in fact the Chronicler has followed the order of Num. 26.

(a) Judah is placed first in the genealogy, against Num. 26, and the reason for this given in 5: 1–2. This shows that concerns of theology were predominant on this occasion at least.

(b) The position of the next few tribes is peculiar too. We should have expected either Judah, Reuben, Simeon, Gad (i.e. simply putting Judah first and then continuing as before), or Judah, Simeon, Gad, Reuben (i.e. with Judah and Reuben exchanging places). In fact we have neither, which is an embarrassment to Noth. He suggests, therefore,

[1] H. G. M. Williamson: 'A Note on 1 Chronicles VII 12'.
[2] Noth accepts that this chapter is in substantially the form that the Chronicler gave it (*US*, p. 117).

that originally Simeon followed Reuben. When the section was secondarily expanded by the addition of geographical material, the influence of this latter drew it up to follow Judah immediately (p. 120). Rudolph, however, observes (p. 38) that even in the genealogical material, a comparison is drawn between Judah and Simeon (4: 27). It is therefore probable that this consideration influenced the Chronicler from the first.

(c) Further difficulty is raised by Gad in 5: 11–17. Because in the present text the genealogy is explicitly joined (*lngdm*) to what precedes, Noth feels obliged to dismiss the whole as secondary, since on his hypothesis 5: 4–10 must be a later expansion of the original Chronicler's work, which only had material from Num. 26. He thinks that the original reference to Gad came later (as in the Gen. 46 list), but was completely lost, as was the reference to Zebulun. However, in that case, this represents yet a further deviation from Num. 26, where Gad is third in the list.

(d) Noth nowhere seems to recognize that Levi should not feature in these lists at all if Num. 26 is being followed, unless it be at the end. However, the fact that the Chronicler includes both Levi and Ephraim/Manasseh merely demonstrates again his lack of concern for the tidiness that Noth is concerned to impose upon him.

The weakness exposed in Noth's initial conjecture about 1 Chr. 7: 12 and these other arguments do not enable us to accept his reconstruction of 1 Chr. 1–9. Though he makes no clear reference to the fact, Noth's starting point would appear to have been an attempt to set these chapters within the context of his wider examination of tribal lists in the OT.[1] There he traced two basic forms of the list, and sought to categorize the others under one of these two types. However, as there are in fact seventeen variations in the OT's presentation of this material, greater care should be exercised before any particular pattern is imposed on another, especially in the case of so late a book as Chr.

B. THE POSITION OF W. RUDOLPH

As was mentioned above, Rudolph has argued that most of this list originally followed the order of 1 Chr. 2: 1–2, apart, of course, from the appearance of Judah in the first place. There are two aspects to his argument in favour of this view, and both are indispensable if it is to be upheld. First, he has to demonstrate that the original order of ch. 7 was Issachar, Zebulun, Benjamin, Dan, Naphtali, Gad, Asher, Manasseh, Ephraim. Secondly, the reference to Gad and the half tribe of Manasseh in ch. 5 must be shown to be secondary to the Chronicler's original work.

---

[1] M. Noth: *Das System der zwölf Stämme Israels*. For criticism of other aspects of Noth's treatment of the tribal lists, cf. A. D. H. Mayes: *Israel in the Period of the Judges*, pp. 16–34.

The Start of the Chronicler's Work

1. The Original Order in Ch. 7

Rudolph deals with this question on pp. 65 and 66 of his commentary. His argument in brief is that vv. 6–12 in particular show signs of heavy textual corruption. It is therefore not surprising that all traces of Zebulun should have been lost after the genealogy of Issachar (1–5). Whilst vv. 6–11 are mostly secondary material, v. 12a shows signs of the original Benjamite genealogy, based on Num. 26: 38ff. Dan can be restored, Rudolph claims, in v. 12b, and that is followed in v. 13 by an undamaged reference to Naphtali. However, the Manasseh fragment (14ff.) is in such a confused condition that clearly the textual corruption postulated earlier did not end with Naphtali. It is therefore not too bold to suggest that Gad and Asher may have been lost between Naphtali and Manasseh. (The genealogy of Asher in 7: 30ff. is considered secondary.) The position of the Joseph tribes at the end of the list can easily be explained on the basis of the Chronicler's anti-Samaritan *Tendenz*.

It must be stated at once that of course all this is possible. Rudolph's reconstruction, being so largely from silence, is by its very nature incapable of being either proved or disproved. Nevertheless, there are some important factors that at the very least throw the burden of proof on to Rudolph in such a way that his argument may be deemed unable to support it. First, Rudolph's starting point is a postulated textual corruption between vv. 5 and 6 such that no trace whatever of Zebulun remains. If we then ask why Zebulun should have originally come at this point, Rudolph answers that we expect it on the basis of 2: 1; but since that is the very point at issue, the argument has become circular. Furthermore, the corruption for which Rudolph claims evidence need not quite start between these two verses, but rather in the middle of v. 6 after Bala, where the genealogy first deviates from Num. 26: 38ff. Thus from a textual point of view it *is* surprising that Zebulun should have dropped out here. Secondly, we have already noted that v. 12b need not be part of the Dan genealogy. It could be, but that is not strong enough evidence when the case under review is precisely to find out whether Dan should be recorded after Benjamin or not. If the MT of 2: 1–2 is correct, we should in fact expect Dan (on Rudolph's view) before Benjamin. Thirdly, the suggestion that Gad and Asher have dropped out after Naphtali is again entirely from silence. There is no textual evidence for such a loss, and both feature elsewhere in the genealogies, though Rudolph's claim that their appearance there is secondary remains to be considered. Fourthly, though the Joseph tribes were the dominant members of the Northern Kingdom, most of the other tribes of this list also took part in the break away from Judah. The position of Manasseh and Ephraim at the end of the list for polemical purposes thus appears arbitrary.[1] Finally, it should be noted that nearly the whole of Rudolph's case rests on the postulation of this extensive corruption, beginning with the loss of Zebulun. If that is rendered doubtful for the reasons suggested, then indeed the whole of his position becomes very weak indeed.

2. *Secondary material in 1 Chr. 4: 24 – 5: 26*

For Rudolph to assert that the order of tribes in 1 Chr. 2–8 originally followed the list in 2: 1–2, it is equally important for him to establish that certain parts of our present text are secondary to the Chronicler's original work. It will not be our purpose in the following discussion to examine every verse or list that has been thought to show later expansion; of all the Biblical material, a genealogy lends itself most readily to such expansion, and it would indeed be surprising if there were not some such additions in these chapters. Our attention rather must be directed towards Rudolph's more drastic suggestion that all reference to Gad and the half tribe of Manasseh in ch. 5 is secondary, for if he is mistaken here, then his whole case may be said to have failed.

Rudolph's discussion of Gad (pp. 46–9) is not self-contained, but explicitly builds on arguments developed earlier. In brief outline, Rudolph is satisfied that part of the genealogy of Simeon (4: 24–43) is secondary, and that the genealogy of Reuben (5: 1–10) was expanded by analogy with this. Since v. 11 introduces the Gadites in apparent dependence upon this secondary material (*wbny gd lngdm*), it too must be a later addition. Similar results are produced for the notice about the war of the two and a half tribes with Arab peoples in 5: 18–22, since it is a development of v. 10, but added at a time when vv. 1–17 were already a unit, and for the notice about the half tribe of Manasseh in 5: 23–6, since it is a development of vv. 18 and 22b. This peeling off of literary layers thus starts back in the treatment of Simeon in 4: 24–43, discussed by Rudolph on pp. 38–42.

In the first place, difficulty has been found with the form of the genealogy as a whole. The usual list of names is followed by some geographical details (vv. 28–33), and then by snatches of information concerning pasturing of flocks and tribal strifes (vv. 34–43). Rudolph objects, however, that the Chronicler had no particular geographical interest, and that the list of names in vv. 34ff. is too abrupt to be anything other than additional or corrupt.

Johnson[2] has replied to this kind of criticism, however, by referring

---

[1] It is unlikely, in addition, that the Chronicler's work was anti-Samaritan in intention; cf. Willi, pp. 190–3; Kippenberg, pp. 49f.; Japhet: *Ideology*, pp. 329–37, and below, Part Two.

M. D. Johnson: *The Purpose of the Biblical Genealogies*, pp. 61f.

to the light thrown on the nature of genealogies in the Ancient Near East generally by the publication of the Safaitic inscriptions. A survey of nearly 1500 of these graffiti has shown me that they indeed throw considerable light on our problem.[1]

They were discovered mainly at camping places of the Bedouin in the Ḥarrah and Ruḥbah, a basaltic area to the south east of Damascus. The Safaites themselves were South Arabian nomads who penetrated the whole of the Syrian desert during the Roman period. The texts can sometimes be dated by historical references, and are thus placed mainly in the last century B.C. and the first century A.D. Whilst this is somewhat later than the composition of Chr., there is no reason to suppose that these people changed much in their outlook and manner of life during the intervening centuries.

The texts are mainly lists of names arranged in genealogical form. These are not usually very extensive (four or five generations only), but sometimes there are found mentioned nine, ten or even eleven generations.[2] Dussaud, indeed, has said that the genealogies 'comptent souvent une dizaine de générations, parfois quatorze ou quinze',[3] but I have not found examples of this as yet. The concern of these nomads for their ancestry is shown not only by the fact that they were clearly so fond of recording it, but also by the placing of a curse on anyone daring to efface it, and by the evident emotion caused on finding a written record of a member of the family; e.g., Littmann no. 259, p. 63: 'By Ḥufāl b. 'Asad b. Gu'al b. Hag-Gamal. And Ba'al-Samāy gave him booty from the enemy; and he found the inscription of Dād and longed (for him).' There is evidence too that these people were interested in more than just their direct ancestry: sometimes they mention the tribe of which they are a member, as, for instance, in 'By 'A'dag b. Ma'n b. 'A'dag of the tribe of Khuṣmān, etc.'.[4] Finally, we may note in

---

[1] For the general background to the discovery of the inscriptions, descriptions of the terrain and people who produced them, etc., cf. R. Dussaud and F. Macler: *Voyage Archéologique au Ṣafâ et dans le Djebel Ed-Drûz*; R. Dussaud: *La Pénétration des Arabes en Syrie avant l'Islam*, pp. 135–40; E. Littmann: *Thamūd und Ṣafā*.

For publication and discussion of the texts, cf. E. Littmann: *Safaitic Inscriptions* (citations will be from this work unless otherwise stated). The publication of new finds of Safaitic texts is still proceeding, so that a full bibliography at this point would not be helpful. The history of their decipherment is told in E. Littmann: *Zur Entzifferung der Ṣafâ-Inschriften.*

The first systematic attempt to relate these inscriptions to Biblical material seems to be G. Ryckmans: 'Les Noms de Parenté en Safaïtique' (1951), followed by O. Eissfeldt: 'Das alte Testament im Lichte der safatenischen Inschriften' (1954), in which parallels are drawn in particular with the Biblical portrayal of Jacob's way of life.

[2] Littmann: no. 18, p. 6; 87, p. 19; 233, p. 53; 244, p. 59; 399, p. 104.

[3] R. Dussaud: *La Pénétration des Arabes*, p. 139.

[4] Littmann: no. 281, p. 69; cf. no. 325, p. 80; 349, p. 90; 701, p. 179.

passing that there is good reason for trusting the accuracy of these lists. Littmann[1] argues for this conclusion on the basis of a game that he discovered in North Abyssinia in which Bedouin boys compete to see who can remember his ancestors back the furthest, whilst adults check the accuracy of the recitations. More significantly, however, it is possible to collate the information from a number of such inscriptions to form a more involved genealogical tree, as Littmann does on several occasions.[2] This would not be possible if the pedigrees were inaccurate.

Whilst all this is of interest as general comparative material, these Safaitic inscriptions become of direct relevance when we find that they often contain additional fragmentary information in a way that closely parallels the section of the Chronicler's genealogy under review. Thus sometimes, the writer notes his place of origin, for instance: 'By Mālik b. 'Awīdh b. ha-Wālī. And he came from the Ruḥbat which was covered with herbage.'[3] Frequently, there are references to details of grazing, tending flocks and so on; thus for instance: 'By 'Auwaḵ-'ēl b. Haudhat. And he tended the flocks in this valley (and) slaughtered, in the year in which Ma'n was killed.'[4] Furthermore, details are sometimes supplied of tribal conflict: 'By Mughaiyir b. 'Audh b. 'Audh. And he was present in the year in which the tribe of (Ḵum)air did injury to the tribe of Ḥumaiy. And he laid a stone on the tomb of the friend.'[5] Sometimes, we note, this tribal war may even be connected with concern for the flocks, which provides an especially close parallel to 1 Chr. 4:41, as for instance: 'By Fāliṭat b. Taim b. Fāliṭat b. Buhaish. And he encamped at this place and tended the camels. So, O Allāt and Ba'al-Samīn, help the troop that persecutes (*sic*!) in order to recapture.'[6] Johnson further refers to Littmann no. 435, p. 116 as providing an illuminating parallel to Chr.: 'By Garam-'ēl b. Dhi'b b. Kaun. And the torrent drove him away at the watering place of camels in the year in which the tribe of Ḵadam drove away the tribe of Harim. So, O Allāt, (give) peace!' Finally, it would seem that an extraordinary occurrence often prompted the recording of an otherwise normal event, as for instance: 'And he tended the camels in the year in which the Nabataeans passed by this valley',[7] or 'And he journeyed with the camels in the

---

[1] Littmann: *Thamūd und Ṣafā*, p. 98.

[2] Cf. Littmann, no. 136, p. 27; 186, p. 43; 366, p. 96; 390, p. 102; 574, p. 148; 638, p. 163.

[3] Littmann: no. 7, p. 3; cf. no. 217, p. 50; 299, p. 73.

[4] Littmann: no. 297, p. 72; cf. no. 4, p. 2; 90, p. 20; 146, p. 30; 155, p. 33; 157, p. 34; 159, p. 34; 357, p. 93; 419, p. 112; 701, p. 179, etc. Cf. G. Ryckmans: 'Inscriptions Safaïtiques', no. 34, p. 517: 'A Burd, fils de Kayḥ, fils de Zammân. Et il a fait paître dans le pâturage (?) les chameaux(?).'

[5] Littmann: no. 255, p. 62; cf. no. 254, p. 61; 360, p. 95.

[6] Littmann: no. 146, p. 30.

[7] Littmann: no. 4, p. 2.

year in which the heat of the sun was intense ',[1] or ' In the year in which he walked the whole night in the mire '.[2]

This survey enables us to say that from an area and a way of life that may not be so remote at least from the two and a half Transjordanian tribes, we have closely parallel material written in a manner of which it would be absurd to postulate literary layers or layers of tradition.[3] As Johnson summarizes: ' To be sure, these inscriptions are much more crude than the passages from Chronicles, but this simply reflects the relative sophistication and literary aims of the writers. The salient point is that in this genealogical material the same kind of historical notes are included.'[4] We conclude from this, therefore, that the form of the Simeonite genealogy need not rouse suspicion, and indeed the tendency of this comparative material is rather to suggest that it is a likely form.

Secondly, we must go on to consider Rudolph's literary objections to the Simeonite genealogy, bearing in mind now that we are not looking for support for a case already established, but for positive reasons to demand attributing some of the material to a later hand. Rudolph is happy to allow that the Chronicler drew on a source otherwise unknown to us for that part of the genealogy which is not taken from Num. 26: 12–14. This agrees with Gray's conclusion that the ' absence of compounds with יה and the presence of מבשם and משמע – names which only recur as those of Ishmaelitish clans – favour the genuineness of these names.'[5] Rudolph then thinks that the note in v. 27b that Simeon did not increase as much as Judah marks the end of what the Chronicler originally had to say about Simeon. This seems quite arbitrary, however. The note is certainly appropriate as the summary of the strictly genealogical section, but that has no bearing at all upon whether the Chronicler continued with other information. Indeed, it would suit his theology well if he did so continue,[6] and the nature of the geographical section which follows (vv. 28–33) also favours this view.

This list of cities clearly has some connection with Josh. 19: 2–8 and 15: 26–32, but the number of slight variations suggests that there may not be direct literary dependence. Albright has argued that these variations are merely matters of pronunciation and so on,[7] but that of

---

[1] Littmann: no. 701, p. 179.   [2] Littmann: no. 288, p. 71.

[3] Cf. G. Ryckmans: 'Ils (the inscriptions) constituent de véritables feuilles d'état civil qui nous renseignent sur la généalogie et les liens de parenté de plusieurs milliers de bédouins qui vivaient en bordure du désert de Syrie', 'Les Noms de Parenté en Safaïtique', p. 379.

[4] M. D. Johnson: *The Purpose of the Biblical Genealogies*, p. 62.

[5] G. B. Gray: *Studies in Hebrew Proper Names*, p. 236.

[6] Cf. Johnson: *op. cit.* pp. 57f.

[7] W. F. Albright: 'The Topography of Simeon'.

course would not be sufficient to account for such differences at the literary level. Cross and Wright[1] explain the differences as due to 'the different stages in the transmission of the original Simeonite list'. Aharoni,[2] however, whilst accepting that the lists are to be dated differently,[3] argues that in fact

> the true explanation of the composition of the two lists seems to be their difference of purpose: the list of the cities of Simeon gives the cities of that tribe only, whereas the list of the Negeb of Judah contains all the cities in that administrative district, including those of other families and tribes.[4]

It is thus less likely that a redactor simply added in what seemed to him appropriate at this point from another Biblical source, but rather that it shows that same kind of collection from source material as is admitted on all sides for the genealogy proper of vv. 24–7.

Next, Rudolph objects to the originality of the material in vv. 34–43. He thinks that the expression at the end of v. 3 – *whtyḥśm lhm* – stresses the suffix of *htyḥśm* because it was originally followed by a genealogical register from which the phrase has now been separated. In consequence 'auf 4: 33 folgte von Haus aus 5: 1ff., und 4: 34ff. ist ein noch späterer Nachtrag als 4: 28ff. Ist also schon 28–33 sekundär, so 34–43 erst recht' (p. 39). This, however, would be to contradict the Chronicler's normal procedure in this section of his work, where the hithpa'el of *yḥś* is used at the end of a genealogical section, as here (cf. 5: 17, 7: 5.7.9.40; 9: 1.22).[5] The only exception to this seems to be 5: 7, where it does precede the list of names. Myers (p. 31) thinks that the phrase simply points to 'the existence of an official register'. We may suggest, then, that the suffix could be explained in a quite different way: Aharoni's study of the boundary lists of the Negeb of Judah and the Simeonite tribal lists leads him to conclude: 'the term "Negeb of Judah" as used in the time of David, was actually identical with the tribal area of Simeon'.[6] If that is so, the Chronicler may well in his schematic presentation have wished to maintain with emphasis the separate identity of the tribal area of Simeon.

As far as the genealogy of Simeon goes, therefore, I find no evidence

---

[1] F. M. Cross and G. E. Wright: 'The Boundary and Province Lists'.

[2] Y. Aharoni: 'The Negeb of Judah'.　　　　　　　　　　　[3] *Ibid.* p. 31:

The list of Joshua 15 cannot be earlier than the division of the kingdom of Solomon; but as regards the cities of Simeon, 1 Chr. 4: 31 states that 'these were their cities unto the reign of David' and we have no reason to doubt this incidental statement, which occurs within the body of the list.

[4] *Ibid.* p. 32.

[5] Which Rudolph, *ad loc.*, along with most other commentators, argues should be taken as a summary of chapters 2–8.

[6] Aharoni: 'The Negeb of Judah', p. 31.

that compels a division into the literary layers postulated by Rudolph. The individual sections are all most easily explained if a single compiler gathered various pieces of information from the diverse kinds of sources that we have discussed. Much of the information, particularly in the last section, could well have come from a type of material similar to the Safaitic inscriptions analysed above, where interests are so closely parallel. Indeed, the form of such material may well have governed the Chronicler's own, for though the latter is more developed from a literary point of view, in outline it is almost exactly the same.

If this position is acceptable, then a similar position can be adopted towards the material in ch. 5. We noticed earlier that Rudolph (p. 46) thinks that vv. 1–10 (Reuben) were finally brought to their present state by following the pattern of the Simeonite material. However, we would wish to turn this argument from similarity of form to argue for the integrity of the Reuben material.

Again, the internal arguments that Rudolph brings to bear here are not sufficient to uphold his case. For instance, he finds the beginning of v. 4 too abrupt, being genealogically unconnected with what precedes it, but this in itself is no reason why the original compiler should not have brought it in here. Verses 4–6 as a section are again in form precisely parallel to the Safaitic inscriptions, and they were inserted here because their primary importance to the Chronicler was genealogical. Verses 7 and 8a continue this interest. Then, in 8b, follows the geographical section, as in the case of Simeon, and it refers to the whole tribe. Its position here is thus determined by an established form, and so cannot be evidence of a later addition at a time when vv. 1–8a were already a unit, which Rudolph thinks accounts for its not being attached directly to the catch-word 'Reubenites' in v. 6.

In v. 11, the details about Gad are very securely attached to the preceding verses by the geographical reference *wbny gd lngdm*. Just as for Rudolph this is sufficient to make the whole section secondary, so for us, in view of our discussion so far, it means that the reference here to Gad must be attributed to the Chronicler. In the next section (vv. 18–22, dealing with the two and a half tribes as a whole), we should notice in particular not only the same interest in flocks and herds as we have seen earlier (v. 21), but also a reflective, editorial phrase concerning a tribal war:

> They made war with the Hagrites, with Jetur, Naphish, and Nodab. And they were helped against them, and the Hagrites were delivered into their hand, and all that were with them: for they cried to God in the battle, and he was intreated of them; because they put their trust in him (vv. 19–20).

This so completely conforms to the theology of the Chronicler as reflected later in the major part of his work that it is indeed hard to relegate it to a secondary, or even a tertiary layer, as Rudolph's purely literary critical arguments oblige him to do.

In the last paragraph of this chapter (vv. 23–6), there do seem to be reasons for doubt. The references are altogether of a more general nature than in what precedes, and the interests are international rather than inter-tribal. Furthermore, they look like an expansion of earlier references, such as the mention of the exile in v. 22, whilst the tribe of Manasseh is dealt with later, in ch. 7. Finally, such detail about the fate of the Northern tribes seems foreign to the Chronicler. On the other hand, it must be acknowledged that the two and a half tribes are so closely linked in Israelite tradition, that a reference to the half tribe of Manasseh here is very likely. The repetition of reference to a tribe is not really a problem, as it happens also in the case of Benjamin, and in any case we should expect details of the other half tribe. Finally, even if the material is an expansion of earlier references, there is no compulsion to attribute this to a separate hand; it may just reflect tidy editorial work. Thus the evidence concerning this paragraph is ambiguous.

C. CONCLUSIONS

We may then conclude that Rudolph's arguments for a substantial amount of secondary addition to these genealogies are not convincing. We have not, of course, been able to examine every verse and list, but it is hoped that enough has been said to justify a position which treats a passage as integral to Chr. until weighty arguments are brought against its authenticity. That this position does not arise from any form of dogmatism about the original state of the text may be seen from the suggestion above that 1 Chr. 5: 23–6 may well, in fact, be secondary.

Others too have argued along more general lines to reach similar conclusions. Both Johnson[1] and Japhet,[2] for instance, have demonstrated that the Chronicler was indeed interested in geographical matters, so that it is in no way surprising to find allusions of this sort in these chapters. Again, information for a number of the tribes may well have been drawn from a military census list.[3] Liver has argued well that such lists may have been included in a book during the period of the monarchy, and that the Chronicler was able to draw from this.[4] These suggestions, by showing threads that unite various parts of the genealogies into possible sources, make use of them by the Chronicler himself more plausible, and reduce the probability that they were all attached piecemeal and separately in a haphazard way.

[1] M. D. Johnson: *The Purpose of the Biblical Genealogies*, pp. 57–60.
[2] S. Japhet: *Ideology*, pp. 355–66.
[3] Johnson: *op. cit.* pp. 63–8, developing the views of G. E. Mendenhall: 'The Census Lists of Numbers 1 and 26'. [4] J. Liver: 'And all Israel'.

EXCURSUS   *The Date of Chronicles*

Dates of over 300 years apart have at various times been suggested for the books of Chr. No useful purpose would be served merely by repeating the main points at issue, which may be found in most of the standard Introductions and Commentaries. Furthermore, inasmuch as many of these points concern Ezr.-Neh., they have no bearing on the question if Chr. is a separate work. However, in order to study the Chronicler's thought against its historical background, it is necessary to come to some decision within general limits on this matter. Therefore, though this excursus will not make any new contribution to the debate, some indication must be given of the reasons that have led to accepting here the late Persian period as the most probable time for the composition of Chr.

(a) If, as has been argued, the work ended at 2 Chr. 36: 21, it would appear that the author's perspective did not reach further than the Persian period.

(b) There is no indication, linguistic or ideological, of any Hellenistic influence whatever.[1] Whilst this on its own is admittedly an argument from silence, it carries some weight in view of the very considerable impact (both positively and by reaction) of Hellenism on Jewish religion and literature.[2]

(c) There are some indications that point to a later, rather than an earlier, date within the Persian period. Since we have argued for the inclusion of the substance of 1 Chr. 1–9 within the original composition of Chr., the evidence of 1 Chr. 3: 17–24 may be adduced here. The genealogy is difficult to reconstruct in detail, so that the simpler version of the LXX is probably to be rejected as a secondary rationalization.[3] The MT is generally thought to give six generations after Zerubbabel, providing a *terminus post quem* of *c.* 400 B.C.

An alternative interpretation was proposed by Keil,[4] however, pointing out that the families listed in vv. 21bff. are not attached to the line

[1] This point is put forward in more detail, though not without reservations, by P. R. Ackroyd: *The Age of the Chronicler*, pp. 7f.; cf. S. Japhet: 'Chronicles, Book of', col. 533.

[2] For both discussion and bibliography, cf. M. Hengel: *Judentum und Hellenismus*, and cf. E. Bickerman: *From Ezra to the Last of the Maccabees*, p. 30: 'The whole conception of the Chronicler shows that he wrote when Persian rule seemed destined for eternity.'

[3] Cf., *inter alia*, W. F. Albright: 'Date and Personality', pp. 108–12, and Rudolph and Myers, *ad loc.*

[4] C. F. Keil, *ad loc.* Keil has been followed by E. J. Young: *Introduction*, p. 391 and R. K. Harrison: *Introduction*, p. 1155.

of Zerubbabel. The list might then end at an even earlier date. It should be pointed out in reply, however, that the affinity of these names with some recorded in Ezr.-Neh. makes it likely that even though they may not be direct descendants of Zerubbabel, they still would bring us to approximately the same date. This (together with the next point) excludes the very early date for Chr. proposed by Welch[1] and Freedman.[2]

(d) Two anachronisms point towards the same conclusion. The *'drknym* of 1 Chr. 29: 7 are generally understood to be Persian darics, a coin first minted by Darius I.[3] Chr. would then have to be dated sufficiently after his reign to allow for the anachronism. However, in view of the political importance of coins in the ancient world, it is unlikely that it would have occurred long after the fall of the Persian empire.[4]

Secondly, it is generally agreed that the association of Tadmor and Hamat-Zobah in 2 Chr. 8: 3f. reflects the Assyrian-Babylonian-Persian system of provincial administration.[5] If this association is the work of the Chronicler himself, it will set a lower limit for his date within the period of influence of the Persian empire.

A number of scholars have wanted to date Chr. later than this, but their reasons do not seem compelling.

(a) Often, the case is maintained on the basis of data found only in Ezr.-Neh.[6] In the light of our previous discussion, this carries no weight.

(b) A late date is also sometimes suggested because of the anti-Samaritan polemic in Chr.[7] In common with most modern works on Chr.,[8] however, it will be argued below that this represents a mistaken understanding of the Chronicler's purpose, so that the question of Samaritan origins will have no bearing on the date of Chr.

---

[1] A. C. Welch: *Post-Exilic Judaism*, pp. 241f.

[2] D. N. Freedman: 'The Chronicler's Purpose'.

[3] Cf. Herodotus: *Histories* IV, 166 and VII, 28.

[4] If, by contrast, the less probable explanation of *'drknym* as a corruption of *drknym*, 'drachmas', were correct (so W. F. Albright, in a review of A. Robert and A. Feuillet (eds.): *Introduction à la Bible*, in *Bi. Or.* 17 [1960], 242b, reversing his opinion given in *JBL* 40 [1921], 113), then this would not exclude a Persian date, since Greek drachmas were common at that time, but it would also allow a date in the Hellenistic period.

[5] Cf. M. Noth: 'Das Reich von Hamath'. He has been followed most recently by Welten, pp. 35f.

[6] Mainly the list of high priests in Neh. 12, the time needed for the chronological confusion to arise in Ezr. 4 and in the dating of Ezra, and the use of the title 'king of Persia'. This latter phrase is found at 2 Chr. 36: 22 and 23, but we have seen that these verses are only a later addition from Ezr. 1.

[7] E.g. by Galling, pp. 14f. and Mowinckel: *Studien I*, pp. 59–61.

[8] E.g. Willi, pp. 190–3; Japhet: *Ideology*, pp. 329–37; Mosis, *passim*, and Welten, pp. 172f.

Excursus: The Date of Chronicles

(c) Particular mention must here be made of Welten's recent study, for he argues that many of the notes in Chr. concerning building, the army and the course of battles reflect the conditions of the Chronicler's own day. The implications of this for dating the Chronicler are drawn out in an excursus.[1]

It may be observed that in the course of his discussion, Welten explicitly refers to the Persian period as providing the most satisfactory background to the data he has adduced.[2] To that extent, his conclusions would agree with our own. There are two details, however, which he thinks demand a date within the Hellenistic period. The first concerns the Chronicler's representation of the Judean army, said to be based on the Greek model.[3] However, even if we allow for the moment that this was the source of the Chronicler's description, we must observe that Welten himself shows that this model would have been well known in Palestine during the latter part of the Persian period from the many Greek mercenary soldiers involved in the campaigns of the fourth century. A date for Chr. later than 333 B.C. is thus not demanded.

The second detail on to which Welten fastens is the reference in 2 Chr. 26: 15 to Uzziah's 'engines, invented by skilful men, to be on the towers and corners, to shoot arrows and great stones'. He follows those who argue that such catapults were unknown in the eighth century B.C.,[4] that their origin should be traced to Syracuse about 400 B.C.,[5] and that their development into defensive weapons would probably not have been known in Judah until the third century.[6]

In reply, it should be said that this is a rather uncertain detail on which to rest the whole case for a late date for Chr., for it is probable that Welten has misunderstood the passage in question. Without discussion, he assumed that the reference must be to 'Torsionsgeschütze'.[7] In doing so, he completely ignores the alternative view, which sees in the verse a reference to defensive constructions on the walls that enabled soldiers to shoot at attackers from a position of safety. Yadin has developed this case from both textual and military points of view,[8] re-

---

[1] Welten, pp. 199f.
[2] E.g. on pp. 35f., 36f., 46f., 139, 153, 159, 166 and 169.
[3] Welten, pp. 110f.
[4] For the contrary (unconvincing) view, cf. L. Alexander: 'The Origin of Greek and Roman Artillery'.
[5] Following a note to that effect in Diodorus Siculus XIV, 42, 1.
[6] Welten, pp. 111–14. The fullest recent presentation of the evidence to this effect is E. W. Marsden: *Greek and Roman Artillery*, pp. 48–64 (apparently unknown to Welten).
[7] Cf. Welten, p. 113.
[8] Y. Sukenik: 'ḥšbnwt mḥšbt ḥwšb'.

ferring in particular to the Assyrian reliefs of the siege of Lachish which, from a period only two generations after Uzziah, portray just this kind of construction, with hardly any other known parallels. If he is right, as seems likely, Welten's argument loses its force.

We may thus conclude that there is no compelling evidence for dating Chr. later than the Persian period, or at least for a date later than the time at which the impact of Hellenism was first felt in Judah. Chr. should thus be dated at some point within the fourth century B.C.

PART TWO

The Concept of Israel in the Books of Chronicles

It was seen above (pp. 1–3) that studies of Israel in the books of Chronicles have usually started from an analysis of Ezr.-Neh.[1] We might summarize them by saying that in the view of these books, true Israel is made up alone by those of Judah and Benjamin who had returned from the exile in Babylon, together with 'every one who had joined them and separated himself from the pollutions of the peoples of the land' (Ezr. 6: 21). None of the other (northern) tribes is ever mentioned, nor is the possibility conceded that some true Israelites might have continued to inhabit the land during the period of the exile. Von Rad can thus concisely say: 'Israel ist jetzt Juda und Benjamin.'[2]

Our interest here is in how these conclusions have usually been traced also in Chr. Since von Rad's understanding is typical, and largely formative, of this modern scholarly consensus, we must first outline his position.

He agrees that the first nine chapters of 1 Chr. indeed present the genealogies of the full twelve tribes, but the real centre of interest is in Judah, Benjamin and Levi alone. He acknowledges, however, that sometimes the presentation of the genealogies conflicts rather sharply with the ethnic purity insisted on by Ezr.-Neh.

To determine the Chronicler's attitude in the rest of his work, von Rad states that all the material that is parallel to Sam.-Ki. must be ignored, as should all stereotyped expressions such as 'God of Israel' and 'King of Israel' and phrases that are influenced by earlier Israelite history (though even then it is admitted that the remaining material is uneven). The important section is that which follows the division of the monarchy: often the Chronicler is found to follow the usage of the Deuteronomist, but sometimes 'Israel' is applied to the Southern Kingdom, and in this the Chronicler's own attitude finds expression.

Especially significant are two verses that follow closely on the account of the division of the monarchy: 2 Chr. 11: 3 – 'all Israel in Judah and Benjamin' – where 'all Israel' is additional to the Kings *Vorlage*, thus

---

[1] G. von Rad: *Geschichtsbild*, pp. 19–25; G. A. Danell: *Israel*, pp. 281–6; H. C. M. Vogt: *Studie*, especially pp. 47–65.
[2] von Rad: *Geschichtsbild*, p. 24.

showing that 'Juda und Benjamin sind jetzt das wahre Israel',[1] and 2 Chr. 12: 1 – 'He (Rehoboam) forsook the law of the Lord, and all Israel with him' – whose significance lies in showing that Rehoboam's kingdom was Israel. Similar passages are then adduced: 2 Chr. 24: 5.16, 20: 29, 28: 19.23, 21: 2.

Von Rad thinks that the strongest argument in his favour is the fact that the Chronicler ignores the history of the Northern Kingdom, which is noteworthy in a religious history, where purely provincial considerations are out of place. Abijah's speech in 2 Chr. 13 reinforces this view. Thus even though in David's time, and to a lesser extent under Hezekiah and Josiah, the concept of all Israel is used to express the dogma of 'Israel = Israel + Judah' (p. 37), yet the practicalities of the post-exilic situation and complete apostasy of the Northern Kingdom lead him to betray his own view that Judah = Israel.

It will be apparent at once that von Rad's treatment of the material is highly selective. In what follows, we shall attempt to give a more comprehensive survey in order to arrive at firmer conclusions. We cannot accept that all parallel passages must be ignored, for if, as von Rad does, we find significance in the small changes that the Chronicler introduces, then it ought to be equally significant that he leaves other passages unchanged. Moreover, as is well known, we can no longer assume that the Chronicler's *Vorlage* was precisely the same as the MT of Sam.-Ki.[2] There is thus the danger that changes which appear to us to be especially indicative of the Chronicler's viewpoint will turn out in fact to be already found in his *Vorlage*. Since, however, we do not possess a full copy of this, the only way to avoid the danger is to make our analysis as comprehensive as possible.[3]

[1] *Ibid.* p. 31, followed most recently by T. Willi, p. 162.

[2] W. E. Lemke: 'The Synoptic Problem'.

[3] S. Japhet is quite correct in her observation (*Ideology*, p. 275) that a study of the word Israel in Chr. is insufficient in itself, since the Chronicler uses the course of events itself to convey his meaning. However, it has seemed simplest, most orderly, and from the point of view of method most sound to start on the basis of a word study, and to work thence towards an examination of the Chronicler's less direct means of expression. It may further be indicated at this point that it has not seemed necessary to devote a special section to the study of the expression 'all Israel'. Despite the fascination that this expression seems to hold for some commentators (notably Myers), it is evident that it is used in a wide variety of ways, just as is the word Israel by itself. Therefore, it has been treated equally along with other occurrences of Israel, and those passages noted where a particular emphasis is present. Japhet's study of *kl yśr'l* in isolation (pp. 275–83) only serves to support this approach.

7

1 Chronicles 1 – 2 Chronicles 9

A. GENERAL USES AND THE PRE-MONARCHIC PERIOD

Of the 300 occurrences of the name Israel in Chr., we have already noted that twelve refer to the patriarch Jacob (above, p. 62), a possible indication of the Chronicler's view that Israel was expressed through the full twelve tribes.

Thirty-five times the word is used in the expression '(the Lord) the God of Israel', and twenty-one times it is used for the corresponding idea that Israel is his people.

Finally, the Chronicler uses Israel twenty-seven times to refer to various aspects of the period prior to the monarchy, and shows thereby his knowledge of all the main Israelite traditions for that early period.[1]

Whilst most of these references are insignificant in the present context, they include one passage that deserves more detailed attention: in 1 Chr. 5: 1–2, the Chronicler explains why he has not listed Reuben first in his genealogies of the tribes of Israel, and further why Judah, not Joseph (as might apparently have been expected), is given that place of honour:

And the sons of Reuben the firstborn of Israel, (for he was the first-born; but, forasmuch as he defiled his father's couch, his birthright was given to the sons of Joseph the son of Israel; and the genealogy is not to be reckoned after the birthright. For Judah prevailed above his brethren, and of him came the prince; but the birthright was Joseph's:) . . .

The older commentators found no difficulty with this verse, for they could point to Gen. 48: 5 as the source of the tradition that Reuben's birthright passed to Joseph, with Dt. 21: 15–17 explaining how the adoption by Jacob of Ephraim and Manasseh was equivalent to giving Joseph a double portion as the legitimate inheritance of the firstborn.[2] More recently, however, a different attitude has been taken by some;

[1] Cf. von Rad: *Geschichtsbild*, pp. 64–80.
[2] Cf. the comments *ad loc.* in C. F. Keil, R. Kittel, CM, W. E. Barnes and I. Benzinger.

von Rad,[1] for instance, points to three problems in these verses: the triple occurrence of *bkrh* is hard; nowhere else in the OT is Joseph given the birthright; the LXX reads *eulogia* (thus presupposing *brkh*) for the first and third occurrences of *bkrh*. Maintaining that the creative contribution by the Chronicler was to combine the theme of blessing that underlies Gen. 48 with the 'cursing' of Gen. 49: 3–4, von Rad adopts the Greek rendering (though not in its rendering of *lbnw* for *lbny ywsp* in v. 1). Rudolph (p. 43) espouses a comparable position, but finds it curious that the rights of the firstborn should be transferred to more than one person. He therefore adopts the LXX reading for v. 1. Verse 2, on Rudolph's understanding, should then go on to explain how, despite the fact that the sons of Joseph received the blessing, Judah adopted the rights of the firstborn, as the emergence of the *ngyd* showed. Verse 2b deviates from this, however, and even contradicts the reconstruction of v. 1. The LXX is of no help here (*contra* von Rad), since it merely repeats its earlier position. Moreover, the present text contradicts what Rudolph supposes to be the Chronicler's attitude towards the Northern Kingdom. He therefore proposes that the words *lô lo'* have fallen out – a readily understandable error before *lywsp* – and translates the whole of v. 2 thus: 'denn Juda wurde der mächtigste unter seinen Brüdern, und aus ihm ging ein Führer hervor, so dass ihm, nicht Josef, das Erstgeburtsrecht zustand'. If we ask why, then, the Chronicler bothered to introduce Joseph into the passage at all, Rudolph replies that it was necessary within the context of the debate in his time with the Samaritans. They based their claims on Gen. 48, 49: 22ff. and Dt. 33: 13ff.; the Chronicler does not deny, therefore, that the blessing passed to Joseph, but he nevertheless maintains that the Davidic monarchy proves the pre-eminence of Judah over Joseph.

This discussion raises a number of issues.

(a) Paramount is the question as to whether the OT anywhere suggests that Joseph or his sons inherited the rights of the firstborn. Mendelsohn argues that it does,[2] and that this is fully in accord with Ancient Near Eastern laws and customs. Texts from Nuzi, Ugarit, Babylonia (in some periods), Mari and Alalakh all show both that a father had the right to disregard the law of primogeniture by 'choosing' a firstborn, and that the firstborn would receive two shares of the inheritance, whilst all his brothers received one each. Applying this background material to our specific instance, Myers (pp. 35f.) then argues that the double share of Joseph is reflected in the fact that he constituted two tribes, Ephraim and Manasseh. This rather generalized

---

[1] von Rad: *Geschichtsbild*, pp. 72ff. A. Klostermann: 'Chronik', pp. 91f., had earlier preferred the Greek text to the Hebrew, but not for the rather specific reasons that von Rad and Rudolph set out.
[2] I. Mendelsohn: 'Preferential Status'.

approach, however, runs ahead of detailed examination of the relevant texts.

Gen. 48 describes the adoption by Jacob of Joseph's two sons, Ephraim and Manasseh. By itself, this has nothing to do with the question of the firstborn. Two verses, however, have stimulated the belief that this further matter is in view. Verse 5 reads 'And now thy two sons, which were born unto thee in the land of Egypt before I came unto thee into the land of Egypt, are mine; Ephraim and Manasseh, even as Reuben and Simeon, shall be mine.' It might appear from this that Ephraim and Manasseh are being given the status of Reuben as firstborn and Simeon as the second brother. However, a moment's reflection will show that this cannot be. If Joseph is granted the position of the firstborn, with Ephraim and Manasseh as representative of his double portion, then the reference to Simeon in this verse is quite out of place, for Ephraim and Manasseh would jointly replace Reuben only. It is thus evident that Jacob cites Reuben and Simeon as mere examples of his full sons. Since they are his two eldest, they make with most emphasis the point that from now on, Ephraim and Manasseh's adoption grants them full filial status. This excludes an allusion to the status of firstborn, however, since obviously there can be only one firstborn, whereas here both boys are dealt with equally.

Conversely, this cannot reflect a tradition of Joseph's adoption as firstborn. If it did, his double portion would be represented by Ephraim and Manasseh (so Myers). In fact, however, these two are elevated to full status as sons, and thus would each receive a portion in their own right. This conclusion is supported by v. 6: *wmwldtk 'šr hwldt 'ḥryhm lk yhyw 'l šm 'ḥyhm yqr'w bnḥltm*, for which we should follow Speiser's translation:[1] 'But progeny born to you after them shall remain yours; they shall succeed their brothers in their inheritance', with the explanation: 'Concurrently, Joseph's younger sons will move up, in terms of inheritance, to the senior spots left vacant by their older brothers.' Speiser offers no particular support for this suggestion, but reference to Dt. 25: 6 shows that he has given the correct rendering of the words that have given rise to misunderstanding, *'l šm*. In this regulation concerning levirate marriage, we read:

whyh hbkwr 'šr tld yqwm 'l-šm 'ḥyw hmt wl'-ymḥh šmw myśr'l.

And it shall be, that the firstborn which she beareth shall succeed in the name of his brother which is dead, that his name be not blotted out of Israel.

Our passage in Gen. is analogous to this situation, the difference being that Ephraim and Manasseh have not died, but been raised to a new

[1] E. A. Speiser: *Genesis*, pp. 355 and 357, followed by J. R. Porter: 'Son or Grandson?', p. 59, n. 1.

status within the family. Joseph's subsequent sons, therefore, take their place (*'l šm 'ḥyhm*) as far as the inheritance is concerned. It follows, then, that in this passage Ephraim and Manasseh do not 'replace' Joseph, which might have been taken as evidence of a double share if he were the firstborn. Rather, if his subsequent sons are to inherit from him instead of Ephraim and Manasseh, he must still be being reckoned within the family in his own right.

We may therefore conclude that Gen. 48: 5f. deals only with the adoption by Jacob of Ephraim and Manasseh as full sons, and the re-arrangement of status within Joseph's family that this necessitates. There is no reference either direct or indirect to the question of the firstborn's status.

The other verse which has been thought to imply Joseph's elevation to the position of the firstborn is Gen. 48: 22:

> Moreover I have given to thee one portion above thy brethren, which I took out of the hand of the Amorite with my sword and with my bow.

If this implies that Joseph was granted a double portion, then we might deduce that he is here being treated as the firstborn. There are two grounds for caution, however.

First, the meaning of the text is far from clear. Though *škm* was certainly understood as 'portion' in later Jewish literature,[1] and this verse even taken in the Midrash as implying possession of the birth-right,[2] there is no evidence for its use in this sense as early as the Biblical period. The later use is an intelligible semantic development (compare *mś'*, *load*, which can also have the meaning *tribute*), possibly under the influence of the difficulty of this very verse. Of the alternatives that remain, though the proper name would in many ways be attractive here, the use of *'ḥd* makes that difficult. It is therefore probably best to translate *škm* here by 'ridge of land' (cf. RSV, NEB), in which is involved a conscious allusion to Shechem. This, however, would not in itself constitute a 'portion', and therefore the precise significance of this verse, as most commentators agree, remains obscure.

Secondly, even if this verse did refer to Joseph's receiving a double portion, it would be strange that the significance of this is not drawn out anywhere. This is not a decisive difficulty, but it nevertheless needs to be explained by those who hold that this chapter refers to the treatment of Joseph as firstborn.

---

[1] Cf. Targum Onkelos: *w'n' yhbyt lk ḥwlq ḥd ytyr 'l 'ḥk* (Sperber's edition, p. 84).

[2] 'R. Judah maintained: The portion (Shechem) means the birthright (*škm zw hbkwrh*) and the raiment of Adam', H. Freedman: *Midrash Rabbah*, II, 943. For the text, see E. E. Hallevy: מדרש רבא, II, 753, and cf. Jastrow, p. 1575 A.

Finally, it should be remembered that the order of tribes in the Biblical lists nowhere betrays knowledge of a tradition that places either Joseph or Ephraim and Manasseh first. We therefore conclude that the MT of 1 Chr. 5: 1f. is unique in the OT in making an *explicit* reference to the concept of the birthright passing to Joseph and the sons of Joseph. Does this then mean that we should assume, as von Rad and Rudolph do, that the text is at fault?

(b) As was mentioned above, Rudolph seeks to avoid the difficulties that he finds in these verses providing the only explicit references to the birthright passing to Joseph by eliminating the first (reading *birkātô* for *bekōrātô*) and applying the second to Judah, not Joseph. Against this, however, we may raise precisely the same objection that Rudolph places against the present text, namely that the OT nowhere speaks of Judah in these terms. Only Ps. 78: 67f. (which Rudolph and Myers both compare at this point) could furnish a possible parallel to the thought that Rudolph finds in 1 Chr. 5: 1f.:

> Moreover He refused the tent of Joseph,
> And chose not the tribe of Ephraim;
> But chose the tribe of Judah,
> The mount Zion which He loved.

Here, however, the chiastic structure of the verses (contrasting 67a with 68b) makes clear[1] that the election is in terms of the sanctuary only: it is the tent of Joseph that is refused, as in v. 60: 'He forsook the tabernacle of Shiloh, the tent which He placed among men'. That need not affect the question of the birthright, but, as with the MT of 1 Chr. 5: 1f., it merely observes that the pre-eminence had passed to Judah, a common enough thought in the OT writings as a whole.

We may thus judge that Rudolph's reconstruction is unconvincing because it removes one difficulty only to introduce another comparable one that does not even enjoy the support of the text or the versions.

(c) We have already had occasion to note that the LXX rendering of 1 Chr. 5: 1f. speaks of the blessing, rather than the birthright, passing to Joseph.[2] Klostermann and von Rad follow this change consistently in both verses. Rudolph accepts the change for v. 1, but retains *bkrh* in v. 2, attributing it, however, to Judah, not Joseph.

Three considerations may lead us to question the judgment of these scholars at this point. First, the present Greek text contains a difficulty of its own which looks like a clumsy attempt by the translator to avoid what he felt to be a problem. Verse 1 states that the birthright in fact passed to the sons of Joseph, which superficially is a curious concept.

---

[1] Cf. A. A. Anderson: *Psalms*, II, 576.
[2] The Vulgate and Peshitta support the MT, as also do some LXX mss: b y e₂.

The Concept of Israel in Chronicles

The LXX seeks to soften the phrase: *edōke tēn eulogian autou tō huiō autou Iōsēph (nātan birkātô libnô yôsēp* for MT *ntnh bkrtw lbny ywsp);* however, it then retains *huiō Israēl* with the Hebrew, a phrase which makes for nonsense after the initial alteration. This small point suggests that the translator was here not above introducing slight changes into the text to ease what he found difficult. But if he could do it once, why should we rule out the possibility of his having done it twice?

A second consideration makes this the more likely. The whole purpose of the comment in these two verses is to explain why the Chronicler did not list Reuben first in the genealogies. For this purpose, the effective statement is 'and the genealogy is not to be reckoned after the birthright. For Judah prevailed above his brethren, and of him came the prince.' Since there is nowhere any suggestion that the genealogy should be reckoned 'after the blessing', the introduction here of Joseph in the way that Klostermann and von Rad propose is at best an irrelevance. In fact, however, the matter may be pressed further, for in view of the defensive tone of these verses, it may be considered extremely unlikely that the Chronicler would have thus laid himself open to criticism when he could equally well have ignored Joseph at this point altogether.

Rudolph tacitly concedes the force of this argument, without following it through to its logical outcome. He writes: 'Dass der Chr. nicht sofort von Ruben auf Juda überlenkt, sondern dazwischen die Segnungen Josefs anerkennt, erklärt sich offensichtlich aus der Auseinandersetzung mit Anschauungen seiner Zeit' (p. 43). Precisely! but in terms of his own argument, the Chronicler would only need to make such a concession if in fact the counter-claim concerned Joseph's birthright, not blessing. It would have been pointless for him to put ideas into his opponents' heads.

The third objection to adopting the reading of the LXX is not insuperable, but nonetheless carries a certain corroborative weight. On our understanding, this passage in Chr. is the only one in the OT unequivocally to state that the birthright passed from Reuben to Joseph. If we eliminate even this one, it becomes much harder to understand the united witness to this same tradition in the Targums. The force of this evidence may be gauged from the fact that it recurs in a remarkably similar, yet not identical, form in all four of the Targums to Gen. 49: 3f.[1] This widespread acceptance of the tradition argues for its antiquity; however, the only Biblical source for it is the MT of 1 Chr. 5: 1f. It must be agreed that corruption could have arisen between the LXX and the origins of the targumic/massoretic tradition, but that is less likely in view of the relatively late date of Par.,

---

[1] Cf. M. Ginsburger: *Pseudo-Jonathan*, p. 92 and *Fragmententhargum*, p. 24; A. Sperber: *Targum Onkelos*, p. 85; A. Díez Macho: *Neophyti I*, p. 329. Cf. the Targum to Chr. at this point in R. le Déaut and J. Robert: *Targum*, II, 21.

the early date of the tradition and the improbability of the corruption affecting all texts in the intervening period.

We may therefore conclude that the MT preserves the best reading at 1 Chr. 5: 1f. Moreover, the repetition of the phrase 'the sons of Reuben the firstborn of Israel' in v. 3 argues against its being the insertion of a later editor.

It is precisely the 'difficulties' that these verses raise which make them of such interest. Without the argument necessitating that he do so, the Chronicler has gone out of his way to maintain that Joseph and the sons of Joseph inherited the birthright. Theirs was an honourable part within the nation indeed, and one which nothing in the later narrative appears to have altered.

B. THE UNITED MONARCHY
(1 CHRONICLES 10 – 2 CHRONICLES 9)

The account of the death of Saul and David's assumption of the throne (1 Chr. 10f.) marks the beginning of the Chronicler's narrative proper. Many commentators have observed quite correctly that throughout this section of the work until the death of Solomon, Israel is presented as a fully united kingdom, apparently undisturbed by any serious internal tensions.

Early critical works on Chr. did not observe this trait at all,[1] or were content merely to point out, without explanation or comment, such well-known changes as *wylk dwyd* wkl-yśr'l *yrwšlm* (1 Chr. 11: 4) for *wylk hmlk* w'nšyw *yrwšlm* (2 Sam. 5: 6).[2] Wellhausen first gave the subject serious attention,[3] although inasmuch as he traced the unity of Israel only in the establishment of David as king (1 Chr. 11–12), his treatment fell short of being a full analysis in this regard. However, he had clearly established the direction that later scholarship was to take, and this was exploited by Rothstein–Hänel in their commentary on 1 Chr.,[4] and in a systematized form shortly thereafter by von Rad[5] and Welch.[6]

With the publication of these latter works, scholarship has been

---

[1] W. M. L. de Wette: *Beiträge*, and *Introduction*, II, 253–316; K. H. Graf: *Die geschichtlichen Bücher*, ch. II; E. Bertheau; W. E. Barnes; R. Kittel; W. A. L. Elmslie (1916); it is of interest to note how much Elmslie's position had changed in this very regard (particularly under the influence of Welch's work) by the time he came to write his second commentary on Chr. nearly forty years later (1954).

[2] So, for instance, W. R. Harvey-Jellie; I. Benzinger and CM.

[3] J. Wellhausen: *Prolegomena*, pp. 165ff.

[4] Rothstein–Hänel, e.g. pp. xliii, 207f., 210, 238f., 258ff., 266 and 364.

[5] von Rad: *Geschichtsbild*, pp. 34–6.

[6] A. C. Welch: *Post-Exilic Judaism*, pp. 188ff. and *The Work of the Chronicler*, where much of the first chapter is given over to precisely this theme.

unanimous in its agreement that the facts have been correctly presented,[1] although divided in its assessment of the purpose and significance of those facts.

Exhaustive study of these chapters has convinced me that this scholarly consensus is entirely justified. It is therefore unnecessary to present familiar material over again. We must emphasize, however, that upon this agreed view, all twelve tribes of Israel are regarded as necessary to the fulness of the people. Their role in the establishment of David as king is underlined by the Chronicler (1 Chr. 11–12), as is David's subsequent concern to involve them all in the important events of his reign (e.g. 1 Chr. 11: 4, 13: 1–5, 15: 3, etc.). Full justice must be done to this in any overall assessment of the Chronicler's viewpoint. It is against this background, moreover, that we should study the more controversial narrative of the divided monarchy.

[1] In addition to the modern commentaries, reference may be made especially to Y. Kaufmann: *History*, 4, 461; A.-M. Brunet: 'Sources'; J. Botterweck: 'Eigenart'; W. F. Stinespring: 'Eschatology'; M. Gill: 'Israel in the Book of Chronicles'; R. L. Braun: 'The Message of Chronicles', pp. 505f.; S. Japhet: *Ideology*, pp. 290–6; R. Mosis, pp. 51–5. R. L. Braun: 'Solomonic Apologetic', makes the important point that this unity also continued uninterrupted through the reign of Solomon; cf. H. G. M. Williamson: 'The Accession of Solomon'.

8

The Divided Monarchy (2 Chronicles 10–28)

Following the death of Solomon, the Chronicler records the story of the rebellion of 'Israel' against 'the house of David' (2 Chr. 10: 19). Against the background of his narrative up to this point, it will be at once apparent that this rebellion must have posed him a very real problem. Naturally he could not deny the event, but its consequences were open to interpretation. Concerning this interpretation, a scholarly consensus has arisen. This, however, has never been universally accepted, and recently it has been especially strongly challenged. Yet, as will be shown, none of the positive suggestions made thus far seems to be fully satisfactory.

A. THE SCHOLARLY CONSENSUS

It was de Wette who first emphasized that in his history of the divided monarchy, the Chronicler omits from his Kings *Vorlage* the notices that are favourable to the Northern Kingdom, and adds others that are hostile (2 Chr. 13, 19: 2f., 25: 7.20, 20: 35ff.). This led de Wette to speak of the Chronicler's love for Judah and hatred for Israel.[1] We have mentioned, however, that with the notable exception of Torrey, this standpoint was not widely applied to the Chronicler's post-exilic situation until after the publication of von Rad's monograph. It is now, however, a commonplace for scholars to seize on the catchphrase 'all Israel in Judah and Benjamin' (2 Chr. 11: 3) as underlining the 'Chronicler's view that only those elements of Israel that remained loyal to the Davidic line were the true Israel'.[2]

Without going into details at this point, it will be at once apparent that a rigid and simplistic adoption of this standpoint is unsatisfactory from the fact that of the eighty references to Israel during the divided

---

[1] W. M. L. de Wette: *Beiträge*, ch. II.

[2] J. M. Myers: *II Chronicles*, p. 65, and for similar examples (representative only!), cf. W. Rudolph, p. 227; K. Galling, p. 15 and T. Willi, p. 161. It is evident from this last reference that adoption of this standpoint does not therefore necessarily involve seeing anti-Samaritan polemic in Chr., even though most scholars have in fact associated the two.

monarchy, fifty-one refer without any doubt to the Northern Kingdom
(and in fact it is virtually certain that some of the passages that are open
to doubt should be further added to this). Not all these by any means
are taken from the Chronicler's *Vorlage*, and especially noteworthy in
this connection is 2 Chr. 13. Abijah's speech, which this chapter contains, is often thought to be the clearest indication of the Chronicler's
attitude towards the Northern Kingdom.[1] Yet Abijah addresses himself in fact to 'all Israel' (v. 4), a title used again in the narrative at v. 15,
whilst in vv. 12, 16, 17 and 18, the Northerners are also called 'Israel'.[2]
Von Rad's analysis, however, takes no account of such a passage, and
indeed seems to be incapable of providing it with a satisfactory interpretation.

B. ALTERNATIVE VIEWS

The two works of A. C. Welch in which he dealt with the writings of
the Chronicler were published within the decade following von Rad's
monograph,[3] and as concerns the idea of Israel, both take a quite
different line. In the earlier work, Welch determines on the basis of
2 Chr. 10: 15 and 11: 4 that 'evidently in his (the Chronicler's) view
there were good reasons for Israel having refused to endure the rule of
the Judean king' (Rehoboam), but on the basis of Abijah's speech
agrees that 'apparently the initial and fundamental sin lay in the rebellion of Israel against the divinely ordained unity of the nation
realised in the Davidic dynasty', especially since Jeroboam's erection
of the golden calves is subordinated. Observing that the battle described
in 2 Chr. 13 shows God to have favoured the Judeans, Welch concludes
that God must have tolerated the division for just so long as the un-
worthy Rehoboam was on the throne, but that after his death, the
Northerners should have returned. They did not, however, and so
thereafter the Chronicler's attitude towards them is unfavourable.[4]
Nonetheless, the strong interest in the maintenance of a united Israel
implies a certain sympathy with the men of the North,[5] and indeed
Welch is able to point to certain passages that portray the residents of
the North in a favourable light. We may again use Welch's own words

[1] Cf. Myers: 'Kerygma'.

[2] This chapter also provides strong evidence against M. Gill's conclusions
in his brief study: 'Israel in the Book of Chronicles', for it shows that the
Chronicler had no reservations about using the name Israel for the Northern
Kingdom, that he could further apply the term to a part of the people without
the presence of Levites, and that 'Judah' can be used as a political term quite
as much as a geographical one.

[3] A. C. Welch: *Post-Exilic Judaism* (1935) and *The Work of the Chronicler*
(1939).

[4] Welch: *Post-Exilic Judaism*, pp. 189–91.

[5] *Ibid.* p. 203.

to summarize his view: 'What he (the Chronicler) condemned in the North was the kingdom *qua* kingdom, since it had made a schism in the nation, but this did not involve that the nation itself with its religious leaders was apostate.'[1]

It is very remarkable that at least so far as our particular subject is concerned, Welch's exposition seems to have had hardly any effect upon the work of other scholars.[2] G. A. Danell is also critical of von Rad's understanding of the interpretation of the division in Chr., but not on the basis of Welch's reasoning, and indeed, he comes in the end to the same conclusion as von Rad, arguing that although on the basis of a word study alone it is not possible 'to establish any definite tendency in the Chronicler to make Judah into Israel proper, . . . this does not however prevent the kingdom of Judah from *being* the real Israel in Chronicles'.[3] Again, Kaufmann acknowledged that the division was the result of a divine decree, but explains this fact quite differently from Welch, and without reference to his work.[4]

The only exception to this is Japhet's attempt to develop Welch's and Danell's studies. She first follows Danell in rejecting von Rad's interpretation of 2 Chr. 11: 3 and finding in the Chronicler's formulation only a stylistic change against 1 Ki. 12: 23: the Chronicler means no more than what he has already expressed in 2 Chr. 10: 17: 'The children of Israel that dwelt in the cities of Judah.' Thus in 2 Chr. 11: 3, 'Judah and Benjamin' should be understood geographically, and 'all Israel' as a reference to the members of the various tribes who either lived there or had moved thence following the division, equivalent to 'the house of Judah and Benjamin' and 'the rest of the people' of 1 Ki. 12: 23.[5]

Japhet later returns to a fuller discussion of the division of the monarchy, out of which it emerges that the Chronicler's presentation differs significantly from that in Ki. There, the divergent traditions in 1 Ki. 10–12 all agree in making the expression of division typological, one tribe against ten, and not just historico-political (despite various attempts to justify this from a historical perspective).[6] In Chr., however, all this has disappeared, to be replaced by a purely geographical division of the kingdom into two parts. Certainly the North is in a state of rebellion and apostasy, but nevertheless all the tribes are a necessary part of the complete Israel.[7]

How, then, did the Chronicler solve the problem of the continued existence of the Northern Kingdom? According to Japhet, not only by

[1] *Ibid.* p. 205.
[2] Indeed, only Elmslie (1954) has followed Welch at all consistently.
[3] G. A. Danell: *Israel*, p. 275.   [4] Y. Kaufmann: *History*, 4, 465f.
[5] S. Japhet: *Ideology*, pp. 278f.; Danell: *Israel*, p. 275.
[6] Japhet: *Ideology*, pp. 296f.   [7] *Ibid.* p. 328.

his unquestionably friendly attitude towards its inhabitants,[1] but in particular by a process of steady territorial expansion on the part of the Southern Kingdom that links in closely with the extending composition of its population. Thus in Rehoboam's time, though members of all the tribes join themselves to his kingdom (2 Chr. 11: 16), it remains geographically limited to Judah and Benjamin (2 Chr. 11: 23). Under Asa, there is an influx of 'them that sojourned with them out of Ephraim and Manasseh, and out of Simeon' (2 Chr. 15: 9), whilst the border is correspondingly advanced to include 'the cities which he had taken from the hill country of Ephraim' (2 Chr. 15: 8). Hezekiah's Passover represents a further advance, with the heralds inviting participation reaching as far as Zebulun (2 Chr. 30: 10), and several other tribes also being mentioned in the course of the account. Finally, with Josiah, the expansion is complete, for the reform is shown to cover the area from Simeon as far as Naphtali (2 Chr. 34: 6), removing the 'abominations out of all the countries that pertained to the children of Israel' (2 Chr. 34: 33).[2]

This solution is superficially attractive, but turns out upon examination to fail because of the highly selective nature of the evidence adduced. In the first place, a full survey of the history of the border between the two kingdoms as presented by the Chronicler shows such a changeable line as to defy all systematization in the form proposed by Japhet. Thus, following Rehoboam's reign, we find that already Abijah annexed 'Bethel with the towns thereof, and Jeshanah with the towns thereof, and Ephron with the towns thereof' (2 Chr. 13: 19),[3] but this without any associated additions of population. The fact that in 2 Chr. 15: 8 we read of 'the cities which he (Asa) had taken from the hill country of Ephraim' suggests either a further expansion or, more probably in view of ch. 16, the loss of those same areas to Baasha and their subsequent recapture.[4] In any case, we certainly find that later in Asa's reign, Baasha was able to advance his southern border as far as Ramah[5] (2 Chr. 16: 1), even though Asa retook this again, following his appeal for help to the Assyrians (16: 2–6), so that we find Jehoshaphat fortifying those self-same cities at the start of his reign (2 Chr. 17: 2). The general tendency through the next eight rulers of the kingdom of Judah (Jehoram to Ahaz) is one of territorial decline, with no further reference to hegemony over any part of Ephraim. Jehoram lost

---

[1] *Ibid.* pp. 313–28. [2] *Ibid.* pp. 299–304.

[3] On this verse, cf. especially F. M. Cross and G. E. Wright: 'The Boundary and Province Lists', pp. 222f., where it is agreed that this verse represents an extension of Judahite territory into Benjamin. See also Y. Aharoni and M. Avi-Yonah: *Atlas*, map 121. [4] So Myers, p. 81.

[5] Ramah is situated within Benjamite territory, just five miles north of Jerusalem. On these movements, cf. Aharoni and Avi-Yonah: *Atlas*, maps 121 and 123 and accompanying text on p. 78.

control of Edom and Libnah (2 Chr. 21: 10), as well as suffering defeat at the hands of the Philistines and the Arabians within Judah itself (vv. 16f.). Under Joash, the Syrians penetrated as far as Jerusalem (2 Chr. 24: 23), whilst in Amaziah's reign it was Israel who defeated Judah 'and broke down the wall of Jerusalem' (2 Chr. 25: 23).[1] Finally, Ahaz was again defeated by Israel within the land of Judah (2 Chr. 28: 5b–8), as well as suffering defeat and territorial losses to the Syrians (v. 5a), the Edomites (v. 17) and the Philistines (v. 18). In the face of all this, it seems hard to trace a plan of expansion of the kind Japhet proposes.

Secondly, it seems improbable that Josiah's reform is meant to be a development from this point of view over that of Hezekiah, for in 2 Chr. 30: 5 'they established a decree to make proclamation throughout all Israel, from Beersheba even to Dan'. Evidently, according to the Chronicler, Hezekiah's interests were no less limited than Josiah's. Moreover, 2 Chr. 30: 11 refers to some of the tribe of Asher coming to the celebration of the Passover, but Asher's territory was as far north as that of Naphtali's and formed part of the northern border of the land in its ideal extent,[2] whereas Japhet takes the phrase 'even unto Naphtali' (2 Chr. 34: 6) as expressive of the full geographical extent of Josiah's reform.[3] These references from Hezekiah's reign may be understood in one of two possible ways: they may be a genuine attempt to record the history of the events, in which case, as we have seen, they allow no increase between Hezekiah and Josiah. Alternatively, they may be no more than a random selection of names, as might be inferred from the differences between 2 Chr. 30: 1.5.10.11 and 18. In that case, however, it becomes impossible to use these selfsame names as expressions of a conscious attempt to show a development of territorial expansion. I therefore find myself unable to accept Japhet's attempt to explain how the Chronicler overcame the problem which the division in the monarchy posed him, despite the many penetrating observations which she has made concerning the account of the division itself in 2 Chr. 10–11; these, of course, may still stand, apart from the question of the shape of the subsequent narrative.

In the light of this position of a scholarly consensus which is yet based upon insecure evidence, and the unsatisfying nature of the positions of those who have opposed it, it becomes necessary first to survey the Chronicler's use of the word Israel for this period, and then to see how the results of such a study fit into his overall narrative.

[1] According to Cross and Wright (*op. cit.* p. 223), it was at this time that the Ephraimite cities were recovered for the Northern Kingdom, for it is known from Amos, to go no further, that by the middle of the eighth century, Bethel was once more part of North Israel.

[2] Cf. Aharoni and Avi-Yonah: *Atlas*, pp. 52f.

[3] Japhet: *Ideology*, p. 303.

C. USE OF THE WORD ISRAEL

The Chronicler uses the word Israel eighty times in connection with the divided monarchy, the majority of these references being to the Northern Kingdom. Fifty-one instances are without question so intended. It is true that twenty-nine are drawn from the *Vorlage* in Ki. (2 Chr. 10: 19,[1] 16: 1.3.4, 18: 3.4.5.7.8.9.17.19.25.28.29 twice].30.31.32.33.34, 21: 6, 25: 17.18.21.22.23.25, 28: 2), and two with just a slight, though significant, change (2 Chr. 10: 18, 11: 1),[2] but that still leaves twenty that come from passages peculiar to Chr., of which a number, such as those already noted above from ch. 13, come from passages where such terminology is especially likely to be of significance to the Chronicler's thought (1 Chr. 5: 17, 2 Chr. 11: 13.16, 13: 4.12.15.16.17.18, 17: 4, 20: 35, 21: 13, 22: 5, 25: 6.7 [twice].9, 28: 5.8.13). This alone makes it unlikely that 'hier spricht nicht Polemik gegen eine schismatische Jahwegemeinde, sondern das Interesse an der nachexilischen Diaspora'.[3]

With this must be contrasted, however, those passages where Israel is with equal certainty used of the Southern Kingdom. There are eleven cases where there is no reasonable cause for doubt: 2 Chr. 12: 1.6, 19: 8, 21: 2.4, 23: 2, 24: 5.16, 28: 19.23.27. Some of these have been challenged on textual grounds, the versions and even some Hebrew mss sometimes giving 'Judah' as an alternative. However, as it is very much easier to understand this as a secondary attempt to alleviate a difficulty, sound method demands that we should not adopt these readings without further compelling evidence. Further, concerning the references that are purely political in nature, Rudolph has advanced the view that they derive from an earlier royal chronicle in which, we infer, Israel was the regular name used for the kingdom. Thus, for instance, he comments on 2 Chr. 21: 2 that the information of the first few verses of the chapter 'offenbar in der vom Chr. benützten Königschronik stand, aus der wohl der Sprachgebrauch stammt, Juda ohne einen bestimmten religiösen Grund (vgl. 20$_{29}$) "Israel" zu nennen (2b 4b, vgl. 17$_{1b}$)'.[4]

---

[1] Since by the Chronicler's time both the Northern Kingdom no longer existed, and the house of David was no longer ruling in the South, it is evident that the phrase 'unto this day' is a purely anachronistic relic from his sources. Thus, not only has it 'no reference to the later Samaritan schism' (so correctly Myers, p. 65), but it cannot really even teach us very much at all about his own attitude towards the situation (*contra* Myers: *I Chronicles*, p. xxxii).

[2] Cf. below, pp. 108–10.

[3] R. Mosis, p. 171, with immediate reference to 2 Chr. 11: 16, but characteristic of his attitude towards the Northern Kingdom in Chr. generally; cf. especially pp. 200ff.

[4] Rudolph, p. 265; cf. p. 291, where it is similarly suggested that 2 Chr. 28: 17–19 'stellen sich als Parenthese dar, die v. 20 von v. 16 trennt und deren Inhalt dem "Buch der Könige Judas und Israels" (26) entstammt, wie auch der Titel "König von Israel" für Ahas nahelegt'.

Even if, as seems probable, Rudolph is right in this, it still does not absolve us from the responsibility of seeking to explain what is the intention of such passages. Finally, it needs to be said concerning any such mechanical means to get round these verses that even if some are removed, others remain. Not only does this mean that an explanation is called for, but it makes the attempt itself look less likely, since these verses hold together as a unique witness to apply the term Israel to Judah in a historical narrative whilst the Northern Kingdom was still in existence. Justice must, then, be done to them in any attempt at a synthesis.

Before moving to this, however, it will be as well to look at the remaining eighteen cases where there is room for question as to what Israel refers to, and to clarify the issue where the doubts that have been raised do not seem compelling.

Several of the references are included in the account of the division of the monarchy and its immediate sequel (2 Chr. 10: 1.3.16 [three times].17, 11: 3). In 1 Ki. 12: 1ff., following the prophecy of the division of the kingdom in ch. 11, it is probable that the reader is intended to understand the references to Israel even in vv. 1 and 3 as to the tribes comprising the later Northern Kingdom. Support for this comes further from the analogy with 2 Sam. 5: 1–3, where 'all the tribes of Israel' who came to David at Hebron clearly refers to the tribes of the (northern) kingdom of Ishbosheth, and from the fact that Rehoboam went to Shechem to receive the kingdom.[1] In Chr., however, apart from the reference to Shechem, this situation is altered: no hint of the impending division has been retained in the account of Solomon's reign, and the analogy with the gathering to David at Hebron would now imply that 'all Israel' refers indeed to the full number of the tribes. The stress that we have noticed in Chr. on the unity and comprehensive nature of all Israel demands therefore that it should retain the same meaning too at the start of 2 Chr. 10.

It is equally clear, however, that by the end of the chapter, Israel is used to refer to the Northern Kingdom alone (vv. 18 and 19). Since throughout the chapter the Chronicler is following his *Vorlage* quite closely, there is doubt as to the point at which this change can have occurred. No doubt, however, the Chronicler presupposed in his readers not only knowledge of his *Vorlage* (as v. 15 makes clear) but also common sense to realize that in v. 16, too, the Northern tribes alone are intended, whilst in v. 17 the reference is to the inhabitants of the Southern Kingdom. Here, he needed only to follow his *Vorlage*, but that it coincided exactly with the point of view that he was anxious to express is made clear by his rephrasing at 11: 3 'all Israel in Judah and

[1] Cf. J. Gray: *I and II Kings*, pp. 303f.; Myers: *II Chronicles*, p. 65.

Benjamin' for 'all the house of Judah and Benjamin and (to) the rest of the people' (1 Ki. 12: 23).[1]

2 Chr. 15: 9: there would be no doubt about understanding Israel in this verse as a reference to the territory of the Northern Kingdom (closely parallel to 2 Chr. 11: 13), were it not for the reference to Simeon, which the Chronicler, in conformity with the usual Biblical presentation, had earlier located to the south of Judah (1 Chr. 4: 24ff.). The problem, however, clearly concerns the position of Simeon, and not the definition of Israel. Thus, whilst it is possible to make various suggestions to elucidate this,[2] the difficulty in no way affects the course of our present investigation.

2 Chr. 15: 17: according to 1 Ki. 15: 14, referring to Asa's kingdom of Judah, 'the high places were not taken away'. In 2 Chr. 14: 2–4, however, the Chronicler had already stated that Asa *did* take away the high places. Thus his insertion of *myśr'l* into our verse must be understood in the present form of the book to refer to the Northern Kingdom.[3] Whilst the Chronicler thereby eased a difficulty in his text, he introduced the concept of the ideal rights of the Davidides still over all the territory of Israel. This is the only place where there is a hint of the possible authority of a southern king over the North before the fall of Samaria. It is thus to be seen as arising from the exigencies of consistency rather than as a deliberate attempt to make some sort of positive claim.

2 Chr. 17: 1: it is extremely difficult to decide on the meaning of

[1] The LXX does not support the MT here at the very point that is crucial to the position of von Rad: *eipon pros Roboam ton tou Salōmōn kai panta Ioudan kai Beniamein legōn* ... If this were the correct reading, it would at once close the discussion, but in fact there seem to be no reasons why on the basis of this evidence alone the MT should be emended. The fact that in both 2 Chr. 10: 17 and 11: 3 the use of '(all) Israel' has to be qualified to show who is intended supports the view that it was not meant to be understood in an exclusive sense. Thus Danell (*Israel*, p. 275) and Japhet (*Ideology*, pp. 278f.) are fully justified in their understanding of 2 Chr. 11: 3 (cf. above p. 99).

[2] M. Noth, for instance, seeks an explanation along the lines of influence from Gen. 34, *US*, p. 178. Following the analysis of the extent and fortification of the Southern Kingdom as reflected in 2 Chr. 11: 5–10 by G. Beyer: 'Das Festungssystem Rehabeams', Rudolph (p. 247) and Myers (p. 89) suggest that this might reflect an expulsion of the population at the hands of the Edomites, following the collapse of the united monarchy, though 1 Chr. 4: 41 would imply that this situation was reversed by the reign of Hezekiah (perhaps in the period of Jehoshaphat, cf. 2 Chr. 19: 4). 2 Chr. 34: 6 may also imply a relationship between Simeon and the North, though there it could equally well be included to indicate the southernmost part of the country as a whole. It is worth pointing out that Amos too seems to think of Beersheba as belonging to the North (Amos 5: 5, 8: 14).

[3] Cf. Willi, pp. 59ff., who associates this passage with other harmonizing attempts of the Chronicler, and who also rejects Rudolph's arguments that these verses are added in secondarily to the Chronicler's text; CM, p. 386.

Israel in this verse. Most frequently, it has been understood as referring to the Northern Kingdom, so that the second half of the verse is translated 'and strengthened himself against Israel'. Verse 2 is then an amplification of this statement.[1] This, however, is not the usual sense of *lhthzq 'l* (cf. 2 Chr. 1: 1) and thus Rudolph sees here a reference to the Southern Kingdom. In support of this view he is able further to point out that in 18: 1ff. and 20: 35ff., Jehoshaphat is seen to work in co-operation with the North, that Israel is also used in this sense during Jehoshaphat's reign at 21: 2 and 4, and that the North is referred to in 17: 2 as Ephraim.[2]

This last argument is weak, however, since Ephraim more probably refers to the tribal territory. Nor do Jehoshaphat's later exploits necessarily determine how he should have acted at the start of his reign, which followed a period of trouble between the two kingdoms (cf. ch. 16). Further, in the following verses, Judah (vv. 2.5.6) and Israel (v. 4) are clearly used in their normal sense, and as we have said earlier, this cannot be avoided simply on the basis of the use of sources.

The context, therefore, inclines us to adopt the traditional understanding, whilst linguistic considerations alone would tend to favour Rudolph, though it must be allowed that, though unparalleled, the traditional rendering might be possible if contextual considerations were felt to be compelling. The question must therefore be left open, and should not be used in an attempt to determine the Chronicler's use of Israel.

2 Chr. 18: 16: although this verse comes in the middle of a long section taken over almost identically from 1 Ki. 22, it seems just possible that in the reference here to 'all Israel', the Chronicler may have seen an allusion to both the kingdoms that were engaged in the campaign, rather than just the Northern Kingdom alone.

2 Chr. 20: 29: it is customary to see in this verse another reference to the Southern Kingdom under the title of Israel.[3] The setting, however, deserves careful attention: Moab and Ammon had come in war against Jehoshaphat (v. 1). In his prayer, Jehoshaphat links this with the movements of Israel shortly before their entry into the land after the wilderness wanderings (vv. 10f.), so that the subsequent battle becomes virtually a sequel to that affair, vindicating Israel's mercy towards them at that time. In the account of the battle itself, the Lord's role is highlighted in response to the people's cultic faithfulness. Thus, though as a technical term there was no such expression in ancient Israel, it is possible to see what Myers means when he comments that

---

[1] Cf. the translation of Myers, p. 96: 'He proceeded to fortify himself against Israel by stationing troops in all the fortified cities of Judah . . .'
[2] Rudolph, p. 249.
[3] So, for instance, von Rad: *Geschichtsbild*, p. 30.

'the writer viewed the whole expedition as a holy war' (p. 116). In the verse under discussion, therefore, the Chronicler probably intended Israel to be understood in its original, fully extended sense, rather than pedantically as Judah alone.

The remaining problematic references are all to the annals of 'the kings of Israel and Judah' (or equivalents): 1 Chr. 9: 1, 2 Chr. 16: 11, 20: 34, 25: 26, 27: 7, 28: 26. Despite Liver's excellent arguments that a genuine source is intended thereby,[1] the fact that the word 'and Israel' is added by the Chronicler to his *Vorlage* (or once even substituted for 'Judah': 2 Chr. 20: 34)[2] suggests that even the way he referred to this source was not without significance for him. Here again, however, it is difficult to tie the Chronicler down to precision: on the one hand, the use of 'Judah and Israel' excludes a simple equation of Israel with Judah, and would seem to imply Southern and Northern Kingdoms together; indeed, generally speaking, the source is referred to for the reign of a king where considerable contact with the North is recorded. On the other hand, however, this latter argument is not entirely valid, since no such contact is mentioned for the reign of Jotham (2 Chr. 27), nor is this source referred to for some other kings who did have such contacts (e.g. Abijah, 2 Chr. 13), and in any case it is referred to also after the fall of the Northern Kingdom (against the *Vorlage*) at 2 Chr. 32: 32, 33: 18, 35: 27 and 36: 8. It is thus clear that the word Israel in these expressions cannot be precisely defined.

The important point in this connection is that he never refers to the 'book of the kings of Judah' (and equivalents) alone, but without exception introduces Israel as well. Apparently, by this consistent practice, the Chronicler wished to emphasize that Judah was still an integral part of Israel in its full sense, despite its name Judah. At the same time, however, he made no attempt through the titles to claim that Judah alone was Israel.

After this general attempt to classify from context the objects of the references to Israel during the divided monarchy, we must proceed to ask just what the Chronicler was intending to convey thereby. Naturally, interest falls initially upon the usage in connection with the Southern Kingdom. Of these, a group come together at the end of the reign of Ahaz (2 Chr. 28: 19.23.[26].27), that is to say, on the Chronicler's view, just after the fall of Samaria, and from the worst of the kings of this period. To this we must return later.

Of the rest, a considerable proportion is used, as has been pointed out by Danell, either in titles, or in connection with the cult.[3] The titles

[1] J. Liver: 'And all Israel'.
[2] There is no justification for taking this as a separate case from the other citations (*contra* Rudolph, p. 263 and Myers, p. 116) to argue that this reflects the view that 'Judah is really the true Israel'.   [3] G. A. Danell: *Israel*, p. 274.

are *śry yśr'l* – the princes of Israel – at 2 Chr. 12: 6 and 21: 4,[1] and
r'śy h'bwt lyśr'l – heads of the fathers' houses of Israel – at 2 Chr.
19: 8 and 23: 2. These titles, or close equivalents, are also used in the
period of the united monarchy (e.g. 1 Chr. 22: 17, 23: 2, 27: 1, 28: 1,
2 Chr. 1: 2 and 5: 2), so that Danell is justified in suggesting that 'this
title had lived on in the kingdom of Judah after the division of the
kingdom'.[2] Association with the cult is clear at 2 Chr. 12: 1, 24: 5 and
16, where again continuation from the past is to be suggested, especially
on the basis of 24: 5. Here, Joash commands the priests and Levites to
gather money for the repair of the temple with the words: 'Go out unto
the cities of Judah, and gather of all Israel money to repair the house of
your God from year to year.' When they fail to do this, he rebukes
Jehoiada by relating his command directly to the tax instituted by
Moses, 2 Chr. 24: 6 (and cf. v. 9). It is thus evident that his use of
Israel in v. 5 is not intended as a political expression, but in the sense
of a community that stands in the direct line of the Israel of an earlier
generation.

This feature of the name as a symbol of continuity from before the
political division thus characterizes both groups of references. This is
precisely the use that was determined on other grounds for its occurrence at 2 Chr. 20: 29 (above, pp. 105f.) and seems closely to parallel the
only sense found acceptable for the appearance of Israel in the titles of
the annals he cites (above, p. 106).[3] There can be little doubt, therefore, that the Chronicler used the name Israel for Judah, not to exclude
or contrast with the Northern Kingdom, but to make the positive
point that there was to be found in Judah an unbroken continuation of
the Isrrel of earlier days.

If it is agreed, however, that the Chronicler deliberately used a word
to convey a particular meaning, it seems unreasonable to argue that he
was oblivious to its meaning in the majority of its usages. In other words,
weight must also be given to its application to the Northern Kingdom.
This fact comes particularly to expression in the account of the division
of the monarchy itself. The first, and remarkable, point to observe here
is that, as we have already noted in the detail of 2 Chr. 11: 3, although
sometimes the Chronicler slightly rephrases his *Vorlage*, he has not

---

[1] The parallel expression *śry yhwdh* – the princes of Judah – is used at 2 Chr.
12: 5, 22: 8 and 24: 17.   [2] Danell: *Israel* p. 274.

[3] It thus covers all the occurrences of Israel used of the Southern Kingdom
except those from the reign of Ahaz (on which see below), two from the account
of the division (again, see below), and the title 'Jehoshaphat king of Israel' at
2 Chr. 21: 2. This verse defies all attempts to fit it into any kind of system, a
fact highlighted by the observation that Jehoshaphat is usually called 'king of
Judah'. It seems probable that it reflects the use of a source (so Rudolph, p.
265), and that the Chronicler allowed it to stand because it was not incompatible
with his overall viewpoint.

altered its meaning as he would have conceived it to any appreciable extent. The only real question on the general structure of the passage concerns the role of Jeroboam. On the basis of the order of events in 3 Reigns, several commentators have sought to re-arrange the text in 1 Ki.,[1] explaining its present form as the result of secondary influence from Chr. The result of such a conclusion would be to make Jeroboam's role in the revolt more prominent. This conclusion, however, has been very seriously challenged,[2] and although the issue is still one of lively debate,[3] it would indeed be hazardous to build at all on what have now been shown to be very questionable foundations.

Not only, then, does the Chronicler at this most obvious point in his narrative fail to make any clearer than his *Vorlage* the significance of the division, had he understood it in the way von Rad thinks, but rather, the very slight changes that he does introduce into the text, and which mainly concern the use of Israel, are likely to be of the more significance. There are five such touches that demand our attention:

(a) The beginning of 2 Chr. 10: 16. In place of *wyr' kl yśr'l* (1 Ki. 12:16), Chr. has only *wkl yśr'l*. Commentators are unanimous in wishing to restore *r'w* after *yśr'l*, explaining its loss by haplography.[4] The meaning of the two texts would then be the same. However, it should be urged against this view that there is no apparent reason why the Chronicler should have altered the word order here, whilst the presence of the *w* before the *kl* precludes the explanation that *wyr'* dropped out from its present position in Ki. Furthermore, whilst the versions that support the emendation can be easily explained as secondary attempts to overcome a difficulty, no such reasoning can explain why the LXX follows the MT of Chr. at this point exactly.[5] The verse should thus be rendered in English: '... for it was brought about of God, that the Lord might establish his word, which he spake by the hand of Ahijah the Shilonite to Jeroboam the son of Nebat and all Israel, for the king hearkened not unto them. And the people answered the king ...' The effect of this slight change is to underline that the division was God's will for all Israel as much as for Jeroboam, and draws attention to their involvement in the division.[6]

(b) The end of 2 Chr. 10: 16. The Chronicler adds *kl* before *yśr'l*,

---

[1] E.g. J. A. Montgomery and H. S. Gehman: *Kings*, pp. 248ff.; J. Gray: *I and II Kings*, pp. 299ff. and Rudolph, p. 227.

[2] D. W. Gooding: 'The Septuagint's Rival Versions' and 'Problems of Text and Midrash'.

[3] R. W. Klein: 'Jeroboam's Rise to Power'; Gooding: 'Jeroboam's Rise to Power: A Rejoinder'; Klein: 'Once more: "Jeroboam's Rise to Power"'.

[4] E.g. Rudolph, p. 228 and Myers, p. 65.

[5] *hon elalēsen en cheiri Acheia tou Sēlōneitou peri Ieroboam huiou Nabat kai pantos Israēl, hoti ouk ēkousen ho basileus autōn. kai apekrithē ...*

[6] It is thus in line with Gooding's conclusions noted above.

with reference to the northern tribes only,¹ making an additional reference to them in this way that has so often been thought to be significant to the Chronicler within the crucial account of the division.

(c) 2 Chr. 10: 18 – *wyrgmw bw bny yśr'l* for 1 Ki. 12: 18– *wyrgmw kl yśr'l bw*.² The reference here is to the Northern Kingdom again. That the Chronicler is not seeking to avoid the application to them of the expression *kl yśr'l* is quite clear from what has just been observed at v. 16. The only possible intention at this point, therefore, must be to use of the Northern Kingdom exactly the same expression as is used of the Southern Kingdom in the previous verse. The inhabitants of both kingdoms are still equally 'sons of Israel'.

(d) 2 Chr. 11: 1 – *lhlḥm 'm yśr'l*, omitting the word *byt* which 1 Ki. 12: 21 has before *yśr'l*.³ This change is in line with the Chronicler's practice of avoiding terminology which might be confused with that used elsewhere in the Bible for the later political division.⁴ Paradoxically, even here where this very division is the subject of the narrative, the same considerations may apply. By dropping the word *byt*, the Chronicler maintains with slightly increased emphasis his view that the northern tribes too still remain Israel in a sense that goes beyond merely political terminology.

(e) 2 Chr. 11: 3 – *kl yśr'l byhwdh wbnymyn* – for 1 Ki. 12: 23 – *kl byt yhwdh wbnymyn wytr h'm*. Since we have already agreed with those who argue that no change of essential meaning is intended here, the question arises all the more urgently why, then, the Chronicler did not retain his *Vorlage* unaltered. That he was not afraid to use the expression found in Ki. is shown by v. 1 of this chapter, where in fact, through the omission of the word *šbt* from 1 Ki. 12: 21, he arrives at the same phrase almost exactly: *'t byt yhwdh wbnymyn*. It must therefore have been for a positive reason that he wished to draw the term *kl yśr'l* into association with the Southern Kingdom. The only solution seems to be that, as in the case of the *bny yśr'l* at 2 Chr. 10: 18, he wished to show that each term could equally be used of either kingdom. However, again as with the expression *bny yśr'l* when applied to the Southern Kingdom, a geographical qualification was needed to make clear exactly who was intended.

The results of this survey of the Chronicler's use of Israel during the account of the division of the monarchy and its sequel in the reign of Rehoboam are that, whereas he does not attempt to alter the course of

¹ The LXX supports respectively the MT of both Ki. and Chr. here, as in the previous case, so that there is no need to suggest mechanical explanations in the way Lemke is able successfully to do at other places.
² The same textual considerations apply here again as in the previous note.
³ The LXX again supports the MT.
⁴ Cf. 1 Chr. 13: 8 and 15: 28 with parallels.

events or its outcome, he does introduce slight changes to show that either party has equal justification in terming itself Israel, thus:

	Southern Kingdom	Northern Kingdom
kl yśr'l	2 Chr. 11: 3, 12: 1	2 Chr. 10: 16, 11: 13
bny yśr'l	2 Chr. 10: 17	2 Chr. 10: 18
yśr'l	2 Chr. 12: 6	2 Chr. 10: 16.19, 11: 1

Moreover, at 2 Chr. 11: 1 he avoids the single expression involving Israel (*byt yśr'l*) that could only have been applied to one part. Our conclusion for this important passage, then, is in line with what we have already seen thus far of the Chronicler's attitude to the divided monarchy as a whole, and we may use Gill's words as a succinct summary of it: 'The explanation is not that the author sees all Israel in Judah and Benjamin, but rather that even reckoning with the division, both alike are Israel.'[1]

D. THE NARRATIVE STRUCTURE OF THE HISTORY OF THE DIVIDED MONARCHY

The conclusions of this word study diverge considerably from the positions generally adopted in modern scholarship. It is therefore imperative to establish whether in his narrative as a whole the Chronicler presents the same point of view.

Just as in our word study the striking feature that demanded most attention was the attribution of the name Israel to the Southern Kingdom, so here the pressing question is, of course, the status of the Northern Kingdom. That Judah's faithfulness in Chr. by and large to the foundational traditions of Israel justifies her claim to that name is too well known to need elaboration. But was the state of rebellion of the North not so great as to disqualify her altogether, as so many commentators have held?

At the point of the division itself, this was clearly not the case. Twice, the Chronicler retains statements from his *Vorlage* that the division was brought about by God so that he might establish his word (2 Chr. 10: 15, 11: 4). These statements are so much in contradiction with the Chronicler's previous concern for the unity of all Israel that their retention can hardly be accidental.[2] Moreover, Shemaiah refuses to countenance any attempt by Judah to coerce Israel back into union, whilst retaining for the Northerners the title 'brethren' (2 Chr. 11: 1–4). It seems difficult, therefore, not to agree with Welch that at this

[1] M. Gill: 'Israel in the Book of Chronicles', p. 111. Despite our use of this citation, many of Gill's arguments are quite unacceptable, as was indicated above.
[2] Cf. A. C. Welch: *Post-Exilic Judaism*, pp. 189f.; Y. Kaufmann: *History*, 4, 465f.; S. Japhet: *Ideology*, p. 315; R. Mosis, pp. 169f.

point, in the Chronicler's judgment, 'there were good reasons for Israel having refused to endure the rule of the Judean king'.[1]

By ch. 13, however, this situation has been completely reversed, for here the Chronicler quite evidently sees God's hand in Abijah's victory over the Northerners, and reckons it to be a vindication of the speech of Abijah in vv. 4–12. What events have intervened to justify this drastic change?

First, there is the account of the apostasy of the Northerners (2 Chr. 11: 14f.). Though the substance of this notice has been drawn from 1 Ki. 12: 26–33, it has been reworked by the Chronicler. Several important features are omitted, such as the setting up of the calves specifically at Dan and Bethel, and the calendrical alteration. However, Jeroboam's expulsion of the Levites and appointment of other priests, his worship at 'the high places' and his making of Satyrs (not in Ki.) and calves are all mentioned, and constitute ample grounds in the Chronicler's eyes for severe condemnation. This is only underlined by the immediate sequel of all 'such as set their hearts to seek the Lord, the God of Israel' coming 'to Jerusalem to sacrifice unto the Lord, the God of their fathers' (2 Chr. 11: 16). For the Chronicler, the correct place, as well as the correct form and object of worship, was of overwhelming importance.

Secondly, it is probable that the death of Rehoboam and the accession of Abijah were also seen as significant in this connection. The Chronicler's doctrine of immediate retribution was so rigid that each successive king was judged entirely on his own merits, without reference back to the situation in the previous reign(s). Thus each king starts out with a completely 'clean sheet'. Now for the Northerners to have associated with Rehoboam would have done them no good, in the Chronicler's account, for 'when the kingdom of Rehoboam was established, and he was strong, he forsook the law of the Lord, and all Israel with him' (2 Chr. 12: 1). 'They trespassed against the Lord' (v. 2) and forsook him (v. 5). Moreover, Rehoboam 'did that which was evil because he set not his heart to seek the Lord' (v. 14). At the accession of Abijah, however, as always in the Chronicler's system, a completely new start was made, with the king against whom the Northerners had with apparent justification rebelled now removed from the scene. Although no judgment is passed by the Chronicler upon Abijah, the Chronicler nevertheless presents him as a worthy king in the Davidic succession.

These two changes in the situation between the time of the division of the monarchy and the events of 2 Chr. 13 are the very same two points upon which Abijah bases his condemnation of the Northerners (vv. 4–12). To see anti-Samaritan polemic in this speech, as is cus-

[1] Welch: *op. cit.*

tomary,[1] seems to me to be entirely beside the point, for the question of the legitimacy of the Davidic dynasty would have been an irrelevance in such a post-exilic debate, whilst to single out 'the sons of Aaron' would, as Kippenberg (pp. 48–50) has shown, have been merely to play into the hands of the Samaritans at one of their strongest points. Moreover, the point of deepest division between the two later communities, namely the relative virtues of the locality of the chosen sanctuary, receives no mention here at all. It seems far better, therefore, to seek to understand the speech within its immediate context, with which, as we have begun to see, there are strong contacts.

First, in vv. 5–8a, Abijah deals with the political aspect of the situation. In line with the Chronicler's strong insistence on the Davidic dynasty, he stresses its permanence as a God-given institution for Israel (v. 5). The cause of the division is then traced first to Jeroboam the son of Nebat (v. 6). The manner in which he is referred to thus in the third person makes it clear that the main addressees of the speech are the people of the North rather than Jeroboam himself. This is confirmed by v. 8b: 'which Jeroboam made you for gods', so that by v. 12 Jeroboam has dropped out as an addressee altogether ('O children of Israel, fight ye not . . .').

In v. 7, the division is secondly attributed to 'vain men, sons of Belial'. It is not clear who this is intended to refer to. Quite evidently, a distinction is drawn between these people and the Northerners who are listening to the speech, and the description even suggests a small group of people (cf. 1 Sam. 10: 27). Whoever these people are, the blame for the initial division is being narrowly based.

If *'lyw* (v. 7) has Jeroboam as its antecedent, then the reference will clearly be to a representative group of Northerners. Alternatively, however, *'dnyw* (v. 6) may be intended as the antecedent. Since the Chronicler omitted the account of Jeroboam's rebellion against Solomon (1 Ki. 11: 26–40), this must, within the context of Chr., refer to Rehoboam. In the account of the rebellion against Rehoboam (2 Chr. 10), only one group fits this description, namely the young men by whose advice Rehoboam was persuaded, and on whom much of the blame for the division must rest.[2] *wyt'mṣw 'l* (v. 7) should then be translated not as 'strengthened themselves against' (a meaning not attested elsewhere in any case), but rather 'prevailed over',[3] hence 'persuaded'.

Whichever interpretation is preferred, Abijah has evidently refrained from laying blame on his listeners. Advantage was taken of Rehoboam's weakness (7b), but this was clearly seen as an exceptional circumstance.

---

[1] In addition to the modern commentaries *ad loc.*, cf. M. Delcor: 'Hinweise'; A. Schalit: 'Denkschrift', pp. 180f., n. 97.

[2] Josephus apparently understood the reference in this way: *Ant.* VIII, 277.

[3] Cf. the use of the *qal* with this meaning in v. 18.

The Davidic king would normally have been expected to be able to withstand such pressure. This is the force of the word-play at vv. 7b and 8a: '(Rehoboam) could not withstand them. And now ye think to withstand the kingdom of the Lord in the hand of the sons of David.' Once again, attention is drawn to the abnormality in the situation at Rehoboam's accession, but now, as the play on words shows, that unique situation has returned to normality. The implication, therefore, is that the Northerners should now return to the legitimate Davidic government.

The second half of the speech treats the second change in the situation noted since the division, namely the apostasy of the Northerners. Again, the points of unfaithfulness are listed in conformity with 2 Chr. 11: 15: the golden calves (v. 8b), the non-Levitical priests (v. 9) and the 'no gods' (v. 9b), by which may be intended the Satyrs. All this amounts to forsaking God (v. 11b), whereas the Southerners have not forsaken him (v. 10a), since every detail of their cultic practice conforms with the law.[1] The contrast of this situation with the statement of 2 Chr. 12: 1 again underlines the changed situation with the end of Rehoboam's reign.

On these two overall bases, Abijah then appeals to the Northerners to call off their rebellion, since they are now fighting against 'the Lord, the God of your fathers' (v. 12b). Their refusal to do so demonstrates that they are indeed in a state of genuine rebellion, and their defeat in the ensuing battle confirms God's judgment against them. This remains their status during the subsequent narrative of the divided monarchy, as 2 Chr. 19: 2f. and 25: 7, for instance, demonstrate.

A few features of this status, however, need emphasizing. First, they remain 'children of Israel' (13: 12); secondly, the Lord is still 'the Lord, the God of your fathers'; and thirdly, the accusation against them is summarized in the words 'ye have forsaken him' (13: 11). There is thus no suggestion that they are completely dismissed as heathen people,[2] but rather, they are in a state into which even the South sometimes fell (cf. 2 Chr. 12: 1, 21: 6.10ff., 22: 3–5, 24: 17–20. 24, 25: 14f. 20 and ch. 28, on which see below), although of course their resistance to Davidic rule was not copied there (though cf. 2 Chr. 25: 27f.). From such a state, repentance is always considered a possibility by the Chronicler, as is made clear by his programmatic addition to God's answer to Solomon's prayer (2 Chr. 7: 14), repeated in the later history by men of God (e.g. 2 Chr. 12: 7, 15: 2–7, 30: 6–9 and 18f.), and as is often illustrated in the sudden reversals of fortune that follow upon such repentance. There is thus, furthermore, no question but that any who did repent and come south are commended by the

---

[1] Cf. below, pp. 114f. and 121f. for the significance of the details of cult practice as listed here.　　[2] As Mosis thinks, pp. 68f. and 172f.

Chronicler. By his attitude to them, he shows that such a theoretical possibility as a full return by all the Northerners is not ruled out (cf. 2 Chr. 11: 13–17 and 15: 9). Indeed, Abijah's speech itself should not be understood only in terms of negative polemic, but be seen to contain in its delicate handling of the division and interpretation of the Northerners' apostasy as 'forsaking' God an appeal for just such an act of repentance.

Consequently, in his subsequent narrative, the Chronicler will naturally not include an account of the activities of the Northern Kingdom on its own, but that he records carefully all contacts between South and North, including some not mentioned in his *Vorlage*, has been most convincingly shown by Japhet, whose full treatment of the subject needs no further comment.[1] Thus far, therefore, it is possible to see how the Chronicler was able to reconcile the North being called Israel whilst yet divided from the Davidic kingdom in the South, so that his narrative remains consistent with the results already achieved from our word study.

This state of affairs apparently continues unchanged throughout the whole period of the divided monarchy. However, it is our conviction that the Chronicler also presents a solution to this situation. The first indications of that solution are contained in his reworking of the account of the reign of Ahaz, the last Judean king of the double monarchy (in the Chronicler's view; cf. 2 Chr. 30: 6). To an analysis of that account, therefore, we must now turn.

The reign of Ahaz is treated in 2 Chr. 28. Although much of the substance of the account is found in 2 Ki. 16, the whole narrative has been reworked, in such a way that only the introduction to and conclusion of the reign are parallel from a literary point of view, and even then there are some significant alterations.[2] Furthermore, the story of the good treatment of the Judean prisoners at the hands of their Northern brethren is added in vv. 8–15. To anticipate our analysis, it may be suggested that the force of these changes is first to reverse almost completely the situation between North and South as presented in 2 Chr. 13, and secondly to close the reign with both communities in the same situation of military defeat and partial exile. Moreover, the fall of the Northern regime leaves only one king reigning in Israel.

We may start by noticing how the Chronicler heightens the description of the apostasy of Ahaz. As well as including from his *Vorlage* the condemnation of vv. 1.2a.3b and 4, he adds the remark at 2b that he 'made also molten images for the Baalim' and at 3a that 'moreover he burnt incense in the valley of the son of Hinnom'. Later in the reign,

---

[1] S. Japhet: *Ideology*, pp. 313–28.

[2] This situation can be immediately seen by a synoptic presentation of the material such as is found, for instance, in A. Bendavid: *Parallels*, pp. 136ff.

whereas 2 Ki. 16 shows that Ahaz made an altar in Jerusalem in imitation of the one he had seen at Damascus and had the regular sacrifices offered upon it (vv. 10–16), the Chronicler spells out explicitly that this involved sacrifice to the gods of Damascus, saying 'because the gods of the kings of Syria help them, therefore will I sacrifice to them, that they may help me' (v. 23). Two verses later, moreover, we find that 'in every several city of Judah he made high places to burn incense unto other gods' (v. 25). Finally, again in addition to 2 Ki. 16, the Chronicler has Ahaz 'shut up the doors of the house of the Lord' (v. 24). The consequences of this deed are made clear by Hezekiah in his confession:

> They have shut up the doors of the porch, and put out the lamps, and have not burned incense nor offered burnt offerings in the holy place unto the God of Israel (2 Chr. 29: 7)

whilst 2 Chr. 29: 18 also shows that the shewbread was neglected.

These various points are almost precisely those which Abijah mentioned in his accusation of the Northern Kingdom in 2 Chr. 13. There, in v. 11, Abijah boasts that in Jerusalem

> they burn unto the Lord every morning and every evening burnt offerings and sweet incense: the shewbread also set they in order upon the pure table; and the candlestick of gold with the lamps thereof, to burn every evening.

However, as we have seen, each one of these points is explicitly negated by the Chronicler for the reign of Ahaz. In addition, Abijah accused the Northerners of worshipping the golden calves (2 Chr. 13: 8) and 'them that are no gods' (v. 9). Exactly the same could be said of Ahaz with his 'molten images for the Baalim' and his worship of the gods of the Syrians.

The combination of all these factors, together with the closing down of the temple itself, is sufficient, therefore, to uphold the view that during the reign of Ahaz, the religious faithfulness of the Southern Kingdom as expounded by Abijah was completely overthrown. Thus, just as it was seen above that Abijah summarized his condemnation of the North by saying that they had forsaken the Lord (2 Chr. 13: 11), so the Chronicler attributes Ahaz's failures to the fact that Judah 'had forsaken the Lord, the God of their fathers' (2 Chr. 28: 6).

With this must be contrasted the situation as described in the North. It was shown above that Abijah's speech was so phrased as to leave open the possibility of the repentance, and hence the full restoration, of the people of the Northern Kingdom, but that during the account of the dual monarchy, this was never realized. A step in that direction is clearly taken, however, in 2 Chr. 28: 8–15. The victorious Northerners are met by Oded, 'a prophet of the Lord' (v. 9).[1] He observes that the people's victory was due to the sin of the Southerners, and not at all to their own faithfulness: 'Are there not even with you trespasses of your own against the Lord your God?' (v. 10). With this assessment certain of the leaders concur:

> Ye purpose that which will bring upon us a trespass against the Lord, to add unto our sins and to our trespass: for our trespass is great and there is fierce wrath against Israel (v. 13).

Here, for the first time, the Chronicler gives an account of a confession on the part of the Northerners, and that in terms that clearly recognize not just the sin of a particular moment or action, but of a general state of sin, to which this event has only added (v. 13). It is thus evident that a move has been made that again might reverse the position as set out by Abijah in 2 Chr. 13.

Next, we may observe the reverse in the military fortunes of the two kingdoms. In 2 Chr. 13, the faithfulness of Judah was fully vindicated in battle:

> God smote Jeroboam and all Israel before Abijah and Judah. And the children of Israel fled before Judah: and *God delivered them into their hand*. And Abijah and his people *slew them with a great slaughter* (2 Chr. 13: 15b–17a).

Under Ahaz, however, this situation is turned upside down, with Judah now being defeated at the hands of Israel:

> And *he was also delivered into the hand of the king of Israel*, who *smote him with a great slaughter*. For Pekah the son of Remaliah slew in Judah an hundred and twenty thousand in one day (2 Chr. 28: 5b–6a).

The similarity of the phrases in italics only strengthens the contrast of the two passages. This applies also to the more general, summarizing statements of each chapter:

> Thus the children of Israel were brought under (*wykn'w*) at that time, and the children of Judah prevailed, because they relied upon the Lord, the God of their fathers (2 Chr. 13: 18).

Under Ahaz, however, it is Judah which is brought low (*hkny' yhwh 't yhwdh*, 2 Chr. 28: 19), because far from relying upon him, they forsake the Lord, the God of their fathers (v. 6, and cf. vv. 21 and 23).

The contrast between 2 Chr. 13 and 28, therefore, appears to be

---

[1] It is clear from 2 Chr. 18: 6ff. and 21: 12ff. that the Chronicler recognized that there continued to be faithful prophets in the North, despite their position as 'rebels'.

complete and comprehensive, so that we are not surprised to find that the Chronicler included from his *Vorlage* the general assessment of Ahaz that 'he walked in the ways of the kings of Israel' (v. 2). Whilst the same is certainly said also of other Judean kings (cf. 2 Chr. 21: 6, 22: 3), only the reign of Ahaz is recorded without a single redeeming feature, and in such complete antithesis to the positions described in 2 Chr. 13.

It thus becomes of interest to notice next how the Chronicler presents the fortunes of the two kingdoms at the end of the reign of Ahaz. As concerns the Northern Kingdom, no explicit detail is given in our chapter, but we learn from Hezekiah's letter of invitation to his Passover in Jerusalem that those living in the land at that time are 'the remnant that are escaped of you out of the hand of the kings of Assyria' (2 Chr. 30: 6), whereas their brethren and their children have been led into foreign exile (v. 9).[1] Since this letter is dated to the very start of Hezekiah's reign (2 Chr. 30: 2 with 29: 3), it is evident that the events described are attributed by the Chronicler to the period of the reign of Ahaz. For the Chronicler, however, the point of interest is not the group who had gone into exile, or the foreigners brought in by the Assyrian kings. His omission of 2 Ki. 17 shows that quite clearly. His interest is in the group that remained in the land, decimated and under God's anger indeed (2 Chr. 30: 8), but nonetheless the group through whom the continuity of tradition is seen to run: it is upon their faithfulness that the possible return of those in exile depends.[2]

As regards the Southern Kingdom, the Chronicler has painted a similar picture, adding a certain amount of material to his *Vorlage* in order to attain this effect. Thus, in 2 Chr. 28: 5, he adds the note that 'a great multitude of captives' were exiled to Damascus, and in v. 8 that many were also taken captive to Samaria, even though subsequently released. In v. 17, he adds that the Edomites took captives from Judah, whilst in the following verse, a considerable area is lost to the Philistines. Consequently, it is not surprising that in Hezekiah's confession at the beginning of his reign, he describes the situation with expressions that in other parts of the Bible have very clear overtones of the exile:[3]

Wherefore the wrath of the Lord was upon Judah and Jerusalem, and he hath delivered them to be tossed to and fro, to be an astonishment, and an hissing, as ye see with your eyes. For, lo, our fathers

---

[1] This need not be taken to imply, however, that only the Northerners are addressed in this letter: cf. below, p. 127.

[2] On the Chronicler's diminution of the importance of the exile of the Northern Kingdom, cf. S. Japhet: *Ideology*, pp. 375f.

[3] For use of the vocabulary of these verses in association with exile, cf. Dt. 28: 25.41, Jer. 15: 4, 25: 9.18, 29: 18, 34: 17, Ezek. 23: 46 and 2 Chr. 6: 36–8, and cf. CM, p. 464.

have fallen by the sword, and our sons and our daughters and our wives are in captivity for this (2 Chr. 29: 8f.).

The situation of the two kingdoms at the end of Ahaz's reign, then, is similar. Both stand under God's anger (2 Chr. 28: 9.11.13.25, 29: 8.10, 30: 8), and both are in a position of military defeat, with large numbers of the population in captivity or exile (2 Chr. 22: 5.17, 29: 9, 30: 9). For both, however, attention is directed to those who remain for the possible continuation of the traditions of Israel (2 Chr. 29: 10, 30: 8f.).

We may conclude this analysis of the Chronicler's presentation of the reign of Ahaz by noticing the instances of the word 'Israel' that were earlier held over for discussion (above, p. 106), namely 28: 19.23.26.27. Initially, it is striking to find a king such as Ahaz called 'king of Israel' (v. 19), and so on, but in the light of what we have seen, it may be suggested that for the Chronicler, with the Northerners having begun, at least, on the road to repentance, the fall of the Northern monarchy at this point removed the only other barrier which, according to 2 Chr. 13, still caused them to be regarded as in a state of rebellion. The use of the word 'brethren' three times (2 Chr. 28: 8.11.15) reminds us not only of the accession of David (1 Chr. 12: 40, 13: 2) but more especially of the time of the division itself (2 Chr. 11: 4). Again, it is very noteworthy that in the Northerners' dealing with the Judean captives, no mention is made of the king, but only of 'certain of the heads of the children of Ephraim' (v. 12). Either we must assume that the monarchy has already fallen, or perhaps we see a further reflection of the Chronicler's open attitude towards the people of the North, in distinction from the institution of its monarchy.

9

Hezekiah to the Babylonian Exile
(2 Chronicles 29–36)

It is evident that, with the Israelite population partially reunited in its depressed state, the Chronicler's interpretation of Hezekiah's reign will be of paramount importance. To maintain continuity of argument, therefore, we shall treat this subject first in this chapter, before going on to deal with other aspects of his understanding of Israel during this period.

A. HEZEKIAH IN THE BOOKS OF CHRONICLES

In his recent book *Untersuchungen zur Theologie des chronistischen Geschichtswerk*, R. Mosis has suggested that the Chronicler adopted the reigns of Saul (1 Chr. 10), David (1 Chr. 11–29) and Solomon (2 Chr. 1–9) as paradigms of the three possible situations in which the Israel of later periods might find herself (p. 165). Since the period of Solomon is thought to have been portrayed by the Chronicler as one of final blessing, for the return of which later Israel can only hope in faith, it follows that the subsequent kings of Israel are patterned only on Saul or David. It is not surprising, therefore, that in the course of his analysis of this later period, Mosis should write: 'Wie Ahas als ein zweiter Saul erscheint, stellt der Chr in Hiskija einen zweiten David dar' (p. 189).[1]

This conclusion is based on three pieces of evidence.

(a) 2 Chr. 29:2 says that 'Hezekiah did that which was right in the eyes of the Lord, according to all that David his father had done.'

(b) Hezekiah's cleansing of the temple and his Passover celebration are thought to parallel the restoration of the cult after the exile as described in Ezr. 1–6, which Mosis categorizes as 'Davidic'.

(c) The salvation of Jerusalem from the Assyrians (2 Chr. 32:1–23) is similar to the 'paradigm' of 1 Chr. 14, where victory over foreign enemies is the reward for 'seeking the Lord' (Ark) (pp. 72–4). The Assyrian invasion would be impossible, were Hezekiah's reign to be compared with that of Solomon, 'the man of peace'.

The force of these arguments may be more easily assessed when the substantial body of evidence to the contrary (which Mosis passes over

---

[1] Cf. F. L. Moriarty: 'Hezekiah's Reform', p. 401.

in complete silence) has been presented, for in a considerable number of ways the Chronicler would seem rather to wish to stress the similarities between Hezekiah's and Solomon's reigns, once it is allowed that, even if we were to grant his record virtually no independent historical value, there were certain well-known facts that he could not completely leave out of account.

(a) We may start with the comment (not found in Ki.) that at the celebration of the Passover under Hezekiah 'there was great joy in Jerusalem: for since the time of Solomon the son of David king of Israel there was not the like in Jerusalem' (2 Chr. 30: 26). Three main suggestions may be put forward as to why the Chronicler drew this comparison, and there is no reason to regard them as mutually exclusive:

First, as many commentators have observed,[1] a distinctive feature of this celebration as of the dedication of the temple in Solomon's day, was its duration – a full two weeks rather than one: 'And the whole congregation took counsel to keep other seven days: and they kept other seven days with gladness' (30: 23; cf. 7: 8–9). This in itself is sufficient for Myers (following Rudolph) to observe: 'Hezekiah appears like a second Solomon, who celebrated two weeks when the temple was dedicated' (p. 179).

Secondly, the unprecedented stress that the Chronicler's account lays on Hezekiah's efforts and substantial success in inviting the Northern remnant to participate in the feast make it probable that he saw in this event a return to the days of Solomon when all Israel was united in worship at the temple (7: 8). An indication in support of this interpretation is found in 30: 5, where the reason for Hezekiah's invitation is said to be 'for they had not kept it in great numbers in such sort as it is written'. Moreover, the immediate antecedent to the verse we are considering is the description in the previous verse (30: 25) of the different groups that made up the congregation, including 'all the congregation that came out of Israel, and the strangers that came out of the land of Israel'.

The third reason has been suggested by Gaster,[2] and in more detail (though apparently without knowledge of Gaster's work) independently by both Talmon[3] and Kraus,[4] namely that for the first time since Solomon's reign there was unity in the matter of the date of the Passover. After the division of the monarchy, 'Jeroboam ordained a feast in the eighth month . . . like unto the feast that is in Judah' (1 Ki. 12: 32). Whether, as Gaster thinks, this was an innovation by Jeroboam, or

[1] E.g. CM, p. 476; Rudolph, p. 303 and Myers, p. 179.
[2] M. Gaster: 'The Feast of Jeroboam'.
[3] S. Talmon: 'Divergencies'.
[4] H.-J. Kraus: 'Zur Geschichte des Passah-Massot-Festes'.

whether Talmon is right in arguing 'that in deferring the Feast of Tabernacles by one month he reverted to an established northern calendar'[1] is not so important for our present purposes as the realization that between the two kingdoms there was thereafter maintained a difference of one month in their calendar of religious festivals. The Chronicler is unique in his witness to Hezekiah's deferring of the date of the Passover by one month, for which part of the reason given is precisely that the people might 'gather themselves together to Jerusalem' (30: 3), or, as Gaster has said, to 'bring about a complete religious harmony between the Northern Kingdom and that of Judah'.[2] Talmon explicitly relates this conclusion to the verse under discussion; of the comparison drawn between Solomon and Hezekiah, he writes 'this statement exactly fits our reconstruction of developments, and is definitely not just a remark taken over from the Josiah story (xxxv 18) as implied by commentators'.[3]

(b) The parallels drawn between Hezekiah and Solomon in the Chronicler's work do not stop by any means with the explicit statement concerning the Passover celebration in 30: 26. We may look next at the temple arrangements that the two kings established. In the account of Solomon's building of the temple, the Chronicler singles out certain items and practices as being specifically 'an ordinance in Israel'. In each case, this reference is in addition to the text in Ki. The main list is in 2 Chr. 2: 3 (Ev. 4):

> Behold, (i) I build an house for the name of the Lord my God, to dedicate it to him, (ii) and to burn before him incense of sweet spices, (iii) and for the continual shewbread, (iv) and for the burnt offerings morning and evening, (v) on the sabbaths, (vi) and on the new moons, (vii) and on the set feasts of the Lord our God. This is an ordinance for ever to Israel – *l'wlm z't 'l yśr'l.*

Of all the temple furniture, only the candlesticks with their lamps are said to be *kmšpṭ*: 2 Chr. 4: 7 and 20:

> And (viii) the candlesticks with their lamps, that they should burn according to the ordinance before the oracle, of pure gold

(*contrast* 1 Ki. 7: 49, which comes in a section that the Chronicler has otherwise followed very closely).

In his account of Hezekiah's reformation, the Chronicler (again

[1] Talmon: 'Divergencies', p. 57.
[2] Gaster: 'The Feast of Jeroboam', p. 201. According to Gaster, this attempt by Hezekiah was not finally successful, for he sees in the later Samaritan calendar a direct continuation of the discrepancy between Judah and Israel introduced by Jeroboam.
[3] Talmon: 'Divergencies', p. 62. For a contrasting approach, however, cf. Moriarty: 'Hezekiah's Reform', pp. 404–6 and H. Haag: 'Mazzenfest', p. 91.

without parallel in Ki.) exactly picks up each item of this list. First, in Hezekiah's confession, the sins of the fathers are listed as having (i) shut up the doors of the porch, (viii) put out the lamps, (ii) not burned incense, and not having offered burnt offerings in the holy place (iii–vii generally, but cf. the itemized list below) – 2 Chr. 29: 7.

Secondly, when the priests return from cleansing the temple, they especially single out for mention that they have cleansed (i) all the house of the Lord, (iv–vii) the altar of burnt offering and (iii) the table of shewbread – 2 Chr. 29: 18. Finally, in 31: 3, Hezekiah is said to have provided the sacrifices necessary for the burnt offerings, namely

(iv) for the morning and evening burnt offerings, (iii) and the burnt offerings for the sabbaths, (vi) and for the new moons, (vii) and for the set feasts, as it is written in the law of the Lord.

Thus all the items from the account of Solomon's work for the temple to which the Chronicler draws particular attention against his *Vorlage* find a precise echo in the work of Hezekiah.[1] This is further emphasized by the similarity of the summarizing statements of this aspect of the two kings' work: *wtkn kl ml'kt šlmh 'd hywm mwsd byt yhwh w'd kltw* of Solomon in 2 Chr. 8: 16, and *wtkwn 'bwdt byt yhwh* of Hezekiah in 2 Chr. 29: 35b.[2]

(c) 2 Chr. 31: 2 alludes to Hezekiah's appointment of priests and Levites. The parallel here to 2 Chr. 8: 14 is clear, and has not escaped the attention of the commentators: Rudolph (p. 306) thinks that Hezekiah was reinstating the old order of Solomon, whilst Myers follows him closely in saying 'Hezekiah reaffirmed the old order established by Solomon in accordance with the command of David' (p. 183).

(d) Moving on now from cultic arrangements, we find that another aspect of Hezekiah's reign which the Chronicler emphasizes over against his *Vorlage* is the wealth of the king, itemized in some detail in 2 Chr. 32: 27–9. This too was a characteristic of Solomon's reign (2 Chr. 9: 13ff.).

(e) A closely related theme, and one that is especially important for Mosis' estimate of the Chronicler's unique portrayal of Solomon (pp. 155–62), is the attitude of the gentile nations to the king of Israel. Mosis thinks that by his handling of the dealings between Hiram and Solomon, and the visit of the Queen of Sheba, the Chronicler has

---

[1] That these items occur also, for the most part, in Abijah's speech and later in connection with the reign of Ahaz is only to be expected if our understanding of the Chronicler's structure has been correct.

[2] The Niph'al of *kwn* is not thus used of the rebuilding of the temple or of the re-establishment of the cult in Ezr.-Neh., but compare also the Chronicler's use at 2 Chr. 35: 10.16.

anticipated the prophetic hope of the pilgrimage of the nations to Jerusalem. Hence we find the summarizing statement:

> And all the kings of the earth sought the presence of Solomon, to hear his wisdom, which God had put in his heart. And they brought every man his present, vessels of silver, and vessels of gold ... (2 Chr. 9: 23f.).

Whether or not Mosis has correctly understood the Chronicler's intention here, it must at least be taken in connection with 2 Chr. 32: 23:

> And many brought gifts unto the Lord to Jerusalem, and precious things to Hezekiah king of Judah: so that he was exalted in the sight of all nations from thenceforth.

(f) Finally, the Chronicler regards the period of Hezekiah as one in which the land was restored for the first time to its geographical extent in the time of Solomon. As Japhet has pointed out,[1] the expression '*rṣ yśr'l*, used only ten times in the Bible, is found on four occasions in Chr., once each in the reigns of David (1 Chr. 22: 2), Solomon (2 Chr. 2: 16 [Ev. 17]), Hezekiah (2 Chr. 30: 25) and Josiah (2 Chr. 34: 7). This in itself is suggestive, but we can move on to even firmer ground since the Chronicler gives clear indication of how he defines the land of Israel. In 1 Chr. 22: 2, it is closely associated by context and content with the census of the previous chapter, and for this the land is defined as 'from Beersheba even to Dan' (21: 2). The reference in 2 Chr. 2: 16 is explicitly identical: 'And Solomon numbered all the strangers that were in the land of Israel, after the numbering wherewith David his father had numbered them.'

In Hezekiah's time, the phrase '*rṣ yśr'l* is used in a verse that summarizes the full composition of the congregation that celebrated the Passover (2 Chr. 30: 25). It is therefore integrally linked with the invitation that Hezekiah sent out prior to the Passover, described in 30: 5 as 'a proclamation throughout all Israel, from Beersheba even to Dan'. A return to the Solomonic boundaries is thus clearly envisaged.[2]

The only way in which this conclusion might be challenged is from the reference in 2 Chr. 7: 8 that Solomon

> held the feast at that time seven days, and all Israel with him, a very great congregation, from the entering in of Hamath unto the Brook of Egypt.

[1] S. Japhet: *Ideology*, pp. 365f.

[2] The definition of the fourth use of '*rṣ yśr'l* in Chr. (2 Chr. 34: 7) is not explicitly made, but appears to cover approximately the same area, as the reference to Simeon and Naphtali in the previous verse suggests. However, since Naphtali lies to the south of Dan, I cannot follow Japhet (*Ideology*, pp. 303f.) in her argument that this represents the culmination of the expansion of the Southern Kingdom from the time of the division of the monarchy onwards.

However, whilst the Chronicler envisages Israelites living throughout this larger area,[1] it is not at all clear that he identified it with the actual geographical extent of *'rṣ yśr'l*. In 1 Chr. 13: 5, those invited to assist David in his first attempt to bring up the Ark from Kiriath-jearim are also said to have come from 'Shihor the Brook of Egypt even unto the entering in of Hamath'. Both the geographical reference and the purpose of the assembly are closely parallel to 2 Chr. 7: 8. We must notice, however, that in 1 Chr. 13: 2 this invitation is addressed to 'our brethren that are left in all the lands of Israel (*'rṣwt yśr'l*)'. The use of the plural here suggests that this larger region was not so much thought of as the well defined unit *'rṣ yśr'l*, but rather that it included regions attached to Israel, more in the nature of an empire.[2] As we have seen, even in David's reign, when a precise definition of *'rṣ yśr'l* itself is required, it is said only to extend from 'Beersheba even to Dan' (1 Chr. 21: 2). In 2 Chr. 7: 8 also, there is no indication that the larger definition is territorial, but merely that this was the area from which Israelites came to attend the dedication of the temple.[3]

It has emerged from this survey that in terms of the celebration of the Passover, cultic and priestly arrangements, wealth, external relationships and geographical extent, Hezekiah's reign as portrayed in Chr. parallels, and hence directly continues from, that of Solomon.[4] In the light of all this, we must finally answer Mosis in his claim, outlined above, that Hezekiah is presented rather as a second David. Taking the arguments in reverse order, it is noteworthy that the Chronicler, in his abbreviated account of Sennacherib's invasion, omits the account of Hezekiah's initial capitulation (2 Ki. 18: 14–16), and seems to deny that any of the cities of Judah were actually captured: against 2 Ki. 18: 13, where Sennacherib 'came up against all the fenced cities of Judah, and took them', 2 Chr. 32: 1 merely says that he 'encamped against the fenced cities, and thought to win them for himself'. Since, as in Ki., the victory was won by a direct intervention of the Lord, without

---

[1] For the geography of these definitions, cf. F.-M. Abel: *Géographie*, 1, 299ff.

[2] That the plural *'rṣwt* should be rendered 'regions' seems clear from 2 Chr. 11: 23 and 34: 33. It is taken thus by J. M. Myers: *I Chronicles*, p. 100, *contra* A. Kropat: *Syntax*, p. 9, who takes it as equivalent to the singular *'rṣ*.

[3] It is further in support of our understanding of the Chronicler's view that whilst 2 Chr. 7: 8 is taken over direct from his source (1 Ki. 8: 65), the definition implied in 2 Chr. 2: 16 is peculiar to his account.

[4] I am grateful to Dr S. Japhet for pointing out another possible indication of this interpretation of the Chronicler, namely the echo in 2 Chr. 30: 9 of 1 Ki. 8: 50. The verse in Ki. comes towards the end of Solomon's prayer at the dedication of the temple. The second half of the verse is omitted by the Chronicler in his parallel account. By putting these words instead into the mouth of Hezekiah, there may therefore be a further suggestion that he was regarded by the Chronicler as a second Solomon.

Hezekiah striking so much as a single blow (2 Chr. 32: 21), there is nothing in the Chronicler's account to make him any less a 'man of peace' than Solomon. Moreover, though Mosis passes over this in silence, even the Chronicler's 'man of peace' 'went to Hamath-zobah, and prevailed against it' (2 Chr. 8: 3) and was not above taking other precautionary defence measures (2 Chr. 8: 4ff.), rather as Hezekiah did.

That Hezekiah's cleansing of the temple and his Passover celebration parallel the account of Ezr. 1–6 is fortuitous (if correct), since the accounts come from separate works. Moreover, as we have seen, the Chronicler was fully justified in explicitly drawing the parallels between these events and the celebration under Solomon.

Finally, the remark that Hezekiah did 'according to all that David his father had done' has no force for this particular argument. It is adopted by the Chronicler from his source (2 Ki. 18: 3) as a stereotyped expression of commendation, and has no reference to the detailed characteristics of his reign.

I thus conclude that the Chronicler has gone out of his way to draw out the parallels between the reigns of Solomon and Hezekiah. The implications of this for the Chronicler's understanding of the history of the monarchy are of considerable importance, since, as we have observed, he is the first king to rule after the fall of the Northern Kingdom. It would appear that the Chronicler made a deliberate attempt by this means to show that with Hezekiah the situation prevailing under Solomon was restored, and involved in this would be, of course, the restitution of the unity of all Israel.

B. THE UNIQUENESS OF THE CHRONICLER'S SOLUTION

If our understanding of the Chronicler's resolution of the problem posed by the division of the monarchy be correct, it would be unique in Biblical tradition, for normally speaking the prophets looked for the reunification of Israel and Judah only after the return from exile (e.g. Isa. 11: 11ff., Jer. 31: 4–14, Ezek. 37: 15–22, Zech. 10: 6–12, etc.). This fact is fully borne out by the Chronicler's use of the word 'remnant' in the closing years of the monarchy.

Basing an analysis upon the use of the root *š'r*, we find that the remnant concept in the OT can be applied to many different groups of people. We may cite as relevant to our purposes its frequent application (especially in Jer.) to those who remained in Judah after the fall of Jerusalem and (rather less frequently) to those who were left in the South between the fall of Samaria and the fall of Jerusalem (2 Ki. 19: 4.30, Isa. 37: 4.31,[1] Jer. 6: 9, Ezek. 5: 10). Amongst many other uses, it is also applied, of course, to those of either kingdom who returned

Cf. G. F. Hasel: *The Remnant*, pp. 331–9.

from exile, whether in historical or eschatological passages (e.g. Neh.
1: 3, Isa. 11: 11.16,[1] Jer. 23: 3, 31: 7, Mic. 2: 12, 4: 7, 5: 6f., 7: 18,
Zeph. 2: 7.9, 3: 13, Zech. 8: 6.11.12, etc.).

Uniquely, however, though fully in line with what we have already
seen, the Chronicler uses the expression either for those left in the
North, or for those in both kingdoms, after the fall of Samaria. On the
first occasion (2 Chr. 30: 6), *hplyṭh hnš'rt*[2] occurs in a passage peculiar
to the Chronicler, but one which we have seen to be crucial to the
structure of his narrative. On the second occasion, 2 Chr. 34: 9, he
paraphrases his *Vorlage*, 2 Ki. 22: 4. For *m't h'm* he writes *myd mnšh
w'pr'ym wmkl š'ryt yśr'l wmkl yhwdh wbnymn wyšby yrwšlm*. This, then,
serves as a comprehensive definition of the people at this time in the
Chronicler's view. Thirdly, at 2 Chr. 34: 21, *b'd hnš'r byśr'l wbyhwdh*
is strikingly substituted for *b'd kl yhwdh* (2 Ki. 22: 13).

Clearly, therefore, there is a difference of outlook between Ki. and
Chr. in this matter. For Ki., as for several other Biblical books, it was
possible to speak of those in the South who survived the Assyrian invasion as a remnant, but only the Chronicler uses this terminology of
those left in the North, or of those remaining in the North and South
together.[3]

If, then, the Chronicler sought to bring forward into the historical
arena of the reigns of Ahaz and Hezekiah the prophetic hope for the reunification of all Israel, it will be evident that his approach to the problems confronting the post-exilic community would have been radically
different from that of the exclusivist that he is often portrayed as having
been.

C. USE OF THE WORD ISRAEL

In view of what has already been seen, it will not be found surprising
that almost without exception, the thirty occurrences of the word Israel
in connection with this period of history are either in material peculiar
to the Chronicler, or added by him to his *Vorlage*. Most of these fall
into certain clearly distinguishable categories.

(a) First, the Chronicler uses Israel eleven times to refer to the total
population without regard for the former political division:
2 Chr. 29: 24 (twice): Rudolph (p. 294) thinks that 'all Israel' in this
verse means 'all Judah', because of the apparent statement to this effect

---

[1] Cf. *ibid.* pp. 339–48.

[2] The use of this phrase in such a context is in very stark contrast to its use in
Ezr.-Neh., where it applies to those returning from exile; cf. especially Ezr.
9: 8–15 and H. C. M. Vogt: *Studie*, pp. 28–46.

[3] Ezek. 9: 8 and 11: 13 might perhaps also be added here, but on the question
under discussion, Ezek. 37 demonstrates that the main line of the prophet's
thinking on this issue is the same as the rest of the prophets. On the difficult
question of Israel in Ezek., cf. W. Zimmerli: 'Israel im Buche Ezechiel'.

in v. 21. However, the king's command in v. 24 stresses by word order (*ky lkl yśr'l 'mr hmlk h'wlh whḥṭ't*) that the offering was to cover an unexpectedly wider group of people, implying a correction of what the priests had thought would be the case (v. 21). This would be fully credible in view of Hezekiah's interest in the former Northern Kingdom.[1] Furthermore, it fits the Chronicler's general usage for this period, whereas to call Judah alone 'all Israel' would be to introduce into the Chronicler's own composition an exceptional case, for which one would demand strong evidence.

2 Chr. 30: 6 (second occurrence): it might at first appear from the tone of this letter of Hezekiah that the 'children of Israel' are those of the North only. However, it is clearly stated in vv. 5 and 6 that the addressees live in the area from 'Beersheba even to Dan', further defined as 'all Israel and Judah'. Moreover, there is recorded not only the reaction of the Northern tribes (vv. 10f.), but of Judah too (v. 12). It would thus seem clear that the total population is being addressed. When the letter itself is then examined in this light, its content is found, on the Chronicler's presentation, to be not unsuitable to both Israel and Judah, for we have seen that under Ahaz, Judah both trespassed and was given over to desolation (v. 7), came under God's wrath (v. 8), was partly led captive (v. 9) and, on the basis of 28: 20f., could even be called 'the remnant that are escaped of you out of the hand of the kings of Assyria' (v. 6).

2 Chr. 30: 21: 'The children of Israel' of this verse means representatives of both North and South, as the context of vv. 17f. makes clear.

2 Chr. 31: 1 (twice): the same group is here referred to, once as 'all Israel that were present', and once as the 'children of Israel'. The re-united people is evidently intended again.

2 Chr. 31: 8: although difficulties surround the interpretation of vv. 5f., the summarizing nature of this verse demands that 'his people Israel' refer to the total population.

2 Chr. 34: 33a (first occurrence): this verse again gives us a summary, this time of Josiah's reform, added to his *Vorlage* by the Chronicler. Since in vv. 6f. the Northern tribes are included as part of the area in which this reform was conducted, 'the children of Israel' of our verse must include them as well as the Southerners.

2 Chr. 35: 3 (twice): the usages here ('all Israel' and 'his people Israel') are not specifically defined, but there is no reason whatever to under-

---

[1] Cf. J. M. Myers: *II Chronicles*, pp. 177f.

stand by them anything other than a reference to the full population of Israel.

2 Chr. 35: 17: the following verse explicitly states that 'the children of Israel' here referred to were drawn from all parts of the population.

These eleven occurrences (and perhaps two others, as suggested below) thus show quite clearly that for the Chronicler, to term the community 'Israel' during this period was to refer to the full extent of the remaining population.

(b) Geographical usage: nine times, Israel is used in a purely geographical sense. On several occasions, it refers to the area of the former Israelite kingdom, and the majority of the occurrences of Judah in these chapters is reserved equally for a geographical definition of the South. Although this might be thought to reintroduce old divisions, the usage is, of course, for convenience of reference only, and the purpose, in fact, is always to stress that the whole country is being referred to: 2 Chr. 30: 1 (first occurrence).6 (first occurrence).25 (twice), 34: 21. As if to show his ideal in this connection also, however, the Chronicler once introduces the expression 'all Israel, from Beersheba even to Dan' (2 Chr. 30: 5), and this full definition is doubtless also intended at 2 Chr. 34: 7.33 (second occurrence) and 35: 18 (first occurrence). The effect of this geographical usage, therefore, is to support the Chronicler's view of the population of Israel.

(c) Four times, the word Israel is used in the title of the royal sources that the Chronicler cites for this period; three times it is added to the 'Judah' of his *Vorlage*: 2 Chr. 32: 32, 35: 27, 36: 8, and once it is substituted for Judah: 2 Chr. 33: 18. This is exactly the same situation as was found to prevail during the divided monarchy (above, p. 106). Whether this refers to a genuine source, written in parallel columns, which preserved thereby the claim of the Davidic house to sovereignty over the whole of Israel,[1] or whether it is merely a device of the Chronicler, the effect is the same: Israel and Judah are anachronistic names as far as political considerations are concerned, so that the only point of including both for this period must be to stress that both former kingdoms are now reunited under the single Davidic ruler. Once again it is made clear that the accusation which Abijah could make (2 Chr. 13) is emptied of its force with the fall of the Northern monarchy.

(d) Other: of the six remaining occurrences of the word Israel, two are purely general in nature: 2 Chr. 35: 18 (second occurrence) and 35: 25. One refers to 'the remnant of Israel', whereby those who remained in the North are apparently intended; in that case, Israel becomes a retrospective reference to the kingdom which now no longer exists independently. In 2 Chr. 35: 18 (third occurrence), there is a

[1] So T. N. D. Mettinger: *Solomonic State Officials*, pp. 36–9.

reference to 'all Israel and Judah that were present'. This is the only example of the population of the North alone being called Israel during this period in contrast to Judah. The intention of the verse, however, is to stress their participation in Josiah's Passover. Thus, although this one case is an exception to the Chronicler's usual practice, whereby he attains the same result by reference to the inhabitants of (geographical) Israel, the purpose and effect of the use are in fact to draw attention to the unity of the people in this ceremony.

The remaining two cases (2 Chr. 31: 5 and 6) are difficult on any showing, and there is no general agreement among the commentators as to who is intended. A straightforward reading would seem to demand that in v. 5, 'the children of Israel' are the same as 'the people that dwelt in Jerusalem' (v. 4).[1] In the following verse, 'the children of Israel' would then have to be those of the North who came south during the divided monarchy.[2] In that case, not only has the meaning of the phrase changed from one verse to the next, but this would further be the only reference to this group in the whole of this section. Several commentators seek to ease this difficulty by dismissing the words 'and of Judah' as a gloss,[3] so that country dwellers rather than town dwellers (v. 5) are intended.

In view of these difficulties, a quite different solution may be suggested. Verse 5 starts *wkprṣ hdbr*, the only time when this verb is used in the OT of a command or speech. Since usually this verb is a violent one, the intention may be stronger than that 'the people that dwelt in Jerusalem' heard the king's command, but that it became widely known.[4] Verse 5 will then describe the reaction of the children of Israel in its full sense. Verse 6, however, describes an additional action on the part of those who dwelt 'in the cities of Judah', namely to bring in 'also the tithe of oxen and sheep'. This would then bring the passage into line with the law of Dt. 12: 5–19, 14: 22–7. In 12: 17, it is forbidden to 'eat within thy gates the tithe of thy corn, or of thy wine, or of thine oil', the three commodities which head the list of 2 Chr. 31: 5. These had to be brought in kind to the sanctuary, and so they were. Verse 6, however, shows that those for whom the way was not too long (cf. Dt. 14: 24 with 12: 15f.) brought also the tithe of their livestock, something difficult, if not impossible, for those who lived further afield.

If this is correct, then the children of Israel in v. 5 will refer to the total population, whilst in v. 6 they are defined as that part which dwelt

[1] It is so understood, for instance, by Rudolph, p. 304 and Myers, p. 182. CM, p. 479, lists this as one possibility, the other being that Judeans generally are intended, which is also the understanding of Galling, p. 162.

[2] So Myers, p. 182.

[3] So, for instance, Benzinger, p. 125; CM, p. 479; Rudolph, p. 304.

[4] *Pace* G. R. Driver: 'Some Hebrew Roots', pp. 72f.

in the cities of Judah,[1] exactly as at 2 Chr. 10:17. These two occurrences, then, will be drawn into line with category (a) above.

We may thus conclude that the uses of the word Israel for the closing period of the monarchy are fully in line with the solution that the Chronicler put forward at the end of the period of the divided monarchy in the reigns of Ahaz and Hezekiah. Where it is used as a way of describing the population, it refers almost without exception to the whole of the people. When it is used in other ways, such as to refer to a geographical area, it may either again stress the completeness of Israel on its own, or be coupled with Judah in order to arrive at the same effect. In these latter cases, its use is a matter of convenience only, devoid of any political or similar force.

D. SUMMARY OF PART TWO

(1) Despite a number of attempts to study the concept of Israel in the Books of Chr., none has been found to do justice to the full extent of the material, even though this was a question of great importance in the post-exilic period.

(2) The Chronicler shows by a number of incidental references that he accepts in the main the attitude of later Biblical tradition on the origins of Israel. He introduces three changes of emphasis, however. First, he stresses the importance of Jacob amongst the patriarchs, no doubt as a device for underlining the solidarity of the later nation in that all were 'the children of Israel'. Secondly, after the announcement of a dynasty to David (1 Chr. 17), the importance of the Exodus/Sinai event recedes, even though it does not disappear. That is to say, within the historical period covered, David and his house become a constitutive factor in the life of the nation, as the Exodus has been before (cf. Ch. 5, section B above). Thirdly, explicit reference is made to the transfer of Reuben's birthright to Joseph and the sons of Joseph (1 Chr. 5: 1–2).

(3) During the reigns of David and Solomon, Israel was a fully united nation. As other scholars have often observed, the anticipations in Sam. and Ki. of the later division are passed over in Chr. The composition of Israel by the full number of the tribes is stressed on several occasions.

(4) Following the death of Solomon, though the Northern tribes broke away, they had good reasons for so doing, according to the Chronicler, and did not forfeit their position as children of Israel. That title now came to be applied to either part of the people, since the South remained generally faithful to the older traditions.

(5) By the time of Abijah, however, religious and political rebellion

---

[1] Omitting *wyhwdh* with the commentators cited above.

had been compounded by the Northerners, so that thereafter they are in the position of those who have forsaken the Lord. This is a situation, however, from which it is possible to return, and those who did so were welcomed in the South.

(6) At the end of the divided monarchy, the Chronicler demonstrates the combination of a number of factors: the end of separate political rule in the North, confession of sin by the Northerners, apostasy by Judah, its defeat at the hand of the Northerners and the carrying into captivity of many from both parts. Thus, whilst the situation of 2 Chr. 13 is fully reversed, the status of the population remains low.

(7) In Hezekiah, however, the Chronicler sees a second Solomon, thus restoring fully the position that was lost when the division took place. Not only is the nation brought back to the Lord and its political fortunes restored, but in principle, the whole population is again re-united under the Davidic king in worship at the Jerusalem temple.

(8) This remains the situation until the end of the monarchy, as far as Israel is concerned, even though there are periods of further un-faithfulness. Inasmuch as the term 'remnant' is applied to the sur-vivors of the former Northern Kingdom, the Chronicler presents a unique witness in the Bible to the reunification of the people in the land before the exile. With reference to the population, Israel now refers once again to the whole of the people, as it had under David and Solomon.

(9) Although this people then becomes the subject of the exile with which Chr. closes, indication is clearly given of the future return, when a completely fresh start may be made. Those returning, therefore, are the nucleus of Israel as a whole, though if they are to remain faithful to their history as the Chronicler has presented it, they will welcome others of Israel who seek to join them, and even actively set about the task of regathering them.

10

Conclusions

Two main approaches have been adopted in recent scholarly literature towards the centre of debate within the post-exilic Jerusalem community. The first is advanced by Plöger in his monograph: *Theokratie und Eschatologie*. On this view, there were radical differences of opinion on the attitude that should be taken towards the hopes of restoration. What Plöger terms 'die offizielle Linie innerhalb der Theokratie' (p. 135) was represented in P and Chr. (including Ezr.-Neh.). The primary purpose of these works was to demonstrate the unique legitimacy of the Jerusalem temple in which were fully realized the aspirations and expectations of earlier generations.

The Priestly Writing, regarded as an independent document, is said to show that ordinances originally applicable to all men (such as Sabbath-keeping and the prohibition to eat blood) were fulfilled in the cultic community of Israel as constituted at Sinai. Beyond this, no historical development is possible: 'Israel, in der Form der durch den עדה-Begriff charakterisierten Kultgemeinde, ist nach der Auffassung der Priesterschrift das Ziel der Wege Gottes mit der Menschheit' (p. 44). The post-exilic community, no longer a nation, but now developing into a religious community, would be expected to identify itself with the *'dh*, whose establishment at Sinai marked the culmination of God's dealings with his creation, 'und über dieses Ziel hinaus mit einer grundlegenden Veränderung nicht mehr zu rechnen ist' (p. 53).

The situation is similar in the case of Chr., concerning which Plöger adopts von Rad's analysis of Israel outlined above (pp. 87f.). Here, however, the Samaritan schism meant that the Pentateuch alone was not sufficient to establish the theocratic ideal; it was necessary to introduce the further criterion of adherence to the Davidic covenant. Thus Rudolph's view is explicitly followed which sees in the Chronicler's work a portrayal of the realization of theocracy as it had come to be re-established in Jerusalem under Ezra and Nehemiah. No place is found here for a continuation of eschatological expectation.[1]

This viewpoint was opposed by certain groups, evidence for which Plöger finds particularly in the Isaiah-Apocalypse, Zech. 12–14 and

---

[1] O. Plöger: *Theokratie und Eschatologie*, pp. 51–3; cf. Rudolph, pp. xxiiif

Conclusions

Joel 3–4, and which came finally to expression in the *Hasidim* of Maccabean times. These groups maintained an eschatological faith, whose development can be traced from the older restoration prophecies to the later upsurge of apocalyptic writing. Here a profound dissatisfaction is expressed with the present situation, whilst political events from the unrest of the later Persian period onwards fostered the hope that a time of renewal was yet to come. However, whilst in the fifth century B.C. this would doubtless have included hopes for the full re-unification of Israel (p. 135), this had given way by the Hellenistic period to the view that these groups themselves exclusively represented the true Israel: 'auch die eschatologischen Kreise lebten von dem Gemeindebegriff' (p. 136), which Plöger sees as culminating in the expression of personal resurrection in Dan. 12, where those who reject the eschatological faith, although they share in the resurrection because they are members of the theocracy, undergo a fate worse than the heathen who are excluded from the hope of the resurrection (p. 137). The exclusive claims of the Qumran community, we might add, would also seem to fit into this framework.

Within this hypothesis, as has been indicated, Plöger argues that the Chronicler's work is influenced not only by an outward looking anti-Samaritan aim, but also by an inward looking anti-eschatological point of view (p. 54). Among those who have followed his analysis in general terms may be mentioned Baltzer,[1] Kellermann,[2] Steck[3] and (with reservations) Hengel[4] and In der Smitten.[5]

The alternative approach to our period cannot be identified with a single scholar such as Plöger, but nevertheless acts as a unifying theme between such diverse works (among many others) as those of Schalit,[6] Weinfeld,[7] Vogt,[8] Smith,[9] Kippenberg[10] and Mantel.[11] Here, the centre of debate is traced to disagreements over the question of universalism and exclusivism, whether concerning the present or the hopes for a future restoration.[12] The particular problems that faced the community

[1] K. Baltzer: 'Das Ende des Staates Juda'.

[2] U. Kellermann: *Nehemia* (but cf. the review by J. A. Emerton in *JTS* ns 23 [1972], 171–85, which deals in part with this question); *Messias und Gesetz*, pp. 111–17.

[3] O. H. Steck: 'Das Problem theologischer Strömungen'.

[4] M. Hengel: *Judentum und Hellenismus*, pp. 321f.

[5] W. Th. In der Smitten: 'Aufnahme der Nehemiaschrift', and *Esra*, pp. 25–8.

[6] A. Schalit: 'A Chapter in the History of Party Strife'.

[7] M. Weinfeld: 'Universalism and Particularism'.

[8] H. C. M. Vogt: *Studie*.

[9] M. Smith: *Palestinian Parties* and 'Palestinian Judaism'.

[10] H. G. Kippenberg, pp. 33–59.

[11] H. D. Mantel: 'The Dichotomy of Judaism'.

[12] A brief summary of the issues may be found in H. Ringgren: *Israelitische Religion*, pp. 279f.

Conclusions

from Nehemiah's time onwards enable us to speak for the later part of the Persian period in Smith's more precise terms: separatists and assimilationists.

It is well known that the groups who returned to Jerusalem from exile in Babylon differed widely over the attitude that should be adopted both towards the Judean remnant who had never been in exile and towards those of the surrounding peoples who professed to share their religion.[1] Whilst this came to expression in the Biblical texts in the matter of mixed marriages, this should be seen as but symptomatic of the wider issues, not as an isolated phenomenon. The concern of the reformers to maintain the distinctiveness of the 'holy seed' (Ezr. 9: 2), however, demonstrates that in the mind of some, at least, racial and religious purity had become closely interwoven.

This latter approach has the advantage over Plöger's of being much closer to the surface of the Biblical text. It is no doubt for this reason that, as seen above, Plöger attempts to integrate it into his scheme. This particular point, however, is one of the weakest elements in his reconstruction. First, whilst we must suppose that the theocratic party found its main support amongst the leading priestly families, who appear to have acquiesced most readily in the development of Israel into a religious community under foreign rule, it is at the same time these selfsame families who led the way into mixed marriages. This in turn establishes a tension with the anti-Samaritan attitude that Plöger maintains was one of the characteristics of this group.

Secondly, it is difficult to understand why the eschatological groups, who maintained the prophetic hopes of a full restoration, eventually became the most exclusive groups of all.[2] It is true that certain later apocalyptic writings preserve the expectation of a restoration of all Israel,[3] but in practical terms that had long since given way to these circles regarding themselves as the remnant within Israel. Plöger is aware of a certain ambivalence here (p. 135), but is unable to account for it satisfactorily.

Thirdly, it has been shown that both particularist and universalistic elements are present in the prophetic hopes of restoration which Plöger maintains were taken over by the eschatological groups.[4] Thus, even if we were to adopt Plöger's basic division, we would have to recognize in the alternative approach a dispute which cut right across party lines as he conceives them.

[1] Cf. especially R. J. Coggins: 'The Interpretation of Ezra IV.4', and Vogt: *Studie.*

[2] Cf. G. Fohrer: *Geschichte der Israelitischen Religion*, pp. 344f.

[3] E.g. 4 Ezra 13: 25–53; Testament of Zebulun 9: 8; of Naphtali 4: 3–5; of Asher 7: 7, and cf. the notes in R. H. Charles: *Pseudepigrapha* at Testament of Reuben 7: 8 (p. 300).

[4] Fohrer: *op. cit.* pp. 352f.

Conclusions

Finally, the same point can be made concerning the writings which Plöger designates as theocratic. Though we are not here particularly concerned with P, it is nevertheless worth noting that Plöger's position is only one of a number that recent writers have adopted. There is no consensus as to the precise date of P or its status (whether independent narrative or redactional re-working of older traditions), though these issues might well affect Plöger's case.[1] Most important, however, is the wide-spread view that P's origins should be sought in Babylon, a view which makes it hard to believe that it was written to authenticate a Jerusalem theocracy or to eliminate from it every element of future hope.[2]

In the case of Chr., Rudolph's view has not been universally accepted,[3] and this will be accentuated if we are right in separating off Ezr.-Neh. Whatever may be the merits of Mosis' thesis in detail, his basic contention is surely justified that the Chronicler's glowing presentation of certain phases of Israel's past history could only have been intended to awaken fresh hopes and aspirations in the minds of his readers. Moreover, it is by no means certain that Chr. is completely devoid of all messianism,[4] even though it is clearly subordinated to other themes.

It is further doubtful whether Ezr.-Neh. portray quite so self-satisfied a situation as Plöger suggests, especially once their reconstitution of the temple cult is not thought to express a direct continuation of the first temple as described by the Chronicler. Certainly, the prayers of Ezr. 9 and Neh. 1 and 9 give no indication of a situation beyond which no advance is contemplated,[5] and the work as a whole seems to tail off in Neh. 13 without any suggestion that the problems and abuses have been finally settled. In short, it is doubtful whether any of the relevant OT writings reflect a completely non-eschatological view; we may speculate that the most likely protagonists of such a view would have been certain elements in the ruling priestly and landed classes, but, as we have seen, their close associations with non-Judeans do not enable us to identify them with the theocratic party as described by Plöger.

[1] For a survey of the principal views until 1965, cf. R. J. Thompson: *Moses and the Law*. More recent views that contrast strongly with Plöger's include S. Mowinckel: *Studien III* and K. Koch: 'Ezra and the Origins of Judaism'.

[2] P. R. Ackroyd: *Exile and Restoration*, pp. 91–102; W. Zimmerli: *Der Mensch und seine Hoffnung*, pp. 66–81; F. M. Cross: *Canaanite Myth*, pp. 293–325.

[3] Of more recent writers on Chr. who deal with this issue, cf. Willi, pp. 111ff.; S. Japhet: *Ideology*, pp. 494–6; Mosis, *passim*.

[4] This has been consistently maintained by G. von Rad: *Geschichtsbild*, pp. 119–32, and *Theologie*, 1, 347f., with many others before and since. Particularly opposed to this view has been A. Caquot: 'Peut-on parler de messianisme?'. A mediating position is espoused by J. M. Myers: *I Chronicles*, pp. lxxx–lxxxv.

[5] Cf. P. R. Ackroyd: *The Age of the Chronicler*, pp. 17–19, and W. Th. In der Smitten: 'Aufnahme der Nehemiaschrift'.

Conclusions

On the other hand, these three works do all demonstrate a concern for the definition of the community. This is well known in the case of P and Ezr.-Neh.,[1] whilst an attempt has been made above to establish this too for Chr. understood as a separate work. We may conclude, therefore, that it was this issue that was the primary centre of debate within the post-exilic community.

Whilst the events of the last century of the Persian empire as a whole are reasonably well known,[2] the detailed history of life in Jerusalem is an almost complete blank. According to Bright, 'no period in Israel's history since Moses is more poorly documented' whilst 'as regards the community in Judah, one can say little more than that it was *there*'.[3]

Two points, however, may be made with reasonable certainty on the basis of such evidence as is available. First, the greater autonomy granted to the province of Judah within the Persian empire towards the end of the fifth century B.C.[4] would have greatly increased its problems, both physical and ideological, of maintaining a true self-identity. Moreover, the fact that this autonomy was won from the province of Samaria whilst there is yet attestation for the continuation into this period of ancient cultural ties that linked Judah and Samaria in distinction from the other surrounding peoples[5] makes certain what on other grounds would already suggest itself, namely that it was from the north that the greatest threat to the individuality of the Judean community arose. The reduced population,[6] threatened by powerful neighbours in virtually all directions,[7] devoid of strong leadership so far as we know, must have been strongly tempted to ease its situation by assimilation to such groups as practised at least a recognizable form of its own religion.

[1] Even if Koch ('Ezra and the Origins of Judaism') is correct in his suggestion that 'Ezra was sent "to all his people beyond the river", including the Samaritans. His aim was to establish one Israel out of all 12 tribes' (p. 193), yet it is clear that this aim has been suppressed in the book as we now have it in favour of a more separatist viewpoint. Nevertheless, if Koch's theory could be substantiated, his interpretation of Ezra's mission would provide a highly intelligible antecedent to the Chronicler's history as understood in the present work.

[2] A. T. Olmstead: *History*.   [3] J. Bright: *History*, pp. 407 and 411.

[4] A. Alt: 'Die Rolle Samarias', supported more recently on quite other grounds by E. Stern: 'Seal Impressions'. The evidence from the coins of this period favours the same conclusion; cf. A. Reifenberg: *Ancient Jewish Coins*, pp. 5–9; E. L. Sukenik: 'Paralipomena' and 'More about the Oldest Coins'; Y. Meshorer: 'A New Type'; B. Kanael: 'Ancient Jewish Coins'; L. Y. Rahmani: 'Silver Coins'; J. Naveh: *BASOR* 203 (1971), 30 and *IEJ* 23 (1973), 83.   [5] E. Stern: *The Material Culture of Israel*, ch. 4 and pp. 227ff.

[6] Cf. *ibid.* p. 250; K. M. Kenyon: 'Excavations . . . 1962'; R. Grafman: 'Nehemiah's "Broad Wall"'; N. Avigad: 'Excavations . . . 1969/70' and 'Excavations . . . 1970'; M. Avi-Yonah: 'The Newly-found Wall of Jerusalem'.

[7] Cf. I. Rabinowitz: 'Aramaic Inscriptions'; F. M. Cross: 'Geshem the Arabian'; W. J. Dumbrell: 'The Tell-Maskhuṭa Bowls'; A. Lemaire: 'Un nouveau roi arabe' and B. Mazar: 'The Tobiads'.

Secondly, it seems very probable that the disputes within the Jerusalem community already reflected in Ezr.-Neh. continued through the fourth century B.C., if anything with increased acrimony. Our main evidence for this period comes from Josephus, whose narrative has to be treated with the greatest caution. Nevertheless, Kippenberg[1] has suggested that amidst the legendary material in *Ant.* XI, 303ff., there is one reliable tradition at least which is relevant to our overall purpose.

Kippenberg's starting point here is an attempt to isolate a source in Josephus' narrative on the basis of terminology: in *Ant.* XI, 340, 342, 344f., 346f. and XII, 10, the Samaritans are called 'Shechemites'. Characteristic of this block of material is the fact that the Gerizim cult started with a complete (i.e. priestly and lay) community, not just a priestly group. *Ant.* XI, 312 and 322 are earlier passages that agree with this, but do not fit so well with Josephus' own view that the Samaritans were of heathen origin.[2] This material, however, comes from Jewish circles, as is shown by the way it refers to Mount Gerizim.[3] Finally, Kippenberg draws into this source the account of Sanballat's building of the Samaritan temple. On the basis of this material, Kippenberg suggests that the origins of the Samaritan community are to be sought exclusively within a break-away group of dissident Judeans, rather like the later Qumran sect.

Whilst some aspects of Kippenberg's hypothesis are not altogether convincing,[4] yet he has drawn attention to a most significant feature of this material, namely the tradition of a substantial number of priests who left Jerusalem for Shechem (*Ant.* XI, 312, 322b, 340 and 346) and

[1] H. G. Kippenberg, pp. 50–9; contrast R. J. Coggins: *Samaritans and Jews*, p. 97.

[2] Cf. *Ant.* IX, 288–91; XI, 19 and 302.

[3] In Samaritan sources, the word *hr* is invariably taken as part of the proper name, yielding *hrgryzym* (so SP and ST) and the Greek transliteration *Argarizin* (*-ein, -im*). In Jewish sources, it is always taken as a separate word, yielding in Greek *oros Garizin*, etc. The 'Shechemite' source has *Garizein oros*, thus betraying its Jewish origin; cf. Kippenberg, pp. 54f.

[4] This applies in particular to his attempt to see in this material a separate source. First, as he tacitly concedes, its elements are too fragmentary to stand alone, and therefore have to be drawn into association with other elements which are generally agreed to be historically quite unreliable, such as the connection of Alexander with the founding of the Samaritan temple. This disparity between the various sections of the postulated source renders its existence improbable. Secondly, Kippenberg (pp. 55f.) attributes to his source the following material: *Ant.* XI, 312–17, 321–5, 340, 342, 344–7 and XII, 10. This includes substantial parts from the second source of Büchler's classical analysis ('La Relation'), but nevertheless omits several parts of it, e.g. *Ant.* XI, 302f. and 306–11. It is a serious weakness in Kippenberg's theory that he does not account for these passages, since in their present form they cannot be dissociated from the postulated source.

who were early adherents to its new cult community. There are good reasons for accepting the view that this tradition reflects historical reality.

First, Josephus himself clearly believed the Samaritans to be of Cuthean origin. It is unlikely that he would have invented an account which we can only imagine was distasteful to him.[1] Secondly, Kippenberg has made out a good case for the view that this tradition was transmitted within a Jewish framework. Thus, just as it is unlikely that Josephus would have invented it, so for the same reasons it is hard to believe that those responsible for his sources would have done so either. Moreover, the description of the Shechemites in *Ant.* XI, 340 as 'apostates from the Jewish nation' strongly supports this contention: the statement clearly indicates the Jewish origin of the group, which is later denied in the same story (*Ant.* XI, 344). It is this denial, however, which can be more easily explained as later, anti-Samaritan polemic. We may therefore accept that Josephus has fortunately preserved an authentic element of early Samaritan history.

It is difficult to say much more with any certainty, but one or two observations may cautiously be made. One of the references, *Ant.* XI, 346, looks rather like a generalizing statement of the situation by Josephus on the basis of other material. It is not necessary, therefore, to take too seriously the reasons which he gives there for defection ('eating unclean food or violating the Sabbath'). Furthermore, this is the only one of the references which dates the defection after the founding of the Gerizim cult. Whilst this in itself is not an implausible suggestion, it highlights the fact that the tradition originally dealt with the founding of the cult, and so relates to the very earliest period.

In *Ant.* XI, 312, by contrast, the cause of defection is said to have been mixed marriages. Thus the tradition which we have tried to isolate here suggests that this problem was more widespread, and continued over a longer period, than the Bible narrative on its own would allow us to conclude. Nothing from the present context allows us to be more specific about its date. A recurring situation, stretching from the days of Ezra and Nehemiah until the building of the Samaritan temple, seems to be most likely.

Since, therefore, this tradition, combined with the Biblical evidence, reflects a general difference of opinion within the Jerusalem priesthood whose result was that a number of priests 'defected' to the north, we can assume only that this division centred on the issue of whether the Northerners should be included within the reconstituted Israel. The extremely difficult background (noted above on p. 136) against which Ezra and Nehemiah had to work renders their rigorism intelligible, but there is no record of their attitude towards the position of any remnant

---

[1] Cf. J. A. Montgomery: *The Samaritans*, p. 157.

Conclusions

Israelite population in the north; it was not the central issue in the fifth century. History teaches us, however, that the followers of great leaders or innovators will often press their insights to unintended extremes. Religious exclusivism being no exception here, there may have been a tendency within the Jerusalem community of the fourth century, struggling as it was to maintain its distinctive identity, to close in upon itself in a way that denied any part to others who may themselves have had fully justified claims to a share in the community's traditions. The defection of some of the priests may then be seen as an equally strong reaction to the direction affairs had taken in Jerusalem. We may thus conclude that both the separatist and assimilationist parties had by now become equally rigid and extreme in their views.

No writer of the period, if he was concerned to give direction to the life of his people, could have ignored these issues. Examination of Chr. in this light has suggested that their author firmly plotted a middle course[1] in proposing a certain compromise such as might have attracted the support of all but the most extreme antagonists.[2]

On the one hand, there can be no doubt about his unswerving loyalty to the Jerusalem cult in its every detail. This aspect of his work is so obvious and well-known as to need no further comment. The speech of Abijah (2 Chr. 13: 4–12) is often rightly cited as a succinct expression of this viewpoint. As we have seen, reconciliation with rebels could only be based on their return to complete allegiance to the authority of this cult.

It is the other aspect of the Chronicler's presentation, however, which has not hitherto received the attention which it deserves. As we have attempted to demonstrate, he not only suggests that all the twelve tribes are an integral part of Israel, but also shows that there is nothing to prevent the practical outworking of these conclusions in the community of his day.

Until the reign of Solomon, all Israel had an equal share in the life of the nation. Since it was all Israel which had raised David to the kingship, it is implied that the leader had responsibilities towards all his people, and this is underlined by the care with which the Chronicler represents David gathering the people for all the major events of his reign, most of which were preparatory for the temple building itself.[3]

---

[1] The distinction between Chr. and Ezr.-Neh. on this issue was recognized by Geiger in a work that most scholars have overlooked: *Nachgelassene Schriften IV*, pp. 168f. For other topics on which the Chronicler took a mediating position, cf. P. R. Ackroyd: 'The Theology of the Chronicler'.

[2] If A. Spiro is correct in his argument that Chr. was both more popular than Sam.-Ki. in earlier times and that 'the whole of Samaritan literature was patterned after Chronicles', then it would appear that our author came close to succeeding in this aim; cf. 'Samaritans, Tobiads and Judahites in Pseudo-Philo'.

[3] Cf. Mosis, chs. 2 and 3.

Conclusions

The same emphasis is continued throughout the reign of Solomon.[1] Moreover, the Chronicler's unique (and in the immediate context, strictly unnecessary) introduction of the transfer of Reuben's birthright to Joseph and through him to the sons of Joseph is best regarded as a concession to demonstrate the honourable part which the central tribes of the later Northern Kingdom had in the nation. Nothing in the later narrative indicates that this position has been cancelled.

The restoration of Israel's unity under Hezekiah is a distinctive feature of the Chronicler's narrative. We have noted further that the basis of its rationale is that the future of the nation and the regathering of those in exile is dependent upon the faithfulness of the community that remained in the land. This may be seen as an attempt to counter the exclusivism of those who had returned from Babylon by granting some status to those who had never been exiled. It is true that representatives of all Israel had gone into exile (1 Chr. 9: 1),[2] and that those who returned included members of Ephraim and Manasseh as well as Benjamin, Judah and Levi (contrast 1 Chr. 9: 3 with Neh. 11: 4). But the return of Israelites from other captivities is also envisaged (2 Chr. 30: 9), and one of the marks of David, Hezekiah and Josiah was that they not only were willing to receive, but actively attempted to reach out after, all who could legitimately attach themselves to this nucleus.

We conclude, therefore, that the Chronicler sought to redress the balance with those who, concerned to avoid the dangers of syncretism and assimilation, had allowed the Jerusalem community so to close in on itself as even to exclude some who had a rightful claim to participation. He achieved this by demonstrating from the history of the divided monarchy that a faithful nucleus does not exclude others, but is a representative centre to which all the children of Israel may be welcomed if they will return.

[1] R. L. Braun: 'Solomonic Apologetic', and cf. his 'The Message of Chronicles', pp. 511–13, for a similar appraisal of the Chronicler's attitude to that suggested here.

[2] It is difficult to decide, however, whether to retain the MT, and translate with Myers (p. 59): '. . . kings of Israel and Judah (when) they were exiled . . .', or, with CM, p. 169, to start a fresh sentence with *hglw*: 'They were carried away, . . .', or whether to postulate that a further mention of Israel and Judah has dropped out by haplography.

Bibliography

Abel, F.-M. *Géographie de la Palestine* (Paris: 1933).

Ackroyd, P. R. *The Age of the Chronicler* (The Selwyn Lectures. Supplement to *Colloquium – The Australian and New Zealand Theological Review*. Auckland: 1970).

I and II Chronicles, Ezra, Nehemiah (Torch Bible Commentaries. London: 1973).

Exile and Restoration. A Study of Hebrew Thought of the Sixth Century B.C. (OTL. London: 1968).

'History and Theology in the Writings of the Chronicler', *CTM* 38 (1967), 501–15.

'The Theology of the Chronicler', *Lexington Theological Quarterly* 8 (1973), 101–16.

Aharoni, Y. 'The Negeb of Judah', *IEJ* 8 (1958), 26–38.

Aharoni, Y. and Avi-Yonah, M. *The Macmillan Bible Atlas* (New York: 1973).

Albright, W. F. 'The Date and Personality of the Chronicler', *JBL* 40 (1921), 104–24.

'The Topography of Simeon', *JPOS* 4 (1924), 149–61.

Review of A. Robert and A. Feuillet (eds.): *Introduction à la Bible*, in *Bi. Or.* 17 (1960), 241f.

Alexander, L. 'The Origin of Greek and Roman Artillery', *The Classical Journal* 41 (1945–6), 208–12.

Allen, L. C. 'Further Thoughts on an Old Recension of Reigns in Paralipomena', *HTR* 61 (1968), 483–91.

The Greek Chronicles. The Relation of the Septuagint of I and II Chronicles to the Massoretic Text. Part I: The Translator's Craft (SVT 25. Leiden: 1974). *Part II: Textual Criticism* (SVT 27. Leiden: 1974).

Allrik, H. L. '1 Esdras according to Codex B and Codex A as appearing in Zerubbabel's list in 1 Esdras 5: 8–23', *ZAW* 66 (1954), 272–92.

Alt, A. 'Die Rolle Samarias bei der Entstehung des Judentums', *Festschrift Otto Procksch zum 60. Geburtstag* (Leipzig: 1934), pp. 5–28, reprinted in *Kleine Schriften zur Geschichte des Volkes Israel*, II (München: 1953), 316–37.

Bibliography

Anderson, A. A. *The Book of Psalms* (CB ns. London: 1972).

Anderson, B. W. *The Living World of the Old Testament* (Second edition. London: 1967).

Anderson, G. W. *A Critical Introduction to the Old Testament* (London: 1959).

Avigad, N. 'Excavations in the Jewish Quarter of the Old City of Jerusalem, 1969/70 (Preliminary Report)', *IEJ* 20 (1970), 1–8.

'Excavations in the Jewish Quarter of the Old City of Jerusalem, 1970 (Second Preliminary Report)', *IEJ* 20 (1970), 129–40.

Avi-Yonah, M. 'The Newly-Found Wall of Jerusalem and its Topographical Significance', *IEJ* 21 (1971), 168–9.

Baltzer, K. 'Das Ende des Staates Juda und die Messias-Frage', *Studien zur Theologie der alttestamentlichen Überlieferungen* (Festschrift G. von Rad), hrsg. von R. Rendtorff und K. Koch (Neukirchen: 1961), pp. 33–43.

Barnes, W. E. *The Books of Chronicles* (The Cambridge Bible for Schools and Colleges. Cambridge: 1899).

Barr, J. 'Daniel', *Peake's Commentary on the Bible*, edited by M. Black and H. H. Rowley (London: 1962), pp. 591–602.

Barthélemy, D. *Les Devanciers d'Aquila* (SVT 10. Leiden: 1963).

Batten, L. W. *A Critical and Exegetical Commentary on the Books of Ezra and Nehemiah* (ICC. Edinburgh: 1913).

Bayer, E. *Das dritte Buch Esdras und sein Verhältnis zu den Büchern Esra-Nehemia* (BS 16/1. Freiburg: 1911).

Bendavid, A. *Biblical Hebrew and Mishnaic Hebrew* (Hebrew. Jerusalem: Vol. I, 1967; Vol. II, 1971).

Parallels in the Bible (Jerusalem: 1972).

Bentzen, A. *Daniel* (HAT. Tübingen: 1952).

Introduction to the Old Testament (Copenhagen: 1948).

Benzinger, I. *Die Bücher der Chronik* (KHAT. Tübingen und Leipzig: 1901).

Bertheau, E. *Die Bücher der Chronik* (Leipzig: 1854).

Bevan, A. A. *A Short Commentary on the Book of Daniel* (Cambridge: 1892).

Beyer, G. 'Beiträge zur Territorialgeschichte von Südwestpalästina im Altertum. I. Das Festungssystem Rehabeams', *ZDPV* 54 (1931), 113–34.

Bickermann, E. 'The Edict of Cyrus in Ezra 1', *JBL* 65 (1946), 249–75.

From Ezra to the Last of the Maccabees. Foundations of Post-Biblical Judaism (New York: 1962).

Bloch, H. *Die Quellen des Flavius Josephus in seiner Archäologie* (Leipzig: 1879).

Botterweck, J. 'Zur Eigenart der chronistischen Davidgeschichte', *Festschrift für Prof. Dr. Viktor Christian*, gewidmet von Kollegen

Bibliography

und Schülern zum 70. Geburtstag, hrsg. von K. Schubert in Verbindung mit J. Botterweck und J. Knobloch (Wien: 1956), pp. 12–31.

Braun, M. *Griechischer Roman und hellenistische Geschichtsschreibung* (Frankfurter Studien zur Religion und Kultur der Antike 6. Frankfurt am Main: 1934).

History and Romance in Graeco-Oriental Literature (Oxford: 1938).

Braun, R. L. 'The Message of Chronicles: Rally Round the Temple', *CTM* 42 (1971), 502–14.

'Solomonic Apologetic in Chronicles', *JBL* 92 (1973), 503–16.

Briggs, C. A. *A Critical and Exegetical Commentary on the Book of Psalms* (ICC. Edinburgh: 1907).

Bright, J. *A History of Israel* (OTL. Second edition. London: 1972).

Brockington, L. H. *Ezra, Nehemiah and Esther* (CB ns. London: 1969).

Brown, F. 'Chronicles, I. and II.', *HDB*, I, 389–97.

Brown, F., Driver, S. R. and Briggs, C. A. *A Hebrew and English Lexicon of the Old Testament* (Oxford: 1907).

Brunet, A.-M. 'Le Chroniste et ses Sources', *RB* 60 (1953), 481–508; 61 (1954), 349–86.

'La Théologie du Chroniste. Théocratie et Messianisme', *Sacra Pagina. Miscellenea Biblica Congressus Internationalis Catholici de Re Biblica* (=*Bib. Eph. Th. Lov.* 12–13), ed. J. Coppens, A. Descamps, É. Massaux (Paris: 1959), I, 384–97.

Büchler, A. 'Das apocryphische Esrabuch', *MGWJ* 41 (1897), 1–16, 49–66 and 97–103.

'La Relation de Josèphe concernant Alexandre le Grand', *REJ* 36 (1898), 1–26.

Cadbury, H. J. *The Making of Luke-Acts* (London: 1927).

Caquot, A. 'Peut-on parler de messianisme dans l'œuvre du Chroniste?', *RTP*, 3me série, 16 (1966), 110–20.

Charles, R. H. *The Apocrypha and Pseudepigrapha of the Old Testament in English, with Introductions and Explanatory Notes to the Several Books, Vol. II: Pseudepigrapha* (Oxford: 1913).

A Critical and Exegetical Commentary on the Book of Daniel (Oxford: 1929).

Coggins, R. J. 'The Interpretation of Ezra IV.4', *JTS* ns 16 (1965), 124–7.

Samaritans and Jews: the Origins of Samaritanism Reconsidered (Oxford: 1975).

Cohen, N. G. 'Josephus and Scripture: Is Josephus' Treatment of the Scriptural Narrative Similar Throughout the Antiquities I–XI?', *JQR* ns 54 (1963–4), 311–32.

Cowley, A. *Aramaic Papyri of the Fifth Century B.C.* (Oxford: 1923).

Cowley, A. E. (ed.). *Gesenius' Hebrew Grammar* as edited and enlarged

Bibliography

Cowley, A. E. (*cont.*)
 by the late E. Kautzsch (2nd ed., Oxford: 1910=28th German ed.: 1909).

Cross, F. M. *Canaanite Myth and Hebrew Epic: Essays in the History of the Religion of Israel* (Cambridge, Mass.: 1973).

'Geshem the Arabian, Enemy of Nehemiah', *BA* 18 (1955), 46f.

'A Reconstruction of the Judean Restoration', *JBL* 94 (1975), 4–18.

Cross, F. M. and Wright, G. E. 'The Boundary and Province Lists of the Kingdom of Judah', *JBL* 75 (1956), 202–26.

Curtis, E. L. and Madsen, A. A. *A Critical and Exegetical Commentary on the Books of Chronicles* (ICC. Edinburgh: 1910).

Danell, G. A. *Studies in the Name Israel in the Old Testament* (Uppsala: 1946).

Davidson, A. B. *Hebrew Syntax* (Edinburgh: 1896).

Déaut, R. le and Robert, J. *Targum des Chroniques* (Rome: 1971).

Delcor, M. 'Hinweise auf das samaritanische Schisma im Alten Testament', *ZAW* 74 (1962), 281–91.

Le Livre de Daniel (Sources Bibliques. Paris: 1971).

Díez Macho, A. *Neophyti I. Targum Palestinense MS de la Biblioteca Vaticana. Tomo I: Génesis* (Madrid-Barcelona: 1968).

Driver, G. R. 'Some Hebrew Roots and their Meanings', *JTS* 23 (1922), 69–73.

Driver, S. R. *An Introduction to the Literature of the Old Testament* (Ninth edition. Edinburgh: 1913).

Notes on the Hebrew Text of the Books of Samuel (Oxford: 1890).

'On Some Alleged Linguistic Affinities of the Elohist', *Journal of Philology* 11 (1882), 201–36.

A Treatise on the Use of the Tenses in Hebrew and Some Other Syntactical Questions (Oxford: 1892).

Dumbrell, W. J. 'The Tell El-Maskhuṭa Bowls and the "Kingdom" of Qedar in the Persian Period', *BASOR* 203 (1971), 33–44.

Dussaud, R. *La Pénétration des Arabes en Syrie avant l'Islam* (Paris: 1955).

Dussaud, R. and Macler, F. *Voyage Archéologique au Ṣafâ et dans le Djebel Ed-Drûz* (Paris: 1901).

Eissfeldt, O. 'Das alte Testament im Lichte der safatenischen Inschriften', *ZDMG* 104 (1954), 88–118=*Kleine Schriften III* (Tübingen: 1966), pp. 289–317.

Einleitung in das alte Testament (3., neubearbeitete Auflage. Tübingen: 1964).

Elmslie, W. A. L. *The Books of Chronicles* (The Cambridge Bible for Schools and Colleges. Cambridge: 1916).

'The First and Second Books of Chronicles', *IB*, III, 341–548.

Emerton, J. A. A Review of U. Kellermann: *Nehemia*, in *JTS* ns 23 (1972), 171–85.

Bibliography

Epstein, I. (ed.). *The Babylonian Talmud. Seder Nezikin II: Baba Bathra* (London: 1935).

Ewald, H. *Ausführliches Lehrbuch der hebräischen Sprache des Alten Bundes* (Göttingen: 1870).

Fohrer, G. *Einleitung in das alte Testament* (begründet von E. Sellin, völlig neu bearbeitet von G. Fohrer. 10. Auflage. Heidelberg: 1965).

Geschichte der Israelitischen Religion (Berlin: 1969).

Freedman, D. N. 'The Chronicler's Purpose', *CBQ* 23 (1961), 436–42.

Freedman, H. *Midrash Rabbah: Genesis II* (London: 1939).

Galling, K. *Die Bücher der Chronik, Esra, Nehemia* (ATD 12. Göttingen: 1954).

Gaster, M. 'The Feast of Jeroboam and the Samaritan Calendar', *ET* 24 (1913), 198–201.

Geiger, A. *Nachgelassene Schriften IV* (Berlin: 1876).

Gerleman, G. *Studies in the Septuagint II. Chronicles* (Lunds Universitets Årsskrift. N.F. Avd. 1. Bd 43. Nr. 3. Lund: 1946).

Giesebrecht, F. *Die Hebraeische Praeposition Lamed* (Halle: 1876).

Gill, M. 'Israel in the Book of Chronicles' (Hebrew), *Beth Miqra* 13 (1968), 105–15.

Ginsburger, M. *Das Fragmententhargum* (Berlin: 1899).

Pseudo-Jonathan nach der Londoner Handschrift (Berlin: 1903).

Gooding, D. W. 'Jeroboam's Rise to Power: A Rejoinder', *JBL* 91 (1972), 529–33.

'Problems of Text and Midrash in the Third Book of Reigns', *Textus* 7 (1969), 1–29.

'The Septuagint's Rival Versions of Jeroboam's Rise to Power', *VT* 17 (1967), 173–89.

Graf, K. H. *Die geschichtlichen Bücher des alten Testaments* (Leipzig: 1866).

Grafman, R. 'Nehemiah's "Broad Wall"', *IEJ* 24 (1974), 50f.

Gray, G. B. *Studies in Hebrew Proper Names* (London: 1896).

Gray, J. *I and II Kings. A Commentary* (OTL. Second, fully revised, edition. London: 1970).

Grintz, J. M. 'Aspects of the History of the High Priesthood' (Hebrew), *Zion* 23–4 (1958–9), 124–40.

Haag, H. 'Das Mazzenfest des Hiskia', *Wort und Geschichte. Festschrift für Karl Elliger zum 70. Geburtstag*, hrsg. von H. Gese und H. P. Rüger (AOAT 18. Neukirchen-Vluyn: 1973), pp. 87–94.

Hallevy, E. E. מדרש רבא, 8 vols. (Tel Aviv: 1956–63).

Harrison, R. K. *Introduction to the Old Testament* (London: 1970).

Harvey-Jellie, W. R. *Chronicles* (CB. London: 1906).

Hasel, G. F. *The Remnant. The History and Theology of the Remnant*

Bibliography

Hasel, G. F. (*cont.*)

    Idea from Genesis to Isaiah (Andrews University Monographs 5. Berrien Springs: 1972).

Hengel, M. *Judentum und Hellenismus. Studien zu ihrer Begegnung unter besonderer Berücksichtigung Palästinas bis zur Mitte des 2. Jh.s v. Chr.* (Wissenschaftliche Untersuchungen zum neuen Testament 10. 2. Auflage. Tübingen: 1973).

Hölscher, G. *Die Quellen des Josephus für die Zeit vom Exil bis zum jüdischen Kriege* (Leipzig: 1904).

Howorth, H. H. 'A Criticism of the Sources and the Relative Importance and Value of the Canonical Book of Ezra and the Apocryphal Book known as Esdras 1', *Transactions of the Ninth International Congress of Orientalists*, 11 (London: 1893), 68–85.

    'The Real Character and the Importance of the First Book of Esdras, I', *The Academy* 43 (1893), 13f.

    'The Real Character . . ., II', *The Academy* 43 (1893), 60.

    'The Real Character . . ., III', *The Academy* 43 (1893), 106.

    'The Real Character . . ., IV', *The Academy* 43 (1893), 174f.

    'The Real Character . . ., V', *The Academy* 43 (1893), 326f.

    'The Real Character . . ., VI', *The Academy* 43 (1893), 524.

    'The Septuagint versus the Hebrew Text of the Bible, I', *The Academy* 44 (1893), 233f.

    'The True Septuagint Version of Chronicles-Ezra-Nehemiah', *The Academy* 44 (1893), 73f.

    'Some Unconventional Views on the Text of the Bible, I', *PSBA* 23 (1901), 147–59.

    'Some Unconventional Views . . ., II', *PSBA* 23 (1901), 305–25.

    'Some Unconventional Views . . ., III', *PSBA* 24 (1902), 147–72.

    'Some Unconventional Views, . . . IV', *PSBA* 24 (1902), 332–40.

    'Some Unconventional Views, . . . V', *PSBA* 26 (1904), 25–31, 63–9 and 94–100.

    'Some Unconventional Views, . . . VI', *PSBA* 27 (1905), 267–78.

    'Some Unconventional Views, . . . VII', *PSBA* 29 (1907), 31–8 and 61–9.

Hunger, H. *Babylonische und assyrische Kolophone* (AOAT 2. Neukirchen-Vluyn: 1968).

Hurvitz, A. 'The Evidence of Language in Dating the Priestly Code', *RB* 81 (1974), 24–56.

    The Transition Period in Biblical Hebrew. A Study in Post-Exilic Hebrew and its Implications for the Dating of Psalms (Hebrew. Jerusalem: 1972).

    'The Usage of שש and בוץ in the Bible and its Implication for the Date of P', *HTR* 60 (1967), 117–21.

Bibliography

In der Smitten, W. Th. *Esra. Quellen, Überlieferung und Geschichte* (Studia Semitic Neerlandica 15. Assen: 1973).
'Die Gründe für die Aufnahme der Nehemiaschrift in das chronistische Geschichtswerk', *BZ* 16 (1972), 207–21.
'Zur Pagenerzählung im 3. Esra (3 Esr. III 1 – V 6)', *VT* 22 (1972), 492–5.

Japhet, S. 'Chronicles, Book of', *Encyclopaedia Judaica* (Jerusalem: 1971), Vol. 5, cols. 517–34.
The Ideology of the Book of Chronicles and its Place in Biblical Thought (Hebrew. Doctoral Thesis submitted to the Hebrew University, Jerusalem: 1973).
'The Supposed Common Authorship of Chronicles and Ezra-Nehemiah Investigated Anew', *VT* 18 (1968), 330–71.

Jastrow, M. *A Dictionary of the Targumim, the Talmud Babli and Yerushalmi, and the Midrashic Literature* (London: 1903).

Jellicoe, S. 'Some Reflections on the καιγε Recension', *VT* 23 (1973), 15–24.

Johnson, M. D. *The Purpose of the Biblical Genealogies* (Society for New Testament Studies. Monograph Series 8. Cambridge: 1969).

Kanael, B. 'Ancient Jewish Coins and Their Historical Importance', *BA* 26 (1963), 38–62.

Kapelrud, A. S. *The Question of Authorship in the Ezra-Narrative. A Lexical Investigation* (SUNVAO. II. Hist.-Filos. Klasse 1. Oslo: 1944).

Kaufmann, Y. *The History of the Religion of Israel* (Hebrew), Vol. 4 (Tel Aviv: 1972).

Keil, C. F. *Biblischer Commentar über die nachexilischen Geschichtsbücher: Chronik, Esra, Nehemia und Esther* (Leipzig: 1870).
Lehrbuch der historisch-kritischen Einleitung in die kanonischen und apocryphen Schriften des alten Testaments (Frankfurt/Main: 1873).

Kellermann, U. *Messias und Gesetz. Grundlinien einer alttestamentlichen Heilserwartung. Eine traditionsgeschichtliche Einführung* (BS 61. Neukirchen: 1971).
Nehemia. Quellen, Überlieferung und Geschichte (BZAW 102. Berlin: 1967).

Kenyon, K. M. 'Excavations in Jerusalem, 1962', *PEQ* 95 (1963), 7–21.

Kippenberg, H. G. *Garizim und Synagoge. Traditionsgeschichtliche Untersuchungen zur samaritanischen Religion der aramäischen Periode* (Religionsgeschichtliche Versuche und Vorarbeiten 30. Berlin: 1971).

Kittel, R. *Die Bücher der Chronik* (Handkommentar zum alten Testament. Göttingen: 1902).

Klein, R. W. 'Jeroboam's Rise to Power', *JBL* 89 (1970), 217–18.
'New Evidence for an Old Recension of Reigns', *HTR* 60 (1967), 93–105.

Bibliography

Klein, R. W. (*cont.*)

'Once More: "Jeroboam's Rise to Power"', *JBL* 92 (1973), 582–4.

'Supplements in the Paralipomena: A Rejoinder', *HTR* 61 (1968), 492–5.

Klostermann, A. 'Die Bücher der Chronik', *Realencyklopädie für Theologie und Kirche*, ed. A. Hauck (Leipzig: 1898), IV, 84–98.

Koch, K. 'Ezra and the Origins of Judaism', *JSS* 19 (1974), 173–97.

Koehler, L. and Baumgartner, W. *Lexicon in Veteris Testamenti Libros* (Leiden: 1953).

König, E. *Einleitung in das alte Testament mit Einschluss der Apokryphen und der Pseudepigraphen alten Testaments* (Bonn: 1893).

Kraeling, E. G. *The Brooklyn Museum Aramaic Papyri. New Documents of the Fifth Century B.C. from the Jewish Colony at Elephantine* (New Haven: 1953).

Kraus, H.-J. 'Zur Geschichte des Passah-Massot-Festes im alten Testament', *EvTh* 18 (1958), 47–67.

Kropat, A. *Die Syntax des Autors der Chronik verglichen mit der seiner Quellen. Ein Beitrag zur historischen Syntax des Hebräischen* (BZAW 16. Giessen: 1909).

Laqueur, R. 'Ephoros', *Hermes* 46 (1911), 168–72.

Lemaire, A. 'Un nouveau roi arabe de Qedar dans l'inscription de l'autel à encens de Lakish', *RB* 81 (1974), 63–72.

Lemke, W. E. 'The Synoptic Problem in the Chronicler's History', *HTR* 58 (1965), 349–63.

Littmann, E. *Zur Entzifferung der Safâ-Inschriften* (Leipzig: 1901).

Safaitic Inscriptions (Publications of the Princeton University Archaeological Expeditions to Syria in 1904–5 and 1909, Division IV, 'Semitic Inscriptions', Section C. Leiden: 1943).

Thamūd und Ṣafā (Abhandlungen für die Kunde des Morgenlandes XXV 1. Leipzig: 1940).

Liver, J. 'History and Historiography in the Book of Chronicles' (Hebrew), in *Studies in Bible and Judean Desert Scrolls* (Jerusalem: 1971), pp. 221–33.

'And all Israel were reckoned by genealogies; and behold, they are written in the book of the kings of Israel' (Hebrew), in *Studies in Bible and Judean Desert Scrolls* (Jerusalem: 1971), pp. 234–48.

Macdonald, J. *The Theology of the Samaritans* (New Testament Library. London: 1964).

Malamat, A. 'The Historical Background of the Assassination of Amon, King of Judah', *IEJ* 3 (1953), 26–9.

Mantel, H. D. 'The Dichotomy of Judaism during the Second Temple', *HUCA* 44 (1973), 55–87.

Marcus, R. *Josephus: Jewish Antiquities, Books IX–XI* (Cambridge, Mass.: 1937).

Bibliography

Marcus, R. (*cont.*)
Josephus: Jewish Antiquities, Books XII–XIV (Cambridge, Mass.: 1943).

Marquart, J. *Fundamente israelitischer und jüdischer Geschichte* (Göttingen: 1896).

Marsden, E. W. *Greek and Roman Artillery I: Historical Development* (Oxford: 1969).

Mayes, A. H. D. *Israel in the Period of the Judges* (Studies in Biblical Theology. 2nd series 29. London: 1974).

Mazar, B. (Maisler). 'Chronicles' (Hebrew), *Encyclopaedia Biblica*, Vol. 2 (Jerusalem: 1965), cols. 596–606.

'The Tobiads', *IEJ* 7 (1957), 137–45 and 229–38.

Mendelsohn, I. 'On the Preferential Status of the Eldest Son', *BASOR* 156 (1959), 38–40.

Mendenhall, G. E. 'The Census Lists of Numbers 1 and 26', *JBL* 77 (1958), 52–66.

Meshorer, Y. 'A New Type of YHD Coin', *IEJ* 16 (1966), 217–19.

Mettinger, T. N. D. *Solomonic State Officials. A Study of the Civil Government Officials of the Israelite Monarchy* (Coniectanea Biblica. Old Testament Series 5. Lund: 1971).

Meyer, E. *Die Entstehung des Judenthums: Eine historische Untersuchung* (Halle: 1896).

Montgomery, J. A. *A Critical and Exegetical Commentary on the Book of Daniel* (ICC. Edinburgh: 1927).

The Samaritans, the earliest Jewish Sect. Their History, Theology and Literature (Philadelphia: 1907).

Montgomery, J. A. and Gehman, H. S. *A Critical and Exegetical Commentary on the Books of Kings* (ICC. Edinburgh: 1951).

Moriarty, F. L. 'The Chronicler's Account of Hezekiah's Reform', *CBQ* 27 (1965), 399–406.

Mosis, R. *Untersuchungen zur Theologie des chronistischen Geschichtswerkes* (Freiburger theologische Studien 92. Freiburg: 1973).

Moulton, W. J. 'Über die Überlieferung und den textkritischen Werth des dritten Esrabuchs', *ZAW* 19 (1899), 209–58 and 20 (1900), 1–35.

Mowinckel, S. *Studien zu dem Buche Ezra-Nehemia I: Die nachchronistische Redaktion des Buches. Die Listen* (SUNVAO. II. Hist. Filos. Klasse. Ny Serie. No. 3. Oslo: 1964).

Studien zu dem Buche Ezra-Nehemia II: Die Nehemia-Denkschrift (SUNVAO. II. Hist.-Filos. Klasse. Ny Serie. No. 5. Oslo: 1964).

Studien zu dem Buche Ezra-Nehemia III: Die Ezrageschichte und das Gesetz Moses (SUNVAO. II. Hist.-Filos. Klasse. Ny Serie. No. 7. Oslo: 1965).

Myers, J. M. *I Chronicles. Introduction, Translation, and Notes* (AB. Garden City: 1965).

Bibliography

Myers, J. M. (*cont.*)

II Chronicles. Introduction, Translation, and Notes (AB. Garden City: 1965).

I and II Esdras. Introduction, Translation and Commentary (AB. Garden City: 1974).

Ezra. Nehemiah. Introduction, Translation, and Notes (AB. Garden City: 1965).

'The Kerygma of the Chronicler', *Interpretation*, 20 (1966), 259-73.

Naveh, J. 'An Aramaic Tomb Inscription Written in Paleo-Hebrew Script', *IEJ* 23 (1973), 82-91.

'Hebrew Texts in Aramaic Script in the Persian Period?', *BASOR* 203 (1971), 27-32.

Nestlé, E. 'Zur Frage nach der ursprünglichen Einheit der Bücher Chronik, Esra, Nehemia', *Theologische Studien und Kritiken* 52 (1879), 517-21.

Marginalien und Materialien (Tübingen: 1893).

Newsome, J. D. 'Toward a New Understanding of the Chronicler and his Purposes', *JBL* 94 (1975), 201-17.

Noordtzij, A. 'Les Intentions du Chroniste', *RB* 49 (1940), 161-8.

North, R. 'Theology of the Chronicler', *JBL* 82 (1963), 369-81.

Noth, M. 'Das Reich von Hamath als Grenznachbar des Reiches Israel', *PJB* 33 (1937), 36-51 = *Aufsätze zur biblischen Landes- und Altertumskunde, 2: Beiträge altorientalischer Texte zur Geschichte Israels* (Neukirchen: 1971), 148-60.

Das System der zwölf Stämme Israels (BWANT 4/1. Stuttgart: 1930).

Überlieferungsgeschichtliche Studien I (Halle: 1943).

Oesterley, W. O. E. *An Introduction to the Books of the Apocrypha* (London: 1935).

Oesterley, W. O. E. and Robinson, T. H. *An Introduction to the Books of the Old Testament* (London: 1934).

Olmstead, A. T. *History of the Persian Empire* (Chicago: 1948).

Pavlovsky, V. 'Die Chronologie der Tätigkeit Esdras. Versuch einer neuen Lösung', *Biblica* 38 (1957), 275-305 and 428-56.

Pfeiffer, R. H. *History of New Testament Times with an Introduction to the Apocrypha* (London: 1949).

Introduction to the Old Testament (New York: 1948).

Plöger, O. *Theokratie und Eschatologie* (WMANT 2. Neukirchen: 1959).

Podechard, E. 'Le Premier Chapitre des Paralipomènes', *RB* 13 (1916), 363-86.

Pohlmann, K.-F. *Studien zum dritten Esra. Ein Beitrag zur Frage nach dem ursprünglichen Schluss des chronistischen Geschichtswerkes* (FRLANT 104. Göttingen: 1970).

Porteous, N. W. *Daniel. A Commentary* (OTL. London: 1965).

Porter, J. R. 'Son or Grandson (Ezra X.6)?', *JTS* ns 17 (1966), 54-67.

Bibliography

Rabinowitz, I. 'Aramaic Inscriptions of the Fifth Century B.C.E. from a North-Arab Shrine in Egypt', *JNES* 15 (1956), 1–9.

Rad, G. von *Das Geschichtsbild des Chronistischen Werkes* (BWANT 4/3. Stuttgart: 1930).

'Die levitische Predigt in den Büchern der Chronik', *Festschrift Otto Procksch* (Leipzig: 1934), pp. 113–24 = *Gesammelte Studien zum alten Testament* (München: 1958), pp. 248–61.

Theologie des alten Testaments, Band I: Die Theologie der geschichtlichen Überlieferungen Israels (München: 1958).

Rahlfs, A. *Septuaginta-Studien 3: Lucians Rezension der Königsbücher* (Göttingen: 1911).

Rahmani, L. Y. 'Silver Coins of the Fourth Century B.C. from Tel Gamma', *IEJ* 21 (1971), 158–60.

Rehm, M. *Textkritische Untersuchungen zu den Parallelstellen der Samuel-Königsbücher und der Chronik* (Alttestamentliche Abhandlungen 13/3. Münster: 1937).

Reifenberg, A. *Ancient Jewish Coins* (2nd and revised edition. Jerusalem: 1947).

Ringgren, H. *Israelitische Religion* (Stuttgart: 1963).

Rothstein, J. W. and Hänel, J. *Das erste Buch der Chronik* (KAT. Leipzig: 1927).

Rowley, H. H. 'The Chronological Order of Ezra and Nehemiah', *Ignace Goldziher Memorial Volume* (Budapest: 1948), Part I, pp. 117–49 = *The Servant of the Lord and Other Essays on the Old Testament* (2nd edition. Oxford: 1965), pp. 137–68.

The Growth of the Old Testament (London: 1950).

Rudolph, W. *Chronikbücher* (HAT. Tübingen: 1955).

Esra und Nehemia samt 3. Esra (HAT. Tübingen: 1949).

'Problems of the Books of Chronicles', *VT* 4 (1954), 401–9.

Ryckmans, G. 'Inscriptions Safaïtiques du Wâdî Rousheydî', in *Mélanges Syriens Offerts à Monsieur René Dussaud* (Paris: 1939), II, 507–20.

'Les Noms de Parenté en Safaïtique', *RB* 58 (1951), 377–92.

Schalit, A. 'Die Denkschrift der Samaritaner an König Antiochos Epiphanes zu Beginn der grossen Verfolgung der jüdischen Religion im Jahre 167 v. Chr.', *ASTI* 8 (1970–1), 131–83.

'A Chapter in the History of Party Strife in Jerusalem at the End of the Fifth Century and at the Beginning of the Fourth Century B.C.' (Hebrew), in *Commentationes in memoriam Johannis Levy*, edited by M. Schwabe and I. Gutman (Jerusalem: 1949), pp. 252–72.

Seeligmann, I. L. 'Menschliches Heldentum und göttliche Hilfe. Die doppelte Kausalität im alttestamentlichen Geschichtsdenken', *ThZ* 19 (1963), 385–411.

Bibliography

Segal, M. H. 'The Books of Ezra-Nehemiah' (Hebrew), *Tarbiz* 14 (1943), 81–103.

A Grammar of Mishnaic Hebrew (Oxford: 1927).

Smith, M. 'Palestinian Judaism in the Persian Period', in *The Greeks and the Persians from the Sixth to the Fourth Centuries*, ed. H. Bengtson (New York: 1968), pp. 386–401.

Palestinian Parties and Politics that Shaped the Old Testament (New York: 1971).

Speiser, E. A. *Genesis* (AB. Garden City: 1964).

Sperber, A. *The Bible in Aramaic, Vol. 1: The Pentateuch according to Targum Onkelos* (Leiden: 1959).

A Historical Grammar of Biblical Hebrew. A Presentation of Problems with Suggestions to their Solution (Leiden: 1966).

Spiro, A. 'Samaritans, Tobiads and Judahites in Pseudo-Philo', *Proceedings of the American Academy for Jewish Research* 20 (1951), 279–355.

Steck, O. H. 'Das Problem theologischer Strömungen in nachexilischer Zeit', *EvTh* 28 (1968), 445–58.

Stern, E. *The Material Culture of Israel in the Persian Period (538–332 B.C.)* (Hebrew. Jerusalem: 1973).

'Seal Impressions in the Achaemenid Style in the Province of Judah', *BASOR* 202 (1971), 6–16.

Stinespring, W. F. 'Eschatology in Chronicles', *JBL* 80 (1961), 209–19.

Sukenik, E. L. 'More about the Oldest Coins of Judaea', *JPOS* 15 (1935), 341–3.

'Paralipomena Palaestinensia', *JPOS* 14 (1934), 178–84.

Sukenik, Y. '*ḥšbnwt mḥšbt ḥwšb*' (Hebrew), *BJPES* 13 (1946–7), 19–24.

Swete, H. B. *An Introduction to the Old Testament in Greek* (Cambridge: 1900).

Tadmor, H. 'The Campaigns of Sargon II of Assur: A Chronological-Historical Study', *JCS* 12 (1958), 22–40, 77–100.

'On the History of Samaria in the Biblical Period' (Hebrew), *Eretz Shomron. The Thirtieth Archaeological Convention, September, 1972*, edited by J. Aviram (Jerusalem: 1973), pp. 67–74.

Talmon, S. 'Biblical Tradition on the Early History of the Samaritans' (Hebrew), *Eretz Shomron. The Thirtieth Archaeological Convention, September, 1972*, edited by J. Aviram (Jerusalem: 1973), pp. 19–33.

'Divergences in Calendar-Reckoning in Ephraim and Judah', *VT* 8 (1958), 48–74.

Thackeray, H. St J. 'Esdras, First Book of', *HDB*, 1, 758–63.

'The Greek Translators of the four Books of Kings', *JTS* 8 (1907), 262–78.

Bibliography

Thackeray, H. (*cont.*)
Josephus: Jewish Antiquities, Books I–IV (New York: 1930).
The Septuagint and Jewish Worship. A Study in Origins (London: 1921).

Thackeray, H. St J. and Marcus, R. *Josephus: Jewish Antiquities, Books V–VIII* (Cambridge, Mass.: 1934).

Thompson, R. J. *Moses and the Law in a Century of Criticism since Graf* (SVT 19. Leiden: 1970).

Torrey, C. C. 'The Aramaic Portions of Ezra', *AJSL* 24 (1907–8), 209–81.
'The Chronicler as Editor and as Independent Narrator', *AJSL* 25 (1908–9), 157–73 and 188–217.
The Composition and Historical Value of Ezra-Nehemiah (BZAW 2. Giessen: 1896).
Ezra Studies (Chicago: 1910).
'A Revised View of First Esdras', *Louis Ginzberg Jubilee Volume* (New York: 1945), pp. 395–410.

Tov, E. 'Transliterations of Hebrew Words in the Greek Versions of the Old Testament. A Further Characteristic of the *Kaige*-Th. Revision?', *Textus* 8 (1973), 78–92.

Treuenfels, A. 'Über das apocryphische Buch Esra', *Der Orient* XI (1850).

Tuland, C. G. 'Josephus, *Antiquities*, Book XI. Correction or Confirmation of Biblical Post-Exilic Records?', *AUSS* 4 (1966), 176–92.

Vogt, H. C. M. *Studie zur nachexilischen Gemeinde in Esra-Nehemia* (Werl: 1966).

Walde, B. *Die Esdrasbücher der Septuaginta* (*Ihr gegenseitiges Verhältnis untersucht*) (BS 18/4. Freiburg: 1913).

Weinberg, J. P. 'Das $B\overline{E}IT$ '$AB\overline{O}T$ im 6.–4. Jh. v.u.Z.', *VT* 23 (1973), 400–14.

Weinfeld, M. 'Universalism and Particularism in the Period of Exile and Restoration' (Hebrew), *Tarbiz* 33 (1963–4), 228–42.

Weiser, A. *Einleitung in das alte Testament* (6. Auflage. Göttingen: 1966).

Welch, A. C. *Post-Exilic Judaism* (Edinburgh and London: 1935).
The Work of the Chronicler. Its Purpose and Date (The Schweich Lectures, 1938. London: 1939).

Wellhausen, J. *Prolegomena zur Geschichte Israels* (6. Auflage. Berlin: 1905).

Welten, P. *Geschichte und Geschichtsdarstellung in den Chronikbüchern* (WMANT 42. Neukirchen: 1973).

Westermann, C. 'Die Begriffe für fragen und suchen im alten Testament', *Kerygma und Dogma* 6 (1960), 2–30.

Bibliography

Wette, W. M. L. de. *Beiträge zur Einleitung in das alte Testament. Erstes Bändchen: Kritischer Versuch über die Glaubwürdigkeit der Bücher der Chronik mit Hinsicht auf die Geschichte der Mosaischen Bücher und Gesetzgebung* (Halle: 1806).
A Critical and Historical Introduction to the Canonical Scriptures of the Old Testament (Boston: 1843).
Lehrbuch der historisch-kritischen Einleitung in die kanonischen und apokryphischen Bücher des alten Testaments (7. Auflage. Berlin: 1852).
Willi, T. *Die Chronik als Auslegung. Untersuchungen zur literarischen Gestaltung der historischen Überlieferung Israels* (FRLANT 106. Göttingen: 1972).
Williamson, H. G. M. 'A Note on 1 Chronicles VII 12', *VT* 23 (1973), 375–9.
'The Accession of Solomon in the Books of Chronicles', *VT* 26 (1976), 351–61.
Wiseman, D. J. 'Books in the Ancient Near East and in the Old Testament', in *The Cambridge History of the Bible, Vol. 1: From the Beginnings to Jerome*, edited by P. R. Ackroyd and C. F. Evans (Cambridge: 1970), pp. 30–48.
Würthwein, E. *The Text of the Old Testament* (ET by P. R. Ackroyd. Oxford: 1957).
Young, E. J. *An Introduction to the Old Testament* (Revised edition. London: 1964).
Zimmerli, W. 'Israel im Buche Ezekiel', *VT* 8 (1958), 75–90.
Der Mensch und seine Hoffnung im alten Testament (Göttingen: 1968).
Zimmermann, F. 'The story of the three guardsmen', *JQR* ns 54 (1963–4), 179–200.
Zunz, L. *Die gottesdienstlichen Vorträge der Juden, historisch entwickelt. Ein Beitrag zur Alterthumskunde und biblischen Kritik, zur Literatur- und Religionsgeschichte* (Berlin: 1832).

INDEX OF PASSAGES CITED

A. THE OLD TESTAMENT

Index of Passages

Index of Passages

C. JOSEPHUS

INDEX OF MODERN AUTHORS

165

Index of Modern Authors

Index of Modern Authors

GENERAL INDEX

General Index

Israel
  after the fall of Samaria 67, 106, 119–31
  All Israel 88, 98f., 103, 105, 108–10, 120, 125ff., 139
  children/sons of 62, 64, 109f., 113, 127ff., 130, 140
  Chronicler's conception of 1–4, 34, 69, 87–131 *passim*, 132
  early history of 61–6, 87, 89, 105, 130
  in Ezra-Nehemiah 3, 69, 71, 87
  general uses of the word 87, 89, 128
  Jacob as *see* Jacob
  Judah, used of 87f., 102f., 105ff. 109f.
  land of 55, 101, 123f., 128
  Northern Kingdom of 1f., 75, 88, 90, 97–118 *passim*, 121, 125, 127f., 130f., 140; apostasy of 111, 113f.; fall of 62, 66f., 104, 106, 114, 118, 125f., 128
  reunification of 125f., 128, 131, 133
  symbol of continuity 107, 117f., 130
  tribes of 69, 71–82 *passim*, 87, 89, 96, 99, 103, 130, 139
Issachar 74f.

Jacob 62ff., 71f., 77, 89, 91f., 130
Jehoshaphat 100, 104f., 107
Jeroboam 98, 108, 111f., 120
Jerusalem 2, 27, 47, 101, 111, 115, 117, 119; fall of 9, 18f.; post-exilic community of 1, 25, 34, 60, 132–40 *passim*
Joseph 75, 89–95, 130, 140
Josephus 21–9 *passim*, 35, 112, 137f.
Josiah 16–20, 88, 101, 123, 127, 129, 140
Judah 61, 72f., 89f., 93f.
Judah, kingdom of 85, 97–131 *passim*
Judah, province of 55, 60, 136
Judah (tribe) 75, 79f., 87, 140

Levi 74, 87, 140
levirate marriage 91
Levites 33f., 57, 65, 69, 98, 107, 111, 122

Manasseh (king) 18–20, 35
Manasseh (patriarch) 89–93
Manasseh (tribe) 74ff., 82, 140
Medes 21

messianism 3, 135
mixed marriages 25, 34, 53, 60f., 68, 134, 138

names 8f., 79
Naphtali 74f., 100f., 123
Nathan, oracle of 65f.
Nehemiah 25f., 30, 60f., 69, 132, 134, 138; death of 24f.; Memoir of 5, 23, 30f., 41–52 *passim*, 70
Nethinim 32f., 51, 57, 69
Noah 62f.

Osnappar 66

Paralipomena 11–21 *passim*, 35f., 94
Passover: of Hezekiah 100f., 117, 119f., 123ff.; of Josiah 129; of the post-exilic community 21
Persia(n) 2, 10, 21, 83ff., 133f., 136
Peshitta 93
Philistines 101, 117
pilgrimage of the nations 123
Priestly writing 40, 43ff., 47, 53, 57, 132, 135f.
priests 33f., 53, 56, 107, 122, 127, 134f., 137ff.
prophecy, prophets 68, 103, 116, 125, 134
Ptolemaic 15, 21

Qumran *see* Dead Sea Scrolls

Rabbinic literature 45, 48
Rehoboam 98, 100, 109, 111, 113; young men of 112
remnant 69, 117, 120, 125–31 *passim*, 134, 138
repentance 113ff., 118, 131
retribution, immediate 17, 19f., 67f., 111
Reuben 73f., 76, 81, 89, 91, 94f., 130, 140

Sabbath 19, 68f., 132, 138
Safaitic inscriptions 77ff., 81
Samaria 47, 66, 117, 136
Samaritans 21, 63, 90, 121, 134; Chronicles and 2f., 75f., 84, 97, 111f., 133; origins of 1, 102, 132, 136–8
Satyrs 111, 113
Saul 73, 95, 119
seed, holy 69, 134